ROUTLEDGE LIBRARY EDITIONS:
ACCOUNTING

Volume 29

A HISTORY OF FINANCIAL ACCOUNTING

A HISTORY OF FINANCIAL ACCOUNTING

J.R. EDWARDS

Routledge
Taylor & Francis Group
LONDON AND NEW YORK

First published in 1989

This edition first published in 2014
by Routledge
2 Park Square, Milton Park, Abingdon, Oxfordshire OX14 4RN

and by Routledge
711 Third Avenue, New York, NY 10017, USA

First issued in paperback 2015

Routledge is an imprint of the Taylor & Francis Group, an informa business

British Library Cataloguing in Publication Data
A catalogue record for this book is available from the British Library

ISBN: 978-0-415-53081-1 (Set)
ISBN 13: 978-1-138-96553-9 (pbk)
ISBN 13: 978-0-415-85490-0 (hbk) (Volume 29)

Publisher's Note
The publisher has gone to great lengths to ensure the quality of this reprint but points out that some imperfections in the original copies may be apparent.

Disclaimer
The publisher has made every effort to trace copyright holders and would welcome correspondence from those they have been unable to trace.

A History of FINANCIAL ACCOUNTING

J.R. EDWARDS

ROUTLEDGE
London and New York

First published 1989
by Routledge
11 New Fetter Lane, London EC4P 4EE
29 West 35th Street, New York, NY 10001

Printed and bound in Great Britain by Mackays of Chatham PLC, Kent

British Library Cataloguing in Publication Data

Edwards, J.R. (John Richard), *1946-*
A history of financial accounting.
1. Great Britain. Financial accounting,
to 1987
I. Title
657'.48'0941

ISBN 0-415-00432-2

CONTENTS

PREFACE

The amount of published material available on accounting history has increased tremendously since I first gave a short course of lectures on this subject in the mid-1970s. Most of the material deals with specific issues, however, and I therefore reached the conclusion that a more general text which outlined and examined some of the major developments in accounting would prove useful. It is intended that this book should have application as a basic text for courses on accounting history, as background reading for other accounting courses, particularly in the areas of financial accounting and auditing, and to appeal to any accountant who has an interest in the development of his or her discipline. It should also prove useful to the business and economic historian keen to find out more about the financial practices employed by businesses at particular points of time in the past.

Parker defines accounting history as 'The study of the evolution of accounting thought, practices and institutions in response to changes in the environment and the needs of society, and of the effect of this evolution on the environment' (*Macmillan Dictionary of Accounting*, Macmillan Press, London, 1984, p.5). My book focuses principally on the development of accounting practices, and treats accounting thought and accounting institutions as part of the environment which has affected the process of change. The book concentrates on financial accounting, in the main, but also contains an examination of management accounting practices in use in earlier times. This is partly because the distinction was then less clear-cut than is the case today; also because internal reporting procedures formed the basis for choosing methods subsequently adopted for external reporting purposes. The book traces accounting developments in roughly their chronological order. The story starts at the beginning and the early chapters discuss events in various countries as a background to British practices which are the main focus of this study.

I have relied heavily on secondary sources, especially when tracing developments up to the British Industrial Revolution, and a considerable debt is owed to numerous articles, books and treatises whose contribution is, I hope, adequately acknowledged. Primary sources have been used as the basis for much of what I say about the financial reporting practices of the limited liability company, though much of the material has already received some attention in articles written over the last dozen or so years. Present day practices are sometimes used as a convenient reference point for discussing earlier procedures, but I hope to have avoided the mistake of evaluating them on that basis.

Accounting did not develop into its present state in a straightforward and orderly fashion. Major changes have usually been achieved as the result of numerous pragmatic adjustments to new circumstances. Each era produced different environmental conditions and imposed new demands on accounting. A proper understanding of accounting developments therefore requires a careful examination of the interrelationship between accountants and accounting techniques on the one hand and, on the other, the social and economic context in which the changes took place. This is obviously a huge undertaking and my book does not attempt to provide more than broad explanations for *some* of the changes which have occurred. These explanations will no doubt be the subject of reappraisal as more information comes available.

In broad terms, the process of accounting change consists of two elements; an initial innovation followed by the diffusion of new practices. The initial innovation is the result of a complex interplay of circumstances in a particular place at a particular point in time. It may occur, for example, as the result of regulation or as a natural response to meet perceived needs. Diffusion then occurs through the activities of what have been described as 'change agents' and 'targets'. A stimulus for change given particular attention in this book is the 'shock effect' of scandals and other well publicised events, such as the impact of revelations surrounding the 'railway mania' (mid-1840s) on the use of the double account system, the influence of *re City of Glasgow Bank* (1879) on the employment of the independent auditor, the implications of the Royal Mail case (1931) for the popularity of secret reserves, and the significance of the GEC-AEI affair (1968) for the profession's involvement with regulating the form and content of published accounts. In these instances the change agents were practising accountants, professional accountancy bodies, or the legislature; targets were the standards applied by practitioners and the accounting practices which had proved to be deficient in one respect or another.

Change does not, of course, necessarily mean progress. For example, the financial reports published by companies during the 1920s became more secretive and obscure than had previously been the case. This signalled the determined attempt being made by some directors to conceal the effects of general economic recession (and sometimes poor management) on their companies' financial progress and position. These managers were often attempting to buy time until trading conditions improved. We know that steps were taken by practising accountants to counter these activities, but businessmen have displayed an enduring ability to report what they want users to believe rather than what has actually happened. Creative accounting is simply the most recent manifestation of a persistent conflict between management and the reporting accountant.

Much more work is needed from accounting historians before an authoritative history can be written. To help understand the process of accounting change, increased use is being made of what is now described as the genealogical method of enquiry. This promising approach involves looking in detail at a particular time period, company or accounting issue in order to understand developments which have occurred. Loft has warned that this is a 'task of immense proportions' (p.141), but both her own article and others referred to in the *References and Bibliography* prove that the effort is worthwhile. It is also the approach used in Tweedie and Whittington's *The Debate on Inflation Accounting* (Cambridge University Press, Cambridge, 1984), which highlights an important practical application for this kind of work – namely, to improve our knowledge of the past and help in the resolution of present day problems by avoiding the need to reinvent the wheel each time persistent but, possibly, intractable problems recur.

I wish to acknowledge financial support from the ESRC which enabled me to undertake, between 1981–85, an investigation of original sources. I am very grateful to the following colleagues and friends who have read particular chapters and made numerous helpful suggestions for improvement: Roy Chandler, Professor Harold Edey, Professor Charles Magee, Professor Christopher Nobes, Professor Bob Parker, David Pendrill, and Professor Basil Yamey. Errors and inadequacies which remain are my own work. Finally, I must record a considerable debt to my wife, Sandra, who, not only showed considerable patience during a period when the amount of time devoted to the family has been reduced to the minimum, but also typed the manuscript.

John Richard Edwards
Cardiff, June 1988

GLOSSARY OF ABBREVIATIONS

AGM	Annual General Meeting
ASC	Accounting Standards Committee – intially, Accounting Standards Steering Committee
BOT	Board of Trade
CA	Companies Act
CLAC	Company Law Amendment Committee
ICAEW	Institute of Chartered Accountants in England and Wales
JSCA	Joint Stock Companies Act
Recommendation	Recommendation on Accounting Principles
SIAA	Society of Incorporated Accountants and Auditors
SSAP	Statement of Standard Accounting Practice
UK	United Kingdom
US	United States

PART I

INTRODUCTION

I

Why Bother with Accounting History?

There has been an upsurge of interest in accounting history since about 1970. There has also been a massive growth in the available literature thanks to the success of the American *Accounting Historians Journal* (first published in 1977), the willingness of other leading journal editors to publish historical material and the efforts of Richard P. Brief who has edited six major series (published by Arno Press and Garland Publishing) of anthologies and reprints of accounting classics. Five international congresses of accounting historians have been held, beginning with Brussels in 1970, and the subject has increasingly found a prominent place in University degree courses. Why this interest?

For many people the past has a considerable fascination, but is this out of idle curiosity or for more constructive reasons? Perhaps history can tell us. Napoleon viewed history as 'a set of lies agreed upon', the philosopher Herbert Spencer dismissed it as 'worthless gossip' and Henry Ford believed it to be 'more or less bunk'. Aristotle, on the other hand, was much more encouraging – 'if you would understand anything observe its beginnings and its development'. Not only is history attacked but also the historian. According to Samuel Johnson 'Great abilities are not requisite for an historian . . . imagination is not required in any high degree'. Our first appeal to history for enlightenment produces conflicting evidence and seems not at all helpful. Looked at a little more closely it contains an important first lesson, that is, history contains no ready-made answers. We need to delve more deeply.

What is accounting history?

One view is that the historian's job is simply to state the facts and set the record straight. The historian is seen as a kind of record keeper, except that he is expected to reconstruct the facts long after they have occurred. This is an enormous task, in itself, made more difficult by the fact that few records survive from earlier periods in which we have an interest. For instance, one problem which worries accounting historians is the exact date that double entry bookkeeping was first used by Italian merchants. Careful investigation of the surviving fragments of the books of Giovanni Farolfi have proved that the system, which had evolved over an unknown period of time, was fully operational in at least one banking house by 1300 (Lee, G.A.). Discoveries in archives may one day produce an earlier example of 'fully fledged' double entry bookkeeping but it will never be possible to say, with confidence, that we know when double entry was first used.

There are some who criticise 'fact finding' on the grounds that it is concerned merely with trivia. The researcher is dismissed as an antiquarian not deserving the more prestigious accolade 'historian'. The difference is described by the economic historian M.M. Postan as follows:

> whereas antiquarians collect facts historians study problems. To a true antiquary all past facts are welcome. To an historian facts are of little value unless they are causes or parts of causes, or the causes of causes, of the phenomena which he studies (p.25).

The point seems to be that the antiquarian collects data of interest to him, irrespective of their relevance, whereas the historian is concerned with an event only if it helps him to discern some pattern of development. The job of the historian is therefore to seek out events that have taken place in the past, to try to understand why they happened when they did, the way in which they did, and the effect that they had.

The discovery of past events is difficult, but finding out the reasons for them is even more demanding. Any conclusions must be tentative as additional information may lead to different interpretations. Moreover, different people will interpret the same information in a variety of ways. Out of the debate will usually come some form of agreement, and this points to flexibility rather than stubbornness as an essential ingredient in the historian's make-up. As Keynes is alleged to have said when challenged that his present views differed from those expressed some years ago: 'I revise my views in the light of new facts. What do you do?'

Much historical research is of course a gap filling exercise but, contrary to Johnson's assertion, this calls for imagination to make the necessary connections. Indeed it has been suggested that history is like literature, but that probably goes too far; history involves innovation and imagination but, unlike literature, generalisations must be consistent with the evidence for them to be an acceptable interpretation of history. The conclusions are, of course, more likely to be accurate if they are based on a full range of information relating to the topic or period under examination.

Uses of accounting history

Recreational. Pure enjoyment is a quite sufficient reason for studying accounting history. Many accountants dabble in accounting history with no serious intention of learning anything useful or making any written contribution. Nor do you have to be a trained accountant to tackle the subject successfully; a few gifted academics have been sufficiently fascinated by the subject to make major contributions despite the fact it is not their mainstream discipline. These have been attracted to accounting history because, in Yamey's words, he 'enjoyed doing it' (1983, p.8).

One does not have to delve very deeply in the archives to find amusing snippets such as Raymond Chandler's description of an (American) accountant in *The Lady in the Lake*:

> Grayson was a long stooped yellow-faced man with high shoulders, bristly eyebrows and almost no chin. The upper part of his face meant business. The lower part was just saying goodbye. He wore bifocals and he had been gnawing fretfully at the evening paper. I had looked him up in the city directory. He was a CPA [Certified Public Accountant] and looked it every inch. He even had ink on his fingers and there were four pencils in the pocket of his open vest (quoted in Newgarden, p.49).

In a similar vein we may be fascinated by the phrase 'king's eyes and ears', used to describe government auditors in the Persian empire of 500 BC, and find perplexing the quaint nineteenth-century audit custom of confirming obscure and uninformative accounting statements as 'certified and found correct'. More recently, in the 1920s, we encounter the common practice of including all fixed assets under an omnibus heading, and the occasional eccentricity where a single caption and value was given for the entire range of assets belonging to the company.

Intellectual. The study of accounting history helps us to understand our past and gives us an appreciation of how our current practices and problems came into being. For example, the source of the accountant's conservative approach to asset valuation is popularly identified with the late nineteenth-century business environment. Investment in a business, at that time, was an even more speculative activity than it is today; liquidations and bankruptcies were everyday features of business life, creditors were the main users of accounting reports and prices were falling. In these circumstances the development of the concept of conservatism was perfectly natural.

Explanations are, however, rarely straightforward. A series of events may appear unconnected and, only when they are examined in minute detail, does a pattern sometimes emerge. Even then, it may be possible to find only some hint of the reasons for particular changes. For example, we know that consolidated accounts were devised to provide an adequate method for reporting the results of a 'group' of companies. We do not know why the system took so much longer to obtain a foothold in Britain than in, say, the US, although possible influences were the lack of technical expertise, management opposition to their adoption, the 'laid back' attitude of the British accountant, the existence of percieved, if not real, legal barriers to change, the fact that consolidated accounts are of little use to creditors, and the undemanding nature of the investing public (see Chapter 18).

Even where there is a mass of information available, there is likely to be disagreement about how the facts are to be interpreted. Taking an example from economic history, the exact causes of as well known and well documented an event as the British Industrial Revolution are, today, as keenly debated as they have ever been. An example from accounting history is the continued disagreement concerning the exact origin of double entry, despite the fact that this topic has received more attention than any other.

Problem solving. Some argue that the study of accounting history provides insights for the solution of present-day accounting problems and helps predict future likely developments.

These are ambitious claims which must be treated with some caution, but we can probably agree that the subject has some contemporary relevance. For example, accounting history throws light on the origin of particular procedures and practices and, therefore, helps us understand possible limitations on their present and future application, e.g. the weakness of the balance sheet as a measure of value becomes much more easy to understand when we realise that the system of double entry record keeping, on which it is based, was initially devised, not to facilitate the preparation of final accounts, but to enable business transactions to be recorded in an orderly and accurate manner, and to keep track of personal accounts and simple physical objects such as cash. As Baxter has put it:

> He [the accounting historian] will not be surprised if accounting seems to falter when called on to perform new and different tasks – such as predicting future income, and aiding investors to make decisions. If we have such ambitions for accounting, may we not be like a farmer who demands that his faithful old cart-horse learn the violin? (p.5)

Historical enquiry also tells us that certain problems are enduring and may not be capable of a permanent solution, e.g. accounting for intangibles, uncertainty and changing price levels. The lesson would seem to be for us not to become over-anxious if the search for a definitive answer proves unfruitful; in many cases all we can do is devise procedures which work reasonably well in the present circumstances, i.e. we need to learn how to live with our problems, while not giving up the attempt to devise improved methods. Those who look for speedy solutions to what appear to be 'new' problems would find it illuminating to discover the quality and sophistication of the literature on such topics in much earlier times.

A further potential application for accounting history is that it may tell us that an apparently useful idea has been tried in some earlier generation and found wanting. According to the philosopher Santayana, 'those who do not remember their past are condemned to re-live it' (quoted in Baladouni, p.54). But circumstances change, and these need to be examined very carefully before parallels are drawn.

One obstacle in the way of progress is the difficulty of discarding outdated archaic shackles of the past. Historical inquiry can help us to question some of our time-honoured concepts and ideas which, although perhaps quite effective for another age, or another type of economic society, are ill-suited to today's social and economic conditions. For example, the historical cost concept was entirely appropriate when accounting statements were mainly used to keep track of rights and obligations, but the concept's continued application has naturally been called into question now that accounting statements are used as the basis for performance assessment and resource allocation decisions. Demands for fundamental change have of course been made, but these have been successfully resisted by individuals and institutions with a vested interest in maintaining a system with which they are well acquainted (see Chapter 19).

Accounting history as a basis for making predictions is even more problematic. Some very general forecasts, e.g. that the level of corporate disclosure and the number of practising accountants will continue to increase, can be made with a fair degree of confidence, but it is risky to be more specific. The historian E.H. Carr sounds the following cautionary note:

> The historian . . . is bound to generalize; and, in doing so, he provides general guides for future action which though not specific prediction, are both valid and useful. But he cannot predict specific events, because the specific is unique and because the element of accident enters into it (Carr, p.63).

At the same time accountants have used their knowledge of history to forecast accurately future events, see for example Mumford's study of 'A Familiar Inflation Accounting Cycle', which drew close parallels between events in 1948–54 and 1973–78, and led him to the correct conclusion that interest in reform would dwindle with the rate of inflation.

Review

The contribution that accounting history can make to problem solving is a matter for debate. The examination of past events, however, enables us to appreciate the complexity and persistence of many of the problems presently facing accountants. It should therefore help to guard against hasty judgements and the premature adoption of apparently simple solutions. The intellectual value of the subject cannot be seriously challenged. Its recreational value is a matter of personal taste, and for every enthusiast there is at least one who finds it deadly boring. I imagine I am dealing with the converted.

2

Economic Progress and Accounting Change

Need for accountability

In every organised society some goods are held by an individual or a group of individuals on behalf of someone else. Such goods may be held merely for safekeeping, e.g. jewellry deposited with a bank, or it may be the intention that the goods should be used to earn a return for the owner. In Britain today the separation of the ownership and custody of goods occurs in numerous circumstances. Boards of directors have cash entrusted to them by shareholders, while trustees have possession of money placed under their care by, perhaps, a parent for the benefit of an infant child. In the case of thousands of clubs and societies, a committee is appointed to use subscriptions and other funds collected for the benefit of the members. Local and central governments have control over resources collected from members of the community, though the citizens have only a limited say about how much is transferred. Local government's main source of fiscal revenue is rates (to be replaced in England and Wales by the community charge in 1990), while central government benefits from a wide range of taxes among which income tax, national insurance contributions and VAT are, financially, the most significant.

For simplicity we will call the person who owns the resources the 'principal', and the person who is given possession of these goods the 'agent'. The agent is normally expected to account to the principal for the resources in his possession, although the accounting function may be carried out by a third party. Accountability may also include an examination, called an audit, to check the accuracy of the information provided by the agent for the principal. A reason for the growing importance of the accounting function is that the proportion of the gross national product entrusted to agents is continuously increasing.

In earlier, less literate, times, when 'records' were substantially in a non-written form, accountability involved no more than the agent providing an *oral* account of the disposition of resources entrusted to him. This account was listened to (hence the term auditor from the latin *audire*) by individuals sufficiently familiar with the transactions to assess the accuracy of statements made. In the case of tax collected from a local community, members of the public sometimes assembled to hear the list read out by the collecting agent. Today the process is more sophisticated but the essential aim is the same; to ensure an accurate report is made.

Legal regulation of the accounting and audit process is designed to protect the weak principal (e.g. the ratepayer) against the stronger agent (e.g. the city council). The need for protection is a fairly modern development; in earlier times the appointment of a particular individual as agent was often motivated by the degree of control enjoyed by the principal. For example, the use of slaves as record keepers was favoured, in ancient Greece, because their statements, extracted under torture, were judged to be more reliable than those of a free man obtained under oath (Stone, p.287). In medieval times the lord of the manor was no doubt reassured by the knowledge that the reporting agent (called the 'reeve'), who was fraudulent or failed to prepare an account, would be tried in the manorial court.

The relative strength of the principal and agent changed in the nineteenth century with the separation of management from ownership and the growth, in power, of the board of directors. The government initially considered these business 'partners' to possess equal negotiating powers and regulations were kept to an absolute minimum. The twentieth century has seen the end of the *laissez-faire* philosophy and, instead, the development of legal regulations in an attempt to ensure that absentee shareholders are not exploited by a powerful board of directors.

Stages in accounting development

The development of accounting can be conveniently divided, for our purposes, into four periods: the pre-capitalist period, 4000 BC–1000 AD; commercial capitalism, 1000–1760; industrial capitalism, 1760–1830; and financial capitalism, 1830 to date.[1]

Pre-capitalist period, 4000 BC–1000 AD. This period began with the Mesopotamian civilisation and lasted through Greek and Roman times to the end of the 'dark ages'. The need for record keeping initially stemmed, as far as we know, from the extensive trade which grew up within and outside the very fertile Mesopotamian valley. The records quite naturally assumed a form appropriate to an illiterate community, with changes made as society became more sophisticated. One primitive form of record was the knotted cord (see Chapter 3); subsequent improvements included inscriptions on clay tablets, writing on papyrus and paper and, in the period of financial capitalism, typescript generated by typewriters and computer printers. Records were initially expressed in terms of physical quantities; later in financial terms. Their purpose, during the pre-capitalist period, was to keep track of goods and cash, with the occasional attempt made to produce a rudimentary form of profit calculation.

A feature of the pre-capitalist period was that wealth tended to accrue to those who held political, religious or military power or status. It has been called the non-economic period. A vast number of accounts survive from Greek and Roman times and these are mainly stewardship records of such thing as expenditure on public works by the Government, lists of cattle and goods on landed estates, army pay sheets and so on. An interesting Greek custom was for builders to chisel receipts and expenditure on public buildings which they constructed. One such tablet shows that the Parthenon cost 469 talents of silver.

Commercial capitalism, 1000–1750. The essence of commercial capitalism, also called mercantile capitalism, is that money was invested in stock-in-trade and, when sold for cash, the proceeds were used to acquire more stock. More complex, and less common, forms of business operation involved the transformation of raw materials into finished goods and/or the sale of goods on credit. During the period of commercial capital little was invested in what may be broadly described as fixed assets or productive equipment, except perhaps in the shipping and mining industries. The investment was essentially short term – hence the description 'circulating capital'.

The development of Mediterranean commerce during and after the crusades, which lasted from the eleventh to the thirteenth century, signalled the advent of commercial capitalism. Genoa and Venice established themselves as the main intermediaries in trade relations between Europe and the Near East, and the result was a three-hundred-year commercial revolution which foreshadowed the Industrial Revolution of the eighteenth century. The Italians remained the leading merchants and bankers throughout the middle ages (Chatfield, p.33).

In Britain, a new social and economic order began to take shape between 1000–1300 (sometimes referred to as the period of nascent capitalism), with the appearance of itinerant merchants, trade fairs and towns. Merchants and artisans gradually settled and organised themselves into guilds, which were useful not only for business but also for social and political purposes. This gave rise to a new class in society, the bourgeoisie or middle class. Beginning with the fourteenth century we see fully-fledged commercial capitalism in certain parts of Europe, associated with geographical discoveries, colonisation, and a huge increase in overseas trade. Capitalists protected by Government controls, subsidies and monopolies made profits chiefly from the transportation of goods.

This rapidly changing environment created new bookkeeping needs. The rudimentary record keeping systems in use in the eleventh century were based on single entry. Very occasionally they were used to prepare the charge and discharge based stewardship report (see Chapter 4), which had either survived from Roman times or was re-invented at this stage. These methods, which worked well in small businesses, broke down when trading activity became more dynamic and the number of transactions increased at a rate of geometric progression. Indeed, it has been argued that unsystematic records limited the size of a business because, beyond a certain point of growth, increasing disorder caused owners to lose control of distant operations. Accounting innovation resulted in the creation of double entry bookkeeping, which dates from about 1300 and was popularised by Pacioli's *Summa* published in 1494 (see Chapter 5).

The specific advantages of the double entry method were the greater care and correctness it demanded from clerical staff; the increased difficulty of falsifying the books to conceal fraud or theft, particularly where duties were divided among a number of personnel; and the arithmetic check provided by periodically balancing the books and extracting a trial balance. Little use was made of double entry as the basis for preparing financial statements, and surviving examples of profit calculations are few and far between. In Britain, the use of double entry became more widespread with the growth of trade during the seventeenth century (see Chapter 6).

Industrial capitalism, 1760–1830. The Industrial Revolution occurred at different times in different countries but, in Britain, it is conventionally assigned to the period 1760–1830. This revolution was the child of the early eighteenth century – Abraham Derby established his famous works at Coalbrookdale, Shropshire, in 1709, where he pioneered the production of high quality iron ore with considerable new potential for industrial use. But it was the discovery of new energy sources in the second half of the nineteenth century, the use of machines in manufacturing, and the development of the factory system which marked the emergence of industrial capitalism.

Other factors which facilitated industrialisation were the abundance of labour, caused by lower infant mortality and the enclosure acts which freed labour from the fields, and cheap capital available in large quantities. Textiles were first to industrialise, followed by pottery making, mining, iron making and transportation. The eventual outcome was that the manufacturing process rather than land became the chief source of income.

The new industrialists had, in broad terms, two accounting systems to choose from – single entry (including charge and discharge accounting) and double entry. The latter was the eventual winner, partly because it proved better for control purposes, and partly because it facilitated the preparation of final accounts which could be used as the basis for performance assessment and resource allocation decisions. The rate of change was initially slow, however, and single entry remained dominant in England until 1800. As interest in performance assessment increased, after that date, the rate of transition accelerated (see Chapter 8)

Financial capitalism, 1830 to date. Fixed capital was relatively unimportant in financing the Industrial Revolution, and the initial pressure for capital, on a large scale, stemmed from the needs of the public utilities. The Liverpool and Manchester Railway was opened in 1830, and the direct result of its technical and financial success was the promotion and building of railways in the 1830s and 1840s. The significance of the railways for the development of the formal capital market is demonstrated by the fact that the London Stock Exchange, which had previously dealt principally in government stocks, began to shift its emphasis towards company securities in the mid-1830s.

A substantial amount of money was required to finance railway building and, unlike most other industrial developments occurring both earlier and elsewhere at this time, it was not possible to commence activity on a small scale and then expand on the basis of retained profits. A workable section of the line needed to be laid and rolling stock acquired before traffic could commence. Financial data was therefore required, on an unprecedented scale, to help ensure that the planned project was soundly conceived, to monitor costs during the construction stage, and to report results when the line became operational. These developments gave particular emphasis to a wide range of accounting problems, including the following: the separation of capital expenditure from revenue expenditure; the valuation of fixed assets; the calculation of periodic profit; and the appropriate form and content of financial statements published for absentee owners.

Business developments occurred more slowly elsewhere in the economy. Many mechanical inventions of the eighteenth century did not come into widespread use until the move into the factories gained pace in the nineteenth century. A big impetus for industrialisation was the development of new sources of power; steam power based on coal, gas, and electricity. A new surge of technological progress in the third quarter of the nineteenth century, e.g. the invention of the Bessemer process (1856) increased capital requirements and led to the rapid growth of the large scale limited liability company as a means of raising sums of money beyond the amount which businessmen themselves could provide. The kinds of accounting problems which resulted from railway development in the 1830s and 1840s gradually became more broadly based. The development of the accountancy profession was, in part, a natural and spontaneous response to the strong demand for financial expertise.

A feature of the period of financial capitalism has been a change in government attitude towards the regulation of business activity. In line with the ideas put forward by Adam Smith in his *Wealth of Nations,* State intervention was kept to a minimum during the nineteenth century and business affairs were usually the subject of voluntary agreement between contracting parties. Financial reporting procedures therefore developed in a substantially unregulated economy and this meant that management was free to choose the methods which it considered most suitable.[2] Legal intervention of course occurred when a dispute came before the courts but, even then, the inclination was to interfere as little as possible. Since 1900 we have seen, by way of contrast, a considerable growth in the amount of legal regulation, with succesive Companies Acts adding to the accounting and audit obligations imposed on directors. More recent events, such as computerisation and rapid inflation, have given rise to new problems for accountancy and the accountant to cope with.

Continuity, stagnation and change

The prologue to L.P.Hartley's *The Go-Between* asserts that 'the past is a foreign country: they do things differently there'. While this is undoubtedly true, it is also true that the thorough investigation of a particular topic, in history, usually reveals a sequence of inter-related events.

A study of history shows accounting to be both adaptive and persistent. It is adaptive in the sense that it is able to change, and it is persistent because it does not change without cause. The phrase 'continuity and change' has been coined to describe accounting development, and it does the job well. Change has of course occurred at different rates at different times and in different places. This is because accounting has developed in response to business needs, which have themselves not proceeded at a uniform rate. A good example of massive variation in the rate of accounting progress, between one place and another, is the fact that non-written accounting records, extant in Mesopotamia around 5000 BC, were used by the Ashanti kingdom of West Africa as recently as the eighteenth century (Yamey, p.127).

In broader terms, accounting history has been marked by a few periods when fairly rapid progress has been made, followed by periods of relative stagnation. But during these quieter times refinements have usually been made to earlier innovations which have also received more widespread application.

The more advanced accounting systems of the Romans – some believe them to have contained elements of double entry[3] – were needed to control a wealthy and far-flung empire, but this was followed by a long period during which there is little evidence of records having been kept and no evidence of accounting innovations having been made. Indeed, methods in use in feudal times were often no more sophisticated than those used by the Romans more than a thousand years earlier. A further highlight of accounting change occurred in the thirteenth century when, under pressure from rapidly growing trade, Italian merchants expanded single entry record keeping into double entry.

The period 1400 to 1800, by way of contrast, was one of relative stagnation. The system of double entry bookkeeping was adequate to meet business needs for many hundreds of years. The major accounting development during this period was the spread of the 'Italian' system to other countries. Progress was slow in Britain. For example, Richard Grassby, an historian who studied a large number of merchants' records, has reported that 'genuine double-entry book-keeping was extremely rare in practice' in the seventeenth century (p.748).

Not only was double entry slow to develop in areas where it could probably have fulfilled a useful function, it was also used in circumstances where there was no demonstrable economic need. For example, in the Italian City States where double entry first flourished, its use was extended to the keeping of family domestic accounts where it remained in operation despite fluctuations in family fortunes which caused immense reductions in the volume of resources controlled (Hoskin and Macve, p.122). It may well be that non-financial benefits were associated with the maintenance of a system of double entry – perhaps it was a status signal. Inertia was another causal factor, and the continued preparation of irrelevant accounting data is just as common today, e.g. the report which is despatched to the 'right-hand drawer'.

The most recent accounting 'leap forward' began to take place in the second half of the nineteenth century, in response to the growth of the modern business enterprise and the separation of ownership from management. We have seen, since then, a change in emphasis from record keeping to financial reporting and, as regards the function of those reports, from using them as a means of assessing stewardship (i.e. to check whether resources entrusted to an agent can be properly accounted for and have been effectively employed) to their use as the basis for resource allocation decisions.

Even so there has been criticism that change has been too slow or not gone far enough. It is perhaps because the procedures have been adopted slowly that they are not easily discarded. The result is that outmoded ideas often continue in use long after the effects they produce become detrimental rather than beneficial. Reluctance to change is understandable as a degree of inconvenience naturally results. The criticism directed at the British accountancy profession, however, is that it has failed to introduce improved procedures when the need for change was clear and obvious. For example, the profession took action neither to encourage companies to publish group accounts in the 1920s nor, at about the same time, to discourage companies from using secret reserves to conceal their true financial position from shareholders. Indeed the submission made to the Greene Committee (1926), by the Institute of Chartered Accountants in England and Wales (ICAEW), displayed strong approval for the maintenance of secret reserves (see Chapter 16).

A criticism of financial reporting procedures, which still applies today, is that methods initially devised simply as a check on honesty have undergone such little change. The essential problem is their excessive emphasis on past financial developments which are unlikely to recur in a rapidly changing environment and are therefore of limited interest. The information is, of course, relevant from the point of view of assessing financial probity and, to some extent, past performance, but it is an unreliable guide to future performance and, therefore, investment decision making.

Up to the Second World War accounting progressed in response to forces internal to firms; it was an evolutionary process. Numerous individuals, determined to improve accounting practices to meet new needs, made many minor experiments. Where the experiment was unsuccessful it was abandoned and forgotten; if it was a success it was retained and copied by other firms. In a sense it was a matter of the survival of the fittest. The best practices resulted in firms prospering, whereas those employing poor practices were driven to the wall. As Baxter put it 'Accounting has thus grown by small steps and is the creation of countless anonymous innovators' (1981, p.6). Littleton is the best known exponent of this view of accounting change and 'Accounting Darwinism' is the term which has been coined to describe the essence of his ideas.

The success of the unregulated evolutionary process is a matter of some debate. What is certain is that the position is quite different today. Because of various scandals, the involvement of regulatory bodies such as the government, the stock exchange and the accountancy profession has increased significantly during the last 50 years, and the process is accelerating. The result has been, perhaps, a movement away from evolution and towards something a little closer to a revolution of accounting practices, characterised by the issue of a whole stream of regulations which must be obeyed.

This has produced criticisms and doubts of another sort. For example, in some cases the regulations appear to be more in the nature of the 'flavour of the month' than a well-thumbed rule which has achieved widespread acceptance on a voluntary basis. A further contemporary problem, stemming from increased statutory prescription, is the growing conflict between accountants, keen to report the substance of business transactions, and businessmen, egged on by their legal advisers, who are determined to confine attention to each transaction's precise legal form. It may be that we are seeing a revival of the power struggle, first fought in the nineteenth century, for the principal position as business advisers.

Accountancy and economic growth

The previous section shows that accounting processes are reactive, in that they develop in response to business needs. This section demonstrates that the widespread use of particular procedures may, in turn, influence economic development, either by helping or hindering. For example, it is thought that the dominant position achieved by Italian merchants in the early centuries of the present millennium resulted partly from superior business organisation, of which double entry bookkeeping was an important feature. In a similar vein Walter Eucken argued that the 'knowledge of double entry bookkeeping was a precondition for the South German expansion of the beginning of the sixteenth century. Where this knowledge was lacking or slow to penetrate, as in the Hanser towns, economic development was delayed' (quoted in Chatfield, p.61).

Max Weber (sociologist), Joseph Schumpeter (economist) and Werner Sombart (historian) are leading academics who have argued that the facility which double entry provided for the identification of capital and profit may have been a *causal* factor in economic development. An alternative, more modest, claim for double entry is that, by providing a more orderly and comprehensive scheme for recording business transactions and imposing financial control, it improved financial organisation and facilitated business development. The debate about the way in which and the extent to which the adoption of double entry techniques fuelled the growth of capitalism is examined in Chapter 6.

Accountancy was devised and developed as an aid to business and it is therefore natural that the use of more sophisticated procedures should speed up the rate of economic development. What also happens, from time to time, is the use or manipulation of accounting statements with the intention of influencing business decisions and economic consequences. For example, May has argued that the omission of a charge for depreciation when preparing the accounts of nineteenth-century railway companies enabled profits to be reported and dividends to be declared. In his view,

> it is incontestible that the effect of the application of such depreciation accounting would have been that the construction of a large part of our railway mileage would at least have been greatly delayed – if, indeed, some part would ever have been constructed at all (p.174).

Brief (1965) has drawn attention to the need to recognise, and distinguish between, the possibility of either persistent error or bias in the preparation of financial statements. Accounting error may be the result of ignorance concerning the appropriate accounting treatment of a particular item or simply a mistake made when writing up the books; it might increase or decrease reported profit, and the effect sometimes cancels out. Bias, on the other hand, is the intentional under or overstatement of profit. Both error and bias were common features of nineteenth-century financial reporting procedures but, in Brief's view, the net effect was that fixed asset costs were consistently understated, profitability overestimated, and business expectations overstimulated (1976, p.2). Like May he believes that investment was encouraged and nineteenth-century economic development accelerated by the accounting conventions adopted (p.189).

The possibility of accounting error has declined over the years as the result of improvements in accounting procedures. At the same time, the likelihood of systematic bias has probably increased with the greater use of published statements as a means of communicating business facts to the outside world. We know, for example, that in the period 1900 to 1920 British companies often prepared and published financial statements which understated the financial strength of the concern: it was the secret reserves era. As a result management was able to avoid possible demands for larger dividend and wage increases, and undertake business investment without reference to the investing public. In the immediate post-war years, industrial reorganisation was needed to adjust to a peace-time economy and cope effectively with the changing pattern of world trade. Not all company directors agreed with the need for change and the 1920s saw secret reserves used to help conceal declining profitability within the basic industries such as shipbuilding and iron and steel.

There is no doubt that managers sometimes encouraged the publication of misleading financial reports in the hope and expectation that fortunes would improve. This sometimes happened and, in such circumstances, it is possible to argue that the means justified the end. Problems arose where management employed optimistic reporting procedures, and retained the confidence of creditors and shareholders, when the downward trend was irreversible. In such cases the reorganisation of business processes along more modern lines and the transfer of resources from the old declining industries to the new expanding industries was delayed with damaging economic consequences.

PART II

FROM ANCIENT TIMES TO THE INDUSTRIAL REVOLUTION

3

Early Record Keeping

Accounting without money

Today accounting records are typically expressed in cash terms with a succinct caption used to describe the significance of each financial total. By way of contrast, the earliest surviving accounting records ante-date not only money but also the written word.[1]

The first great civilisations of man emerged almost simultaneously in Mesopotamia, Babylon and Egypt. These produced what may have been the first organised governments in the world, several of the most ancient written languages, and the oldest surviving business records. The earliest examples of primitive accounting records, which are believed to date from about 5000 BC, have been found in prehistoric tombs. These 'records' take the form of graphic symbols on such items as shards, vases and stones. They indicate goods, quantities and other business data. In Mesopotamia, in the middle of the fourth millennium BC, a drawing, often of an animal, was repeated to signify a quantity; similarly a Babylonian frieze of water birds had feet omitted or necks extended to indicate some kind of numerical significance. The sequence of events in the evolutionary process seems to have been from pictures to symbols to letters and, finally, to writing.

The name Mesopotamia is Greek and means the land between two rivers, the Tygris and Euphrates. The country covered the Northern half of modern Iraq; Babylonia covered the southern half and was split between Akkad in the North and Sumer in the South. Mesopotamia is a particularly rich source of explanatory material concerning the nature and purpose of early accounting records. The landscape outside Baghdad is today dotted with about 10,000 mounds or 'tells', only a few of which have so far been excavated.

Nevertheless these few have yielded an enormous collection of historical records (Garbutt, 1984, p.84).

The Mesopotamians and Babylonians were obsessive book-keepers (Garbutt, 1981, p.11) and, because they maintained their records in the extremly durable form of stone and clay tablets, a large quantity have survived. In sheer volume the records are unrivalled, and they extend over a period of 3000 years, from approximately 2400 BC to 700 AD. Indeed far more material has already been unearthed than has survived from all Egypt prior to the Persian era (sixth century BC). For this reason it has been suggested that, when the collection is fully examined, we may know a community from the middle of the second millennium BC better than we know most European capitals at the time of Columbus (Garbutt, 1984, p.87).

Early record keeping mainly developed to meet government and business needs, but there were sometimes legal requirements to be satisfied. The code of Hammurabi, named after the King of the first dynasty of Babylonia (2285–2242 BC), required an agent, selling goods for a merchant, to give his principal a sealed memorandum quoting prices. Otherwise the contract, if contested, was unenforceable. It was also common practice for even the smallest business transaction to be put into writing and signed by the contracting parties and witnesses. There existed the office of public scribe (the accountant of the ancient world) who did the written work and ensured compliance with legal requirements.

Chatfield describes the accounting process appropriate to a substantially illiterate community as follows.

> Using as pencil a wooden rod with a blunt, triangular end, the scribe recorded the agreement on a small lump of moist clay . . . The inconvenience of mass illiteracy was circumvented by having each man carry his signature around his neck in the form of a stone amulet engraved with its owner's mark (and buried with him when he died). Each party to the transaction, and the witnesses, affixed their signatures by impressing these seals into the clay tablet . . . The more important commercial tablets were kiln-dried; the rest were allowed to dry in sunlight (p.5).

To prevent forgery, the tablet was sometimes wrapped in an additional layer of clay to act as an envelope. The seals of the contracting parties were impressed on this envelope.

Evidence of government accounting also survives from ancient Babylonia. Taxes were normally paid 'in kind' and the assets were sold to raise finance for the government. The scribes again used clay tablets to record the types and quantities of goods as they arrived; they also supervised their use, accumulation or sale. Periodically accounting reports were prepared. These consisted of inventories of assets on hand, and charge and discharge-type summaries of commodities received and disbursed.

Charge and discharge statements[2] are stewardship reports which start with the opening balance owed by the agent to the principal. In a pre-cash economy the balance of goods on hand was described in physical terms; in a money economy the balance of cash and/or goods could be expressed in financial terms. A mixture of procedures, with goods reported in physical terms and cash in financial terms, was also common. To the opening balance was added any amounts received from the principal and collected on his behalf. This represented the total indebtedness of the agent to the principal. The agent's obligation was partly discharged by transfers to the principal and by making payments on his behalf. The undischarged balance of cash and/or goods, sometimes the subject of an audit, was carried forward to the next period.

A similar system of government accounting operated in Egypt at the time of the Pharaohs, where the introduction of papyrus made records less cumbersome. (Papyrus was made from a reed abundantly available in the Nile Delta, and the earliest surviving example is 2390 BC). The advanced system of stores accounting ('payments' into and out of the treasury involved transfers of a vast range of goods because a uniform medium of exchange had not yet been developed), in operation during the second millennium BC, has been described by Stone:

> Scribes prepared records of receipts and disbursements of silver, corn and other commodities. One recorded on papyrus the amount brought to the warehouse and another checked the emptying of the containers on the roof as it was poured into the storage building. Audit was performed by a third scribe who compared these two records. An official order was required for withdrawals and the scribe in charge of the storehouse recorded the disbursements and retained the order. His records of receipts, disbursements, and inventory balances were periodically audited by another scribe or his superior (p.285).

In ancient Egypt, probably also Babylonia and Crete (the heyday of the last named occurred in the middle of the second millennium BC) 'the profession of scribe was one of great dignity and importance, and the highest offices in the land were open to him' (Woolf, p.7). But it was also important for the bookkeeper to do his work efficiently; accounts were audited by the storehouse superintendents and gross irregularities were punished by mutilation or death.

The accounting records were extremely detailed but never sophisticated judged by modern standards; a major constraint on their development was the lack of coined money. Bookkeepers were therefore unable to express goods in terms of a single substance, making accumulation and summation very difficult.

A later, fascinating, example of a non-written accounting record is the 'quipu' or knotted cord used, at various times, in Peru, China and Hawaii. This record consisted of a main cord to which were attached knotted pendant cords. Knots on these subsidiary strings recorded, for example, the number of people in a village or the quantity of materials in a storehouse. The values of the knots differed depending upon their distance from the main cord; knots at the very end of the subsidiary cord being equivalent to a unit of one. Sometimes different coloured cords were used to indicate different types of items being counted. These counting devices were clearly quite sophisticated, and further knotted strings might be added to the subsidiary cord to provide additional supplementary information. For example, a subsidiary cord might give the number of women living in a village and an attached piece of string the number that were unmarried. In Peru the record keepers were called 'quipuamayus' and there were usually more than one to produce a system of at least double check (Keister, p.415).

The earliest example, presently available, comes from Hawaii and is dated approximately the eighth century AD. Tax gatherers, though they could neither read nor write, kept exact accounts of all kinds of articles collected from the inhabitants throughout the island. The line of cordage used was four to five hundred fathoms in length (a fathom is 6 foot). It was divided into numerous portions corresponding to the various districts in the island, and amounts and quantities were indicated with the aid of loops, knots and tufts of different shapes, colours and sizes. In China use of the knotted cord dates back to ancient times. We know this because Confucius (551–489 BC) refers to these cords being used by 'men of antiquity'.

Clearly these embryonic accounting records were totally different in both form and content from their modern-day equivalent; indeed it is probably more precise to describe the process as counting rather than accounting. However, an important feature of early records, whatever form they took, was that they served two functions which are still central to the accounting process today: they fulfilled a 'reminder' function by providing individuals with a record of their rights and obligations and of assets remaining; also they enabled the principal to exercise a degree of supervision and control over the agent.

Accounting in classical times

Ancient record keeping was based on physical movement of goods. Expressing the transactions in financial terms became possible only when coined money was invented. This seems to have occurred in Lydia (the ancient kingdom of West Asia Minor) in 700 BC. The use of coinage spread to other Mediterranean countries and enabled the development of accounting in its true sense in classical Greece.

During the classical period, which lasted from approximately the fifth century BC until the fourth century AD, the main writing surface was initially papyrus, but it began to be replaced by parchment made from the skins of animals in the second century BC. The papyrus rolls, made by sticking together single sheets, 9–13 inches in height and 5–10 inches in width, were sometimes as long as 40 foot. The practice of fastening sheets of papyrus together, in the form of a book or *codex*, began in the second century AD. For accounts purposes, wooden tablets were often used instead of papyrus. The wood was either whitened to receive ink from a pen or, more usually, covered with wax on which writing could be scratched with a stylus. The data might subsequently be obliterated to enable repeated use of the tablet (de Ste. Croix, p.69). A substantial step forward occurred in the last century BC when the Romans began to use, for accounting purposes, a *codex* made from leaves of parchment.

The use of coins spread slowly in the Greek world and its impact on accounting was therefore gradual. Most business tended to be done in person and settled on the spot; the ordinary Greek found little need for bookkeeping beyond a record of debts owing and owed. Banking, on the other hand, was more highly developed in Greece than in any earlier society. All bankers kept account books which sometimes had to be produced as evidence in court. Functions undertaken included changing and lending money, accepting deposits, acting as intermediaries and trustees, and arranging cash transfers for clients through correspondents in distant cities. Detailed financial records were needed to keep track of these transactions.

The numerous inscribed rolls of the Zenon papyri comprise by far the largest body of surviving accounts from the classical period. In 256 BC Zenon became manager of the great private estate of Apollonius, chief finance minister of Ptolemy II, ruler of Egypt. According to Hain (p.700),

> [Zenon] introduced a clearly defined structure of responsibility accounting. Each section of the estate – the farms, vineyards, herds of livestock, grain stores, household units, and administrative offices – was managed by a supervisor who had to render account daily or at frequent intervals . . . Written documents were prepared for every transaction . . . Items of a similar nature were summarized in paragraphs and only the totals extended.

The essential aim of these records was the protection of property through the control of people. Zenon achieved this by recording and auditing receipts and expenditures in minute detail, 'literally down to the price of used nails' (Chatfield, p.11).

An impetus for the development of record keeping, in Roman times, was the legal requirment for taxpayers to prepare statements of all their property and outstanding debts. The fact that a citizen's rights depended to some extent on the amount of property he declared provided an incentive for those who were well off to maintain detailed household records. The initial entry of transactions was made in an *adversaria* or memorandum book, from which postings were made to the main account book, called the *tabulae*. It seems that this book may have been split into sections, with a *codex accepti et expensi* (a kind of cash book) used to record receipts and payments. Other sections contained accounts with individuals and schedules of property. The banks also maintained books in this form, and, additionally, a *liber rationum* or personal ledger, where data from the memorandum were classified.

The Roman system of accounts contained certain features, in particular the bi-lateral form of account, which have caused scholars to speculate whether a rudimentary system of double entry bookkeeping was in operation. The conclusion that this was not so (see Chapter 5) is based on a detailed analysis of available evidence, and the perceived absence of strong pressure to develop sophisticated double entry procedures. Single entry record keeping was quite adequate to cope with the relatively small number of transactions that had to be processed in order to keep track of goods and to enable the preparation of charge and discharge statements.

Government accounting was again prominent in Roman times. To help control the extensive Empire, quaestors were appointed to carry out a function equivalent to the 'King's eyes and ears' of the Persian Empire. They date from about 200 BC and were required to report periodically to Rome and have their records heard by an examiner. These accounts were not always entirely satisfactory. Cicero described a report received in 84 BC as 'an extraordinary document. It gives no details at all, but simply says, I received 2,235,417 sesterces. I spent on army pay, corn, the legates, the proquaestor and the praetorian cohort, 1,635,417 sesterces. I left at Arminum 600,000 sesterces' (de Ste. Croix, p.45).

The system was, however, in many respects highly developed; the duties of collecting revenue, authorising expenditures, looking after cash, and recording financial transactions were separated. Expenditure could only be authorised on the production of evidence that goods had been received or services supplied. Proquaestors supervised and audited all the government financial transactions.

There is no evidence that accounting records were used, extensively, as the basis for business decision in classical times. Indeed, the form which the records took ensured that they were unsuitable for this purpose. Notable features were the presentation of data as a continuous narrative, and the total absence of summarisation and presentation in, say, a columnar format. There remains, of course, the strong possibility that these records were sometimes used to prepare rudimentary accounting statements on which action was based. The lack of evidence, pointing in this direction, however, has produced the fairly firm conclusion that little use was made of the records, *even indirectly*, as the basis for performance assessment and resource allocation decisions. Their function was to maximise asset protection rather than asset utilisation.

Review

This chapter has given a brief sketch of accounting developments up to and including Roman times. The available material is patchy and detailed claims concerning the contributions of particular civilisations and the date at which a particular practice was first employed are impossible to substantiate and have been avoided. Some accounting historians have been less cautious, prompting one critic to conclude that they concentrate on this period simply because it enables them to exercise their imagination to the fullest without fear of contradiction (Stevelinck, p.7).

In the fifth and fourth millennium BC, records were kept without the aid of writing in certain advanced civilisations. Up to about 600 BC records were based on physical quantities, and their purpose was to keep track of property belonging to the principal. The system of record keeping used in Babylonia and, later, Egypt is best described as a kind of stores accounting. The use of such procedures was made possible, in each of these countries, because promising young people were thoroughly educated in order to achieve the skills required to function as a scribe.

Financial record keeping developing during the Greek and Roman period, and quite sophisticated accounting and audit procedures were in operation by the middle of the fifth century BC. However, the basic purpose remained unchanged. There was little interest in performance assessment; the principal's main interest was the protection of resources entrusted to the agent, and the charge and discharge report was perfectly adequate for that purpose. It should be noted that the accounts and audit procedures discussed in this chapter relate mainly to the affairs of government. There is little surviving evidence of the accounting regulation of private ventures; a famous exception being the Zenon papers.

The Roman Empire fell, in the West, in the fifth century AD when much of Europe was 'overrun by hordes of [Germanic] barbarians, who swept down from the North' (Woolf, p.53). For the next 500 years, Western civilisation was temporarily at a standstill and accounting suffered along with other skills during a period, known as the dark ages, when the economy and government lacked organisation. At the same time, there were exceptions to this general state of affairs. In the sixth century, for example, the properties and revenues of the Roman Church, with its vast domains, were enormous. Sources of income included taxation, fees arising from legal proceedings in the ecclesiastical courts, and the proceeds from farming church lands. The central Papal treasury in Rome was elaborately organised to record these revenues and also payments out of the public treasury for troops, alms to the poor and donations to the clergy. Also of considerable interest is the accounting system of Charlemagne, leader of the Holy Roman Empire, up to his death in 825 AD. In 812 he issued instructions for an annual survey of the Royal Estates, for the maintenance of books of accounts and for the employment of overseers to ensure 'that the King's estates were cultivated to the best advantage and the produce properly utilised' (Woolf, p.61).

4

Charge and Discharge Accounting

Feudal society

Emperor Claudius I began the Roman conquest of Britain in 43 AD. After initial, strong, opposition, Britain settled down to become a model protectorate with a prosperous and thriving business community. When the army of occupation was withdrawn to help deal with threats nearer home, at the beginning of the fifth century AD, the indigenous population was left to the mercy of the invading Angles, Saxons and Jutes. This period was also marked by continuous internal conflict between petty kingdoms. The Saxon kings emerged from this chaos to achieve supremacy, with Egbert crowned king in 802 AD.

In pre-Norman Britain literacy was so unusual that a written system of accounts rarely justified the cost of its preparation. The fact that Alfred, who ruled between 871–99, learned to read and write marks him out as a person of exceptional ability. Also extraordinary is the fact that he arranged for the maintenance of accounting records and for a periodic inventory of his properties. A rudimentary form of record keeping also seems likely to have existed in monasteries where there was a higher level of literacy, but there is no significant evidence of accounts being written-up on any kind of systematic basis in Britain prior to 1100.

After invading England, William the Conqueror took title to all property in the name of the Crown. This enabled him to develop a feudal society consisting of a multi-layered pyramid, with individuals at each lower level guaranteed certain rights in exchange for certain duties. One quarter of Crown lands was kept for William's personal use; the rest was leased to earls and barons on stringent conditions which included the obligation to swear allegiance to the king and to provide military support in times of war. The earls and barons, in turn, distributed land surplus to requirements among knights, with the result that the country was split up into thousands of estates or 'manors'. Further down the pyramid was the villein, who received a parcel of land in exchange for free labour, and the serf who could not even allow his daughter to marry without his lord's permission. For the daughter to marry outside the manor was almost unknown because it depleted the actual and potential work force. The basic accounting problem, which resulted, was one of vertical communication between layers in the pyramid. The charge and discharge system, which had either survived from Roman times or was reinvented at this stage, was eminently suitable in these circumstances.

William recognised the importance of financial information as a basis for sound administration and, in 1086, he arranged a survey from which the Domesday Book was compiled. This book is today remembered mainly as a census, but it also served as a register of land values on which Crown assessments could be based (Chatfield, p.21). The importance of the Domesday Book stems from the fact that it is a rare example of a written record. Financial data was nearly always communicated and verified orally; written documents being merely supplementary to the more important spoken word. The essence of a contract was also the verbal agreement, perhaps because a written document, which could be forged, was considered less reliable than a verbal statement requiring the presence of witnesses to prove its authenticity.

According to Chatfield, the introduction of the abacus, to Britain, and other improvements in arithmetic technique, during the eleventh century, roughly coincided with the re-birth of interest in the written language. The primacy of the spoken word persisted, however, until the fourteenth century.

Features of the system

Charge and discharge accounting is a generic term which covers a range of accounting systems operated on the basis of single entry. More specific terms, which emphasise the subordinate's responsibility to the principal, are agency accounting and stewardship accounting; descriptions which focus on the accounting entity are estate accounting and manorial accounting. Common features of all these systems are that they are accounts of an individual rather than an organisation, they are addressed to a higher authority, they cover the flow of resources over a period of time, and they make no distinction between capital and revenue transactions.

From the principal's viewpoint the purpose of the account was to check the integrity and reliability of the agent, e.g. the treasurer reporting to the guild. From the agent's viewpoint the report served to prove his honesty. There was less interest in performance assessment because activities were repetitive and, usually, followed a fairly consistent seasonal pattern. The system of audit normally involved the charge and discharge statement being read out to the principal. This procedure was based on the following assumptions:

1. Those listening, e.g. members of the guild, broadly knew what receipts and payments were reasonable.
2. Knowledge that the audit would take place acted as a deterrent against fraud.

A further feature of the charge and discharge system was that the agent was obliged to make up any deficit out of his own pocket. A modern parallel is the responsibility of the district auditor to require councillors, or other defaulting officials, to reimburse public funds where a financial loss has been suffered because they have failed to discharge properly their duties. For example, in 1986 the district auditors surcharged the Lambeth councillors £126,947 and the Liverpool councillors £106,103 for loss of interest resulting from their delay in levying the rate for the financial year 1985/6.

The manor

Prior to about 1100 income from land mainly took the form of rent; the amounts were certain and there was little need for accounting records and reports. This changed with the development of demesne farming, whereby the landowner farmed the estate instead of renting it out. The actual job of managing the estate was delegated to a steward who was therefore entrusted with moveable, easily convertible, assets. This provided greater scope for the fraudulent conversion of assets, and the natural response was to develop the accounting function as a check on honesty.

The earliest evidence of systematic estate accounting in England dates from the twelfth century in the case of monastaries, and the thirteenth century in the case of the manor. The system continued in operation for several hundred years. The job of rendering the manorial account was primarily the duty of bailiff or reeve, who were responsible for the day-to-day running of the manor. In practice the account was often prepared by the steward, explaining the popularity of the term 'stewardship accounting' (Noke, p.137).

It is possible to distinguish three methods of presenting the charge and discharge statement.

1. Data presented as a continuous narrative, or in paragraph form, with appropriate references to quantities of goods and amounts of cash.
2. Separate lines for each category of receipt or payment, but figures not extended in columnar format.
3. Separate lines with figures in columns.

In the various sectors of society which used charge and discharge accounting, the presentation involved a gradual transition from method 1 to method 3. An advanced version of the statement approriate for a manor is presented in Figure 4.1.

Figure 4.1
Money Charge and Discharge Account

The Charge		£ s d
1.	Opening balance due to the lord of the manor	
2.	Cash and other property received from the lord	
3.	Rents receivable	
4.	Receipts from sales of produce and livestock	
5.	Receipts in the form of fines imposed by the courts and taxes	
6.	Total receipts	———
The Discharge		
1.	Payment of cash and other property to the lord	
2.	Expenses associated with running the manor	
3.	Expenses unconnected with running the manor, e.g. entertainment of the lord or his officials (called foreign expenses)	
4.	Total payments	———
5.	Closing balance due to the lord of the manor	———

Note. The narrative was often at least partly in Latin, and Roman numerals were used until superceded by the Arabic notation. In Britain this occurred in about the sixteenth century.

The charge and discharge account was usually drawn up entirely on the cash basis. Where the accruals concept was applied, it was to revenues rather than expenditures. Common adjustments were for rents receivable and credit sales uncollected at the accounting date. This resulted in a closing balance which contained a figure for debtors and rent outstanding. In such circumstances the charge and discharge statement was clearly not a cash account, but it was equally clearly not a profit and loss account. It was a stewardship statement, prepared principally on the cash basis, with an element of accruals accounting incorporated in order to make accountability and control more effective, i.e. this early application of the accruals concept had nothing to do with profit measurement; its purpose was to ensure that the full amount due to the landlord was reported.

The basic format of the charge and discharge account changed little over the years, although the number of headings showed a significant increase. Noke tells us that the accounting statements, listed below, were attached to the charge and discharge account in descending order of regularity as early as the thirteenth century (pp. 144–45). Their purpose was to broaden control to other assets.

1. The corn and stock account, which was expressed in quantities and prepared in the classical charge and discharge format.
2. A statement setting out the labour services due from villein tenants and how these obligations were to be discharged.
3. A narrative statement of fixed assets belonging to the manor. No attempt was made at a valuation but a precise description of the type of asset and its condition was given.

The charge and discharge system worked most efficiently where the number of transactions was small, where they were undertaken on the cash basis and, most important, where receipts and payments remained unchanged from one year to the next. In these circumstances the need for underlying records was at a minimum; an important characteristic in a primitive and illiterate society. As the scale of operations increased, and the range of activities undertaken became more varied, the need for a primary record developed. It was first satisfied by the use of tallies; a non-written record (see later in this chapter) which was in common use during the fourteenth century. Additional records, increasingly used for the purpose of preparing the charge and discharge statement, include the previous year's account, a record of rents receivable, a list of recurring payments, and vouchers for irregular receipts and payments. The account was sometimes compiled, in stages, during the year but, more often, as a single exercise immediately prior to the audit.

Many contemporary books were written on estate accounting and these included detailed directions about procedures to be followed. Manorial accounting was also taught as part of the curriculum at Oxford beginning in the thirteenth century. These factors helped to standardise estate accounting practice.

Manorial audit

The audit was an essential element in the system of responsibility accounting. The first half of the charge and discharge statement set out the agent's total indebtedness, and he was required to prove that he could discharge his financial responsibility at the time of the audit. Often the audit took the traditional form, with the lord of the manor and the household hearing the statement read out by the steward, i.e. accounting and audit occurred simultaneously. In the large manors the audit was sometimes a more sophisticated affair; the accounts being examined by a specially appointed audit official.

The manorial audit has the closest links with the present-day method of accountability; transactions were mainly of a recurrent nature, but not as unchanging as in the case of government revenue and expenditure (see below). Close scrutiny was therefore needed to ensure that transactions were not omitted from the account. The accounting period varied although Michaelmas to Michaelmas, the natural agricultural trade cycle, was most common.

Stewards responsible for different aspects of the manor's activities kept their own primitive records and, at the time of the audit, there ensued a familiar contest between the auditor and the audited. The steward, wishing to minimise the balance for which he was accountable, estimated losses generously and revenues and the natural increase in the crops conservatively. In contrast, the auditor's job was to ensure that the lord did not suffer loss from negligence, inefficiency or fraud.

On many estates the auditor began the proceedings by informing the steward of the notional amount for which he stood charged for the year. This was, usually, the recurrent income of the estate. The steward was obliged to account for any differences between expected and actual recurrent income and for any non-recurring items. The steward was also required to produce bills showing his expenses and provide evidence of monies paid over to the lord of the manor. If allowed by the auditor, these items were entered into the account and deducted from the charge. If disallowed, they would be struck out on the face of the statement where a written account was submitted. Any deficiency of cash or other goods under his control, such as the corn stock, would have to be made good by the steward personally. To complete the discharge, the balance outstanding was paid by the steward to the auditor who, in turn, transferred the cash or goods to the lord of the manor.

A distinctive feature of the medieval British audit (compared with those of the Greek and Roman period) was the attention paid by the auditors to what *should* have occurred as well as what had occurred. As a result they would sometimes amend the accounts to reflect expected results and surcharge the bailiff or the reeve for the additional amount due to the lord of the manor.

The auditor also had the job of combining the individual accounts into a charge and discharge statement for the whole estate. A final step was the annual declaration of the audit with 'the charge and discharge statement as verified by the auditor read in the presence of the lord and the assembly of stewards whose discharge of duties was under scrutiny' (Chatfield, p.27).

In most cases the system worked well, but legal regulations were required to deal with agents who were either fraudulent or failed to prepare an account. Where the reporting official was the reeve the position was straightforward; he was tried in the manorial court which naturally put the lord of the manor in a strong position. A free man was subject to common law, however, and it was some time before adequate remedies were developed for dealing with the errant bailiff. Actions could always be brought to recover amounts due, but it was only from the beginning of the thirteenth century that the 'action of account' was evolved to enable the court, on application, to require the defaulting official to prepare an account.

The common law position was reinforced by a statute of 1285 which outlawed accounting officials who would not make an account. It also made the following provision where the official did not pay over the amount due: '[he] shall be arrested, and by the testimony of the auditors . . . [be] imprisoned in iron under safe custody, and shall remain in the same prison at their own cost, until they have satisfied their master fully of the arrearages'. This statute therefore recognised the obligation of the servant to prepare an account and, in addition, placed the auditor in a position of some authority. The accounting party who believed he had been wrongly imprisoned had a right of appeal to the Barons of the Exchequer where the principal was required to attend 'with the rolls and tallies by which he [the servant] made his accompt'. The administration of justice therefore required the presentation of written records, which provided a further strong impetus for their maintenance.

The origin of the legal regulation of accounts and audit, and legal recognition of the need for accounting statements, therefore dates back to the thirteenth century.

Central government[1]

The oldest surviving accounting record, in England, is the pipe roll or 'great roll of the exchequer'[2] compiled annually from valuations in the Domesday Book and from statements of accounts by sheriffs and others bringing payments to the treasury. Each roll consists of a number of pieces of sheepskin stuck together and, beginning in 1130, they comprise a 700-year record of rents, fines, taxes and other fixed levies due to the king, together with a summary of amounts actually received and collection costs. Certain payments could be made directly to the treasury, but in most cases the sheriff, who occupied the principal castle in the county, acted as the local collecting agent. He also administered justice.

At Easter and Michaelmas the sheriff of each county was summoned to Westminster. The purpose of the Easter meeting was to enable the Crown to improve its cash flow. The sheriff brought with him roughly half the total assessments for which his county was liable, and the treasurer ordered a tally stick to be cut as evidence of this payment. The tally stick was than split down three-quarters of its length. The shorter piece, called the foil, was given to the sheriff and served as his receipt for payments rendered; the remainder, called the stock, was retained by the treasury. The position of treasurer evolved, in due course, to become the office now known as Chancellor of the Exchequer.

At Michaelmas the sheriff returned to pay over the balance of Crown revenues and to present himself for the judicial audit which took place before the exchequer; an awesome body of men consisting of many national leaders. The treasurer began by formally asking the sheriff if he was ready to account and, if so, the treasurer read out the amount due as shown by the pipe roll. The sheriff was asked if his expenses were the same as for the previous year; if not, proof of the non-recurring expenditure had to be provided. For example, repairs to castles were vouched both by writ and by two of the king's surveyors who certified the performance and the cost of the work. The sheriff provided details of any miscellaneous receipts, such as voluntary payments to gain the king's favour, murder fines imposed on the county in cases where the murderer could not be found, and any goods confiscated from felons and fugitives.

Final settlement took place across a table laid with the chequered cloth after which the exchequer is named. On the one side sat the sheriff with the amount he had collected, his tally from the interim payment and his disbursement vouchers. On the other side of the table sat an official called the calculator who set out, on the chequered squares, counters representing the total payment due for the year to the Crown. The sheriff's tally was then matched with the tally in the possession of the exchequer; a procedure which caught out more than one rogue who attempted to conceal a shortage by cutting additional notches in the foil. The total amounts owed and 'proffered' were compared to ensure they agreed. The audit was completed by the sheriff swearing to the exchequer that he has made a lawful account according to his conscience.

The exchequer accounting system was essentially visual and oral and, therefore, wholly appropriate for a substantially illiterate society. As is often the case, however, a tried and tested system continued in operation when the reason for its original development no longer existed. It actually lasted until 1780, but it was less effective after 1500 because revenues became less predictable and unchanging.

Tallies

In the twelfth century the tally was a narrow hazel wood stick 8–9 inches long (the length later increased in line with Crown revenue), notched to indicate the amount received. The word tally comes from the French 'tailler', meaning to cut, and different cuts represented different denominations of money. For example, an incision the width of a man's palm represented £1000; a penny was represented by a simple cut with no wood removed. We have seen that tallies were used by the government as receipts for tax collected and paid over by the sheriff. Over the years tallies also became widely used as an acknowledgment of debts. The Plantagenet and Tudor kings, for example, 'first occasionally and then routinely raised money on the security of tallies which gave the lender the right to receive future tax revenues or even, in the Roman fashion, to collect certain taxes himself' (Chatfield, p.24).

Roger North, writing in 1714, considered that their continued use was unjustified, describing them as 'being of ordinary use in keeping accompts with illiterate people' (quoted in Parker, p.80). In 1834 it was decided to destroy the accumulated tallies of centuries. They were burnt in the stoves of the House of Lords, but the fire got out of hand and on 16 October the Houses of Parliament were destroyed.

Local government[3]

From the twelfth to the nineteenth century, agency accounting was used widely by what might be loosely described as organs of local government, namely the parishes, boroughs and counties. At the end of the eighteenth century these comprised over 15,000 separate organisations. The use of double entry, in local government, was not common until the nineteenth century.

Parish accounting. The parish began as an ecclesiastical unit centred around the church. A statutory power to levy rates dates from 1427, although non-statutory rates have been levied since time immemorial. Responsibility for specific functions was usually vested, by the parishioners, in officials such as the church warden and the overseer of the poor. Charge and discharge statements were presented, annually, for approval by the parishioners meeting in the church vestry, and the balance on hand was delivered up or handed over to the new officers. Sometimes the phrase 'examined and allowed by us' was written on the account, and signatures attached. The statement was usually on the cash basis, but outstanding debts were sometimes included. There are even examples of inventories listed in narrative form and, in exceptional cases, with physical quantities and/or cash values provided. For example, the 1509/10 accounts of St Martin's-in-the-Fields contain the following item: 'Arrearages £8.18s.8d, 2½oz. of silver worth 7s.11d. and 14s. in wax' (Jones, p.201).

A legal obligation to prepare an account complying with the accruals concept was imposed by an Act of 1601: 'a true and perfect account of all sums of money by them received, or rated and sessed and not received, and also of such stock as shall be in their hands, or in the hands of any of the poor to work' shall be submitted to the Justices of the Peace within four days of the end of the year (s.2). Agency accounting was naturally appropriate for this purpose.

Borough accounting. The term borough means 'walled town'. This type of community dates from the fourteenth century. The financial affairs of the borough were typically vested in a powerful officer known as the chamberlain (from 1835 called the treasurer). He held office for a year or two and, because the town was often in debt to the chamberlain, it was important for him to be well off. The accounts were again straightforward charge and discharge statements. The earliest, known, surviving accounts are those of the Chamberlain of London for 1334. These records are a mixture of Norman French, abbreviated Latin and early English; the English language being in the course of formation between the twelfth and fifteenth century (Eldridge, p.18).

County treasurer's accounts. After the middle ages the Justices took over the judicial functions previously performed by the sheriffs. Responsibilty for financial matters was also gradually transferred to them. An Act of 1739 created the office of County Treasurer who administered a single rate levied by the Justices. The treasurer was required to keep books and

> to deliver in true and exact accounts upon oath if required . . . of all and every sum and sums of money respectively received and paid by him or them, distinguishing the particular uses to which such sum or sums of money have been applied . . . and shall lay before the justices at such sessions the proper vouchers for the same (s.7).

Accounts were kept on the charge/discharge basis until about 1800 when aspects of double entry bookkeeping began to be introduced in some areas.

Scope and limitations of charge and discharge accounting

Charge and discharge is often dismissed as a primitive system of accounting. However, the best accounts in a given situation are those which provide sufficient information for rational decisions to be reached at the cheapest cost. An elaborate system of accounting is not justified unless it enables significantly better decisions to be made. The accounting systems, employed in feudal times, seem to have been adequate to meet contemporary needs. Indeed, the continued use of charge and discharge accounting, after double entry techniques became available, proves that simpler methods can often yield equally useful results (see Chapter 5). At the same time it should be acknowledged that there has been a traditional reluctance to discard tried and tested accounting method, and this inertia is likely to have delayed change, in certain quarters, until new methods proved irresistably superior.

Charge and discharge accounting is not concerned with profit measurement; even where an element of accruals accounting was applied, no distinction was made between capital and revenue transactions. The general lack of interest in formal performance assessment resulted from the fact that income was fairly fixed and the bulk of the expenditure unavoidable. In these circumstances a system which emphasised supervision and audit was quite adequate. In assessing the usefulness of manorial accounts it should also be recognised that the lord of the manor would have obtained information by direct contact with officials and estate activities.

Accounting innovations were sometimes made, on an informal basis, to provide information for the purpose of performance assessment. For example, expenses were allocated to particular activities to arrive at a profit figure, though overall profit was not normally calculated. Such calculations might be made from the subsidiary records and details appearing in the roll. Indeed, there are surviving examples of such calculations at the foot of the roll itself which bear little relation to the information contained in the money charge and discharge account set out above.

Such information was outside the strict stewardship report, but it is not surprising that such calculations were made. A large landed estate undertook a variety of activities, for example farming, forestry, mining, and the operation of the household itself. Moreover, within each of these units a number of separate and distinct activities took place, which gave rise to the need for information for performance assessment and decision making.

We also know that charge and discharge accounting is itself capable of modification to produce profit figures. According to Baxter a multi-column system of charge and discharge accounting was in use, quite recently, among a small number of solicitors for the purpose of preparing trust accounts (Baxter 1983, p.138). Under this system various types of transactions are painstakingly analysed into their capital and revenue elements so that net income can be calculated. An advantage of presenting the profit calculation in this manner is that it enables the trustee to study all the details; a drawback is that, where there are many transactions, the system grows 'voluminous and clumsy'. We will see, in the next two chapters, that double entry bookkeeping was the system successfully developed to overcome these problems.

5

Origin and Development of Double Entry Techniques

Possible origins

Littleton identified seven preconditions for the emergence of systematic bookkeeping. These are: the art of writing; arithmetic; private property; money as a medium of exchange; credit transactions; commercial activity; and the owner's capital investment. All these features existed in Roman times; an observation which resulted in the hypothesis that double entry developed in that era.

Based on an analysis of surviving records, de Ste. Croix has proved, conclusively, that the Romans were neither aware of nor used the double entry system or anything closely approximating it. He explains these findings in terms of the limitation imposed by the system of Roman numerals which have neither the zero nor place values and therefore do not lend themselves to addition and subtraction in the manner of Arabic numerals. According to de Ste. Croix, these circumstances prevented the concept of debit and credit from emerging and, therefore, inhibited the development of the notion of double entry bookkeeping.

This does not mean that it is impossible to use the Roman system of notation for arithmetic purposes. Sugden (p.10) has drawn attention to the fact that additions and subtractions can be processed using Roman numerals provided the letters are arranged in an appropriate manner and a few simple rules are learned, such as 2 times V makes an X. Moreover, any number can be expressed in Roman numerals and the only requirement for a number system to be used as the basis for double entry is the ability to identify, clearly, debit and credit amounts, maintain equality, and allow arithmetic calculations. All this could be done and, we will see, was done with Roman numerals, although not in Roman times.

However, it is a laborious process when there are columns of figures, and it cannot easily be adapted for division and multiplication. We therefore come back to de Ste. Croix's conclusion that it was not impossible to use Roman numerals as the basis for double entry but, in a society where only these existed, they prevented the necessary conceptual breakthrough from being made.

A contributory explanation for the Romans' failure to develop double entry is the primitive character of their economy in which credit, in particular, was not highly developed. Mass illiteracy was no doubt a further limiting factor. This leads us to the more general conclusion that, although Littleton's seven preconditions for the development of double entry were present in Roman times, they were not present in a sufficiently strong form to stimulate change.

If the Romans did not develop double entry, where did the system come from? One suggestion is that it was invented by an individual, possibly a mathematician. Following this line, some writers suggested that the Franciscan friar, Luca Pacioli (see below), invented the system, but this is nonsense. Pacioli made it clear that he was describing a system already in operation, and research has shown that double entry procedures were in use long before Pacioli was born. It remains a remote possiblility that the system was the invention of some earlier genius; another idea is that it may have been derived from equations developed by the Arabs (Williams).

One further fascinating, but unsubstantiated (see Nobes *Abacus*, 1987), idea is that double entry originated in India prior to Greek and Roman times in the form of the Bahi-Khata system of bookkeeping still practised in most parts of India among the unincorporated enterprise. According to Lall Nigam, Indian traders took this system to Italy and, from there, double entry spread throughout Europe. Bahi-Khata is based on Jama and Nam entries presented the opposite way round to the Italian system with credits on the left and debits on the right.

Computational aids

Two numeric systems – Arabic and Roman – operated alongside one another for 300 or 400 years after the initial development of double entry. The Roman system of notation was developed around 500 BC; the term Arabic numerals is something of a misnomer because this scheme is believed to have originated in India –

certainly the earliest known examples are inscribed on stone columns in India, *circa* 250 BC. The Arabic system was introduced into Europe by the eighth century, at the latest; the Arabs invaded the Spanish peninsula, in 711 AD, and may have brought the system with them at that time.

Both methods of counting are based on the decimal system, i.e. they use multiples of 10 (the Roman equivalent is X) and were probably derived from counting on fingers. The difference between the two systems is, therefore, not the way in which magnitudes were counted but in how the results of the calculations were written down. The system of Roman numerals is of course a little clumsy compared with the more compact system of Arabic notation, and it was no doubt for this reason that the Romans developed the abacus as a practical aid to computation. This Roman ready reckoner was derived from the Greek abax (board) which in turn is thought to have been a development of the Sematic abag (sand), a counting devise still used in oriental countries. One theory is that the Greek abax was invented by Pythagoras around 530 BC. The Roman abacus was in use by the second century BC (Stone, p.345).

Despite the fact that it simplified calculations, Arabic numerals gained acceptance slowly. Their use was resisted on the grounds that they could be more easily changed for fraudulent purposes by adding, removing or altering a single figure. It was also argued that the flexibility of the new system led to inaccuracies and errors due to less need for painstaking effort on the part of the accountant. (Perhaps not surprisingly, similar arguments had been used centuries earlier when Roman numerals were introduced, and have been heard much more recently in an attempt to resist mechanisation and computerisation.)

In 1399 a law was passed in Florence forbidding bankers to use the Arabic numeral system in bookkeeping, prescribing instead Roman figures or the written word on the grounds that the older method was safer for recording important sums. But as Stone has pointed out, we should not be too quick to deride this practice in view of the continued use of written figures, as well as numbers, in cheques and other legal documents (p.348).

The controversy between the two systems raged for centuries, and a measure of the usefulness of Roman numerals, backed by the abacus, is that, during this period, they continued in use alongside Arabic numerals. Gradually the Arabic system won, but for many years it was common practice to use Arabic numerals for book-keeping entries and to include Roman symbols in the explanation of each entry to help prevent fraudulent changes in the record. Indeed, Roman numerals continued to be used as the entire basis for double entry records, here and there, until about the sixteenth century.

A final factor explaining delay in the widespread adoption of Arabic numerals is that it took time to recognise their full potential. The facility of Arabic numerals for arithmetic calculations only becomes clearly apparent when the numbers are neatly arranged in columns. 'Pen-reckoning', as Parker describes it (p.81), became *common* during the seventeenth century and, because of its superiority over the abacus, particularly where there were l.s.d. (from the Latin *librae, solidi, denarii*) to be cast, the Roman ready reckoner was abandoned in Britain between 1668 and 1699 (Sugden, p.17). British businessmen and accountants relied on pen-reckoning during the next two centuries and made virtually no use of mechanical aids to computation. The accounting machine came into widespread use during the first half of the twentieth century, and computers in the period since the Second World War (Parker, p.82).

Early examples of double entry

The view which today receives almost universal support is that double entry evolved among the flourishing city states of medieval Italy. It has been argued that an important enabling event was a series of contemporary innovations in the presentation of written material. This was the work of early scholars (especially clerics) who began to re-write authoritative primary texts, such as the Bible, in a format which improved their accessibility to the interested reader. By 1300 they had invented a variety of devices designed to improve presentation, such as alphabetical order, rubric, paragraph marks, different letter sizes, lists of chapters and cross-references (Hoskin and Macve, pp.109–11).

Differences in form and technique between early double entry systems has led to the conclusion that the system developed, independently, in several trading centres, the most important of which were Florence, Genoa and Venice. The following summary of events suggests a process whereby businessmen were groping towards improved methods of presentation as the basis for a more effective memory aid and means of financial control.

The importance of Florence was that it was Europe's leading banking city; it had 80 banks in 1338 and over 100 by the end of the century. The distinctive feature of Florentine banking organisation was the large merchant banking partnerships which, like today's holding companies, controlled a network of foreign branches and sub-partnerships. The oldest surviving Florentine account book containing elements of double entry – a bank ledger of 1211 – exhibits aspects of contemporary presentational innovations. It is written in paragraph format with loans followed by a space for noting repayments as they occurred. The space often proved insufficient and de Roover described it as a 'clumsy arrangement' (p.117). Nevertheless, using paragraph format, punctuation and a chronological presentation represented an immense step forward.

The accounting records of the Salimbeni company of Siena, located near Florence, are notable for their analysis of transactions into seven different account books, including a cash book, a debtor and creditor book, a sales book, a book containing confidential entries concerning the partners' equity, and a book which records all dealings in foreign exchange. A novel feature of the cash book is that receipts appear in the front and payments at the rear (de Roover, p.122).

The Fini Account Book (*c.*1300), although still in paragraph form, contains a scheme of cross-referencing to corresponding debits or credits. The account books of Giovanni Farolfi, 1299–1300, comprise the earliest known set of comprehensive and fully articulated double entry records (Lee, 1977, p.94). These ledgers also feature cross-references to corresponding debits and credits, but presentation is further developed by placing the amounts, expressed in Roman numerals, in extension columns instead of as part of a continuous narrative (de Roover, p.119).

Genoese and Venetian firms were heavily involved in overseas trade, and they used double entry techniques to help cope with the intricate accounting procedures associated with transactions undertaken through consignment agents and short-term partnerships. The oldest surviving Genoese records definitely displaying all the characteristics of double entry are the Massari accounts of the City of Genoa, 1340. Probably the accounts had been in this form since 1327 when, because of many frauds, it was decreed that the ledgers should be kept 'after the manner of banks' (Chatfield, p.42). A feature of these records is that the bi-lateral or tabular layout was used; a format found earlier, e.g. in Roman times, within systems of single entry record keeping. An advantage of this format was that it reduced the need to make subtractions when standards of numeracy were poor. The oldest known Venetian accounts are contained in the ledgers of Donaldo Soranzo and Brothers, 1410–18, and the earliest Venetian example of mature venture bookkeeping is found in the Barbarigo ledgers, 1431–39 (Chatfield, pp.36–37).

One final collection worth mentioning is the ledgers of Francesco di Marco Datini, a merchant banker, which run continuously from 1366–1410. A full double entry system is in operation from 1390, complete with balance sheets, both for overseas branches and the main Florentine office. The important innovation in these ledgers is the conversion from vertical to bi-lateral account form. Traditionally the debit and credit sections of Florentine ledger accounts had been placed one above the other instead of on opposite pages as in Venice. Following this change the Venetian and Florentine bookkeeping techniques were basically the same (Chatfield, p.40).

Double entry out of charge and discharge

Since few records survive, any explanation of how the mechanism of double entry developed must be speculative. A theory, which appeals to this writer, is that it evolved by a process of adaption and innovation out of earlier bookkeeping techniques which proved inadequate to meet growing business requirements. The process occurred in northern Italy, during the thirteenth and fourteenth centuries, because of the massive increase in the level and complexity of trading operations resulting from the success of Italian merchants and bankers. Lee (1976, p.7) describes the transition from charge and discharge accounting to double entry bookkeeping as follows.

1. The cashier of a firm was treated as the agent and charged with cash received from, say, customers, and discharged by payments to, say, suppliers.
2. In a similar fashion credit customers were charged with goods bought and discharged when payment was received. The converse procedure applied for creditors.
3. By the second half of the thirteenth century, Italian bookkeepers had begun to notice that the receipt of cash from a debtor, for example, resulted in two entries; in the record of the debtor the discharge, and in the record of the cashier the charge. They therefore began to cross-reference these transactions.
4. By 1300 the prefixes *deve avere* (ought to have) and *deve dare* (ought to give) were used to distinguish positive entries in the

form of cash receipts from negative entries such as cash payments. In Britain these words were translated into debitor (an earlier version of debtor) and creditor, shortened to debit and credit and, finally, abbreviated to Dr and Cr.

5. In the fourteenth century the procedure of distinguishing debits from credits by using the bi-lateral format became more widely used.

It was natural that transactions undertaken by Florentine banks should have been the focal point for the above developments. Bank business principally consists of (i)loans and repayments, and (ii)deposits and withdrawals. Double entry procedures are ideally suited to record, for example, the dual effect of credit transactions on the cash position of the bank and the amount due from customers. The general line of argument is that fully articulated double entry then evolved out of cash accounts and personal accounts by adding accounts to cover revenues and expenses (nominal accounts) and other assets (real accounts). In this way double entry developed by trial and error, improvements being imitated from one business and city to another. The new system survived because of its inherent advantages over single entry methods. These are as follows:

1. It enables transactions to be recorded in a more systematic and orderly manner.
2. It provides an arithmetic check on the records by periodically balancing the books and extracting a trial balance.
3. By clearly identifying a sequence of tasks to be performed, it facilitated the division of bookkeeping duties between a number of personnel. The specialisation, which resulted, reduced the risk of error and made it more difficult to falsify the books and conceal fraud.

We can therefore see that, initially, the main virtue of double entry bookkeeping compared with single was that it was a more effective memory aid and system of internal control.

Pacioli's system

Luca Pacioli was born at Borgo San Sepolcro, a small Italian town 80 miles south-east of Florence, in 1445. His family was poor but, during the Renaissance, background was much less important than had been the case earlier in the middle ages. He took orders with the Franciscan friars and soon esablished himself as a highly gifted mathematician. At various times he was professor of mathematics at the universities of Perugia, Milan, Florence, Pisa, Naples and Rome. He met and became friendly with many leading personalities including Leonardo da Vinci. From what we know about him, it is clear that he was totally at ease in the stimulating and exciting Renaissance environment.

Pacioli wrote a number of important books, including his enormously influential *Summa de Arithmetica, Geometria, Proportioni et Proportionalita* (Everything about Arithmetic, Geometry and Proportion). *Summa* was published in Venice in 1494, over two centuries after double entry was first practised in Italy, and it was a further 49 years before publication of the first British text. Pacioli became the 'father of modern accounting' (Hatfield, p.3) quite by chance. He was principally a mathematician and, although he had some early experience of commerce while apprenticed to a local businessman, record keeping does not seem to have been one of his principal interests. Chapters on this topic were included in *Summa* simply because Pacioli was attempting to prepare a work containing material of interest to businessmen.

Under Pacioli's system the books are opened by entering a full inventory of the merchant's assets and liabilities. He makes it clear that the items should first be expressed in financial terms and he also emphasises the need for a full cross-referencing between debit and credit entries. The system advocated by Pacioli is based on three records: the memorandum, the journal, and the ledger. He is fully aware of the need to tailor the system to business requirements and observes that 'because of the smallness of their businesses . . . many make use of [only] the last two' (p.13). More generally, an initial record of transactions in the memorandum is used as the basis for debit and credit entries in the journal and, from there, postings are made to the ledger. Chapter 33 deals with balancing the ledger either because 'you want to change book by reason of its being filled up, or because of the beginning of a new year, as is customary to do in the best known places' (p.90).

The procedure for transferring balances to the new ledger, i.e. 'cash, capital, goods, furniture and buildings, debtors, creditors, offices, brokerages, and dues to public weigher' is carefully described (p.98). 'Accounts which you may not desire to transfer to ledger A [the new ledger], but which you wish to keep privately, and have no obligation to render an account of to anyone' are closed to a profit and loss account, written up within the ledger, and the balance transferred to the capital account. Pacioli also describes a procedure whereby a list of closing balances may be extracted and checked for accuracy before entering them in the new ledger. It is not entirely clear whether this list is prepared *before* preparing the profit and loss account, in which case the document is akin to a modern trial balance, or *after*, in which case the items remaining are those which normally appear in the present-day balance sheet.

We can see that the system described by Pacioli *broadly* resembles that in operation today. The focus of attention is, however, the bookkeeping process which he painstakingly explains. Little attention was given to the preparation of financial statements other than as a check on the accuracy of the ledger. References to performance assessment were confined to comments that, by preparing a profit and loss ledger account, 'you will be able to see succinctly and without delay, whether you are gaining or losing, and how much' (p.82) and that 'you will be able to know your gain or loss' (p.98). Perhaps the greatest tribute to Pacioli's ability to encapsulate the essence of double entry is that for nearly a century, major bookkeeping texts drew heavily on the content of *Summa*, often dealing with material in the same way, and even using similar examples.

The relative lack of interest shown by Pacioli in periodic balancing, the preparation of accounting statements and the calculation of profit was perfectly natural at a time when business operations commonly took the form of a short-term (terminable) venture. The merchant invested capital and, if the project was successful, he ended up with a larger amount. If the activity was undertaken by a number of merchants, acting in partnership, cash and goods on hand on completion of the venture could simply be shared out in proportion to the initial investment. Interim accounting statements and profit calculations served little purpose and were rarely made.

Expansion of the system

The 300 years following the publication of *Summa* has been called accountancy's 'age of stagnation'. In a sense this is true, but the Italian system spread to many parts of the world and was refined and elaborated upon.

The operation of a system of double entry does not necessarily involve a distinction between capital and revenue, but the classification of accounts into these two groups was a natural development which enabled businessmen to calculate profit and prepare the interlocking profit and loss account and balance sheet. In due course, the terms 'real' and 'nominal' were coined, probably by teachers and writers, to underline the difference between impersonal accounts used to record capital as opposed to revenue transactions. The potential of double entry for producing final accounts setting out the financial progress and position of an enterprise began to be more widely exploited toward the end of the fifteenth century. The delay may have been due to ignorance. A more plausible explanation is that, while business activity remained small scale, businessmen simply did not require, for decision making purposes, the kind of information contained in the double entry based profit and loss account and balance sheet.

The organisational aspects of the system of bookkeeping also underwent a series of changes and refinements. These included: the replacement of the memorandum by files of invoices, receipts and other primary documents; the use of books of originating entry, in addition to, or instead of, the journal, e.g. sales daybooks and purchases daybooks; the use of subsidiary account books to release a mass of data from the main ledger and to enable them to be maintained by separate individuals; and the closing of the ledger on a regular basis for the purpose of financial statement preparation. The maintenance of a 'secret ledger' to conceal the owner's personal affairs from the counting-house staff was advocated by Peele in 1569 (Yamey, p.19). Progress also saw the development of a system of internal control by the division of duties between different individuals and the imposition of a requirement for transactions to be authorised and activities to be the subject of a double check.

6

Use of Double Entry Bookkeeping in Britain, 1500–1800

Introduction

Bookkeeping is not a subject which is famous for conjuring up strong emotions, but there are a few notable exceptions. It has been described by a character in Goethe's works as 'among the finest inventions of the human mind' (quoted in Macve, p.257), and by the English scientist Sir George Cayley as 'one of the two perfect sciences' (quoted in Hatfield, p.11). Hatfield's frustration with the derogatory attitude of academic colleagues towards accountancy, as epitomised by the phrase 'that is a mere bookkeeping entry', stimulated him to write a spirited and amusing riposte entitled 'An Historical Defence of Bookkeeping'. A more common characterisation is provided by Drew who observed that 'bookkeeping is at the best of times a subject which few people find attractive' (quoted in Macve, p.257). This lack of respect extends to the bookkeeper. According to the *Spectator's* fictitious eighteenth-century gentlemen Sir Roger De Coverley, 'What can there great and noble be expected from him whose attention is for ever fixed upon ballancing his books, and watching over his expences?' (quoted in Boys, p.25).

We leave aside these disputes and simply start with a definition of bookkeeping as 'the systematic recording of financial and economic transactions and other events' (Parker, p.27). Three methods of bookkeeping were in operation in Britain between 1500–1800; charge and discharge, single entry and double entry. Their relative popularity changed considerably during the period under review.

The description single entry strictly covers any system of accounting which is not double entry, including charge and discharge. In practice, however, the term charge and discharge is usually employed where the record keeping system was designed solely to enable the preparation of a stewardship statement in that form. Tallies were used to provide the initial record of receipts and payments but, as time went by, the tally stick was first supplemented and eventually replaced by written records. The term single entry typically describes a bookkeeping system consisting of a cash book and a memorandum record of amounts due to customers and from suppliers. Sometimes these debts and obligations were recorded in a personal ledger. Under a system of single entry bookkeeping, profit was calculated, if at all, by comparing business valuations based on an inventory of assets and liabilities at the beginning and the end of the accounting period.[1]

Double entry comes to Britain

The distinguishing feature of double entry bookkeeping is that it requires every transaction to be recorded twice, and is epitomised by the slogan 'for every debit there is a corresponding credit'. The system reached Britain via two main routes: British businessmen learning their trade abroad and returning to Britain; and translations of the bookkeeping chapters of *Summa* and other writings becoming available in Britain during the sixteenth century (see Chapter 7). The use of double entry by British offshoots of overseas, say Italian, operations does not seem to have been a material factor. An exception is the London branch of Gallerani, a Sienese banking company. An examination of two surviving account books, for the period 1305–8, has produced the conclusion that they contained 'substantial elements of double entry [but] there is no suggestion that indigenous English records were kept in this advanced way either during or following its presence' (Nobes, p.309).

In Britain the period of commercial capitalism (see Chapter 2) stretched from the beginning of the sixteenth century to the middle of the eighteenth century. It saw business activities, previously centred on the manor, extend to include those of merchants engaged in domestic and overseas trading activities. Such activities were, by their nature, far more dynamic. Investment, disinvestment and reinvestment in different types of stock in trade were essential features of this more rapidly changing environment. Long periods of credit given and received also pointed to the need for a more sophisticated system of financial control. Most firms kept their records by single entry, however, and the rate of adoption of double entry bookkeeping was extremely slow.

What were the reasons for delay – ignorance, lack of expertise, the complexity of the new system, or something else? In truth we do not know the answer, but the absence of a strong demand from business seems the most likely explanation. The vast majority of firms were not large and the number of transactions did not justify the use of double entry procedures. Certainly there were plenty of written expositions of the system, and oral instruction was presumably available at the right price. However, even bookkeeping texts identified double entry's main advantage as its ability to make accounting records orderly and complete, i.e. little or no data was provided that could not be obtained from the single entry system.

Although double entry procedures were used in Britain well before 1600, relatively few systems were in operation before the late eighteenth century. Those in existence were fairly rudimentary. A glimpse of sixteenth-century practices is given by the Flemish merchant, Ympyn (1543). He comments favourably on the neat bookkeeping methods of the Spaniards and the Germans but refers, scathingly, to the fact that many *large* businesses in France and England did not even keep their accounts on a double entry basis (Yamey, 1980, p.82).

An examination of prevailing practices reveals a sharp contrast with the meticulous precision today associated with double entry. Ledgers were often only partially written up and periodic balancing was rare. The most usual reasons for closing the ledger were that it was full or that a change of ownership had occurred. The failure to make what would today be regarded as a proper distinction between nominal and real accounts, when preparing accounting statements, reflected a lack of interest in profit measurement (see Chapter 8). There are, by way of contrast, numerous examples of carefully kept personal accounts, displaying a keen interest in the control of indebtedness. Not until the eighteenth century was much practical recognition given, in Britain, to double entry's potential as a basis for reporting as well as recording business facts.

Record keeping in the early Industrial Revolution

The British Industrial Revolution is conventionally assigned to the period 1760–1830. Of the accounting systems available to the new industrialists, the choice was naturally influenced, to some extent, by the businessman's background and experience. Where industries developed from the estates themselves, particularly mines, canals, and iron works, the tendency was to use the charge and discharge system. This scheme of accountability was, in many respects, entirely appropriate as the manorial steward was usually the industrial manager's superior. The limitation of this method, in the new environment, was that it did not show the amount of capital invested by the owner, and could not easily be adapted to provide profit figures and other data for performance assessment. The British manorial accounting system had worked well when business conditions were stable, but they were now dynamic. But because the system had had such a long period to become established and institutionalised, it was very difficult to shift.

The double entry system used by some merchants had more potential for meeting the needs of industry because there were closer environmental similarities. The accounting requirements of industry were different, however, in two important respects. First, although industry remained predominantly labour intensive, capital expenditure now reached a level, in certain businesses, where its accounting treatment could no longer be dismissed as unimportant. Secondly, the greater continuity of business operations (compared with the merchant's activities which often consisted of individual ventures) increased the need for periodic reporting to owners and managers. We can therefore say that commercial capitalism created the need for double entry bookkeeping as a protection against loss due to error or fraud, whereas industrial capitalism increased the need for double entry bookkeeping as the foundation for financial reports on which better informed business decisions could be based.

The above discussion of single entry and double entry has implied that a clear-cut choice was made in favour of one system or the other. In practice this was not so, and a combination was often used; a finding which is consistent with the view, put forward in Chapter 5, that double entry developed out of charge and discharge accounting. 'Hybrid' systems were found, for example, on the manorial estates where aspects of double entry procedures were adopted to cope with the diversification of activities into separately identifiable areas such as mining, fishing and forestry.

Haydn Jones has drawn attention (p.61) to an unpublished treatise, compiled by Thomas Lovett in the 1760s, which describes an advanced system of landed estate accounting then in use. It combines features of charge and discharge within a system of double entry accounting. The text also covers budgeting and the calculation of the return earned on an investment. Features of the system are that it is not dominated by the rigid technicalities of double entry, as were most contemporary texts, but is instead concerned with devising a system suitable for a situation where profitability, and its measurement, was as important to the gentleman farmer as checks on the honesty and integrity of personnel had been previously.

Jones also gives some interesting practical illustrations of how the mid-eighteenth century transition from charge and discharge to double entry accounting resulted in the integration of one system with the other. These include a 1780 charge and discharge statement prepared to report the accountability of Thomas Beynon (accountant) to John Vaughan, landlord. The account is prepared in bi-lateral format with the columns headed debit and credit (p.42). The accounts of the Mackworth Estate for 1759–60 are another example of a hybrid system which employs the charge and discharge method of accountability, but also generates profit figures based on a system of double entry (pp.52–60).

In a similar vein, Yamey has drawn attention to the Stour Valley Iron company which was organised into a number of iron works, each the responsibility of a separate manager (1982, p.111). In its records for 1668–69, a personal account was opened for each manager. This was debited with amounts received from the owner and collected on his behalf, and credited with money spent on the owner's behalf, transferred to the owner or transferred to the owner's agents. These accounts are therefore reminiscent of the charge and discharge statements submitted by an agent to his principal. A difference is that the accounts were part of a complete double entry system. For instance, sales made by individual managers were debited to the manager's personal account and credited to the profit and loss account. The accounts were balanced intermittently, and a balance account, called 'the proof of the whole accompt' prepared (p.113).

With the increase in trade, during the eighteenth century, we find more firms adopting double entry accounting. As interest in performance assessment increased, the rate of transition accelerated. The Crawshay Ledger Accounts, 1791–98, are an early example of an elaborate double entry system supported by extensive and detailed subsidiary records in use for a large-scale industrial enterprise (Jones, pp.118–41).

Double entry and the growth of capitalism

Sombart's theory. Double entry replaced cruder methods of record keeping at a time when the economy changed from being one which was essentially feudal to one which was commercially based, i.e. economic developments demanded better accounting systems and innovations occurred to meet this need. But accounting is proactive as well as reactive and it has been suggested by Winjum that double entry bookkeeping made a substantial contribution to the economic growth and development of England between 1500 and 1750 (p.246). Certainly this was a period of substantial economic progress in Britain. According to the economic historian Herbert Heaton,

> fifteenth century England was an unimportant, unfortunate country . . . [whereas] . . . By 1750 the population has almost trebled and was growing quickly. Commercial agriculture covered much of the country, some grain was being exported, but wool was kept at home by law for use in a cloth industry which was now the largest in Europe. The production of metal goods was highly developed, and coal fired a wide range of industries. British merchants, using British ships, were firmly established in most European ports, in the oriental and African trades, and in every kind of traffic with the Americas (p.307).

The extent of accountancy's contribution to the development of capitalism has been the subject of healthy academic debate. Sombart sees double entry bookkeeping as the driving force transforming a feudal society into a capitalist society. According to Sombart, 'it is hard to imagine capitalism without double entry bookkeeping: they belong together like form and content' (from translation in Most, p.251). In essence, double entry is seen as the causal factor in the development of capitalism because it 'endows the economic world with accuracy, knowledge and system' (Pollard's synthesis of Sombart's views, 1963, p.75).

The perceived link between double entry and the development of a capitalist society is based on the definition of capitalism as the rational pursuit of profit by the entrepreneur using either his own capital or resources provided by investors. By facilitating the identification of profit and capital, and demonstrating the link between them, double entry focused attention on the potential of business for maximising income instead of just providing a living. Double entry therefore supplied a rational basis on which the capitalist could choose the direction in which to employ his capital to best advantage. Moreover, by impersonalising capital, it facilitated the separation of the business from its owners. In this way the development of the large joint stock company and the economy as a whole was given a strong impetus.

Yamey's rebuttal. Yamey's findings (1949, 1964) may be summarised as follows:

1. The examination of surviving records has proved that double entry bookkeeping was very little used as the basis for decision making during the period of commercial capitalism and the early period of industrial capitalism. The main reason for the initial adoption of double entry procedures was because they provided a better means of keeping track of resources. In other words, capitalist entrepreneurs found double entry bookkeeping useful but not for the reasons postulated by Sombart.
2. Single entry bookkeeping provided early capitalists with the kind of information thought important by Sombart just as efficiently as double entry bookkeeping. Indeed businessmen were probably more adept at producing *ad hoc* calculations of profit from single entry records, than in preparing final accounts based on a fully interlocking double entry system.

For the above reasons Yamey rejects the idea of a causal link between double entry bookkeeping and economic development. Other researchers have even argued that accounting practices exerted a negative influence on economic development. According to Lister, poor methodology resulted in the preparation of inconsistent and disorderly accounting statements containing misleading profit figures and asset values. He therefore concludes that the development of accounting was 'irrelevant to, lagged behind, or even retarded social and economic progress' (p.68).[2] Pollard's investigation of accounting systems used during the Industrial Revolution produced the critical, but less strident, conclusion that, where accountancy was used to provide guidance, 'such guidance was often unreliable' (1965, p.245).

Evaluation of Yamey v Sombart. Obviously capital is at the very centre of the idea of capitalism; the disagreement is about *how crucial* is a financial measure of capital to capitalist development. The essence of the dispute is that, whereas Sombart argues that double entry's main contributions were that it enabled income and capital to be measured and performance to be assessed, Yamey believes the system satisfied the rather more narrow bookkeeping function of checking the accuracy of the ledgers and keeping track of assets and liabilities.

The capitalist era and the development of double entry bookkeeping ran more or less concurrently, and it is probably for this reason that Sombart initially made the link between the two. The time period covered by these two developments begins in the thirteenth century, though there are significant differences in the exact starting date from one place to another, e.g. commercial capitalism and double entry were manifest much earlier in Italy than in England. But whereas Sombart's ideas are derived from abstract reasoning, Yamey's conclusions are based on solid facts obtained by examining the contemporary account books of traders. Nevertheless, Yamey does not deny there is a link between the two, only that the claims for double entry have been exaggerated. Indeed it would be very strange if double entry was not introduced because it made a substantial contribution to business development, since innovation inevitably produces a certain amount of upheaval. But Yamey's point is that insufficient evidence has been adduced to prove that it was the facility provided by double entry techniques for the identification of profit and capital that was particularly important.

Support for Yamey's thesis is provided by the fact that the distinction between real and nominal accounts, to facilitate profit calculation, was a refinement worked out slowly over a number of years, rather than an initial feature of the system. Further reassurance is provided by Baxter who has discovered that colonial merchants, in seventeenth-century America, succeeded with only the 'scrappiest of profit calculations' (p.145), and by Macfarlane (discussed in Yamey, 1981, p.134) who points out that any carefully kept set of accounts has economic and social implications and consequenses similar to those attributed by Sombart to double entry.

It is important to realise, however, that the scarcity of surviving double entry based financial reports does not conclusively prove that medieval businessmen were uninterested in their preparation. It is possible, if unlikely, that numerous capital and profit calculations, and even balance sheets, were prepared outside the ledger on loose paper which has simply not stood the test of time. Even where a system of double entry bookkeeping was in operation, lack of evidence of regular balancing does not necessarily signify anything more than the fact businessmen considered it unimportant to close the accounts before extracting balances for the purpose of preparing accounting statements.

The conclusion here is that double entry bookkeeping was not a precondition for the development of capitalism but it certainly provided capitalists with a powerful tool for organising business activities and, as time went on, providing more precise indicators of business progress as the basis for resource allocation decisions. Progress would have been made in the absence of double entry bookkeeping, and was in many cases, but the rate of overall progress would have been slower. Figures for profit are rarely required in the small firm but they become increasingly important as a firm grows in size. Profit can be calculated where a system of single entry bookkeeping is in use but, as firms become larger, the figure which results is much more likely to be accurate if double entry is adopted. The problems of valuation must still of course be faced, but the possibility of omitting assets and liabilities is much reduced. A further advantage of double entry records is that that they facilitate the preparation of a profit and loss account containing detailed information for use as the basis for business decisions.

Origin of final accounts

The trial balance was clearly in use in 1494; its preparation, usually as a listing at the back of the ledger, was the final stage under Pacioli's accounting system,[3] and its initial purposes were to check the arithmetic accuracy of the underlying records and to enable the transfer of balances from one account book to the other (Peragallo, p.219).

The Flemish writer, Jan Ympyn Cristoffels, made an important contribution to the development of accounting by clearly explaining the method of preparing the balance sheet (then called the balance account). Ympyn's advice was, first to transfer the balances on the various merchandise accounts to a 'remaining goods' account, second to collect together the nominal accounts in the profit and loss account, third to close the balance on the profit and loss account to the capital account (a possibility referred to but not dwelt on by Pacioli). The ledger was then closed by transferring the asset, liability and capital balances to the balance sheet (discussed in Peragallo, p.221). Simon Stevin of Bruges produced a further important breakthrough (1604) by emphasising the importance of producing summarised financial statements outside the ledger.

According to Chatfield, this innovation 'helped bridge the gap between Renaissance and modern accounting' (p.55).

The ranking of the profit and loss account and balance sheet in terms of importance has fluctuated over time, and the focus of attention has also been influenced by the nature of the inquirer's interest.

Profit and loss account. Within the double entry framework, the profit and loss account was prepared by collecting together revenues and expenditures in a separate ledger account long before assets and liabilities were assembled in the balance sheet. As early as 1400 there are examples of profit statements generated, in Italy, by the double entry scheme of record keeping. Indeed Pacioli refers to the need to close 'mercantile expenses, household expenses, or extraordinary expenses, rents, pensions, feudal tributes and similar items' to the profit and loss account, but he does not demonstrate the preparation of this financial statement (p.98).

The fact that Stevin (1604) chose to illustrate the layout of the profit and loss account suggests that some progress was being made in the preparation of periodic financial statements by the beginning of the seventeenth century. According to ten Have, however, Stevin considered that the main function of this document – called 'the proof of the estate' – was to check the accuracy of the profit figure first calculated by comparing the opening and closing balances for net assets (p.244). It is unlikely that much use was initially made of this double entry based profit figure for performance assessment and resource allocation decisions. In Britain, profit calculations derived from double entry systems were of a low standard throughout the period 1500–1800 when, according to empirical evidence assembled by Yamey, the profit and loss account 'served in a weeding-out process, in which detailed and unwanted information in the ledger was removed' (1977, p.23).

As business requirements increased, the development of ledger based profit calculations went through the following broad stages:

1. A separate merchandise account was opened for each bundle of merchandise and, when all the items were sold, the financial balance remaining on the account was carried to the profit and loss account. This was the natural accounting method where the sale of one parcel or consignment of goods generated the cash to make a further purchase. Investment was usually short term; the exception was the long distance voyage where resources might be committed for a number of years.

2. The merchandise account was balanced at fixed intervals, with closing stock valued and carried down to enable the calculation of *periodic* profit.
3. Costs directly associated with stock were also posted to the merchandise account.
4. The separation of transactions, contained in the merchandise account, into the sales account, purchases account and expense accounts. The totals of these accounts were periodically summarised in the trading account.
5. The balance(s) from the trading account(s), together with any unallocated expenses and revenues remaining in the nominal accounts, were collected together in the profit and loss account (this was the presentation illustrated by Stevin).

Balance sheet. By the seventeenth century, some British businessmen had begun to prepare a balance sheet *outside* the ledger. According to Chatfield, 'throughout this period [it] was by far the most important financial statement' and the one emphasised by early British writers such as Dafforne (p.69). Preoccupation with the balance sheet stemmed from the fact that it was more useful in answering traditional stewardship questions, which had their roots long before the introduction of double entry, such as the manorial manager's honesty and ability to account for resources entrusted to him. Even where interest extended to the financial state of business operations, users generally confined attention to assets, liabilities and capital; expenses and revenues were considered merely incidental in an agricultural environment where the rate of change was gradual.

There are plenty of examples of early balance sheets, but their publication and, probably, their preparation was not a common practice, even among the large statutory companies formed to develop the canal and railway networks in the late eighteenth and early nineteenth centuries (see Chapter 13). The so-called balance sheets, often filed by companies under the Joint Stock Companies Act (JSCA) 1844, further indicate the continued lack of accounting expertise and familiarity with this basic accounting statement (see Chapter 15).

The English balance sheet. According to Lisle the 'wrong way round' English balance sheet has 'arisen through the influence of the forms given in Acts of Parliament, chiefly the Companies Act, 1862 [see Figure 15.1], which must have been prepared by those unacquainted with the theory of accounts' (p.205). This is not true. The English format originated much earlier and was used, for example, by the East India Company, 1641 (Baladouni, 1986, p.27) and in the Du Cane ledgers of 1754–58 (Yamey, Edey and Thomson, p.192). A balance sheet in the English format appears in Stevin's famous text of 1604 (reproduced in Littleton and Zimmerman, p.76). The possibility that he influenced the arrangements of assets and liabilities in British balance sheets has been explored and rejected by Yamey (1970). A number of alternative attempts have been made to explain its use.

One idea is that, when the ledger accounts were closed, the balances were listed, to check their accuracy, before carrying them down. A more complicated explanation is based on the idea that preoccupation with double entry required *all* opening balances in a new ledger to appear as both debits and credits. When an old ledger was closed, one method of transferring balances to the new ledger was to reproduce the balance sheet on the first page. It was therefore necessary to list assets, liabilities and capital in the balance sheet, in reverse order, so that the double entry could be achieved by making postings to the relevant ledger accounts. For example, plant would appear as a credit entry in the balance sheet and as a debit entry in the ledger account headed 'plant'. This procedure was recommended in a number of textbooks, including John Weddington's (1567) and used in practice, but it is not known how widespread (Yamey, 1970, pp.72–73).

A variation of this explanation is that a new ledger was sometimes opened by listing each asset and liability in the appropriate ledger account, with the counterpoise credit or debit entry in the owner's capital account. The result was a capital account which resembled the reverse balance sheet, except that there was no explicit entry for the opening capital balance which was simply implied by the excess of credit (asset) balances over the debit (liability) balances. In Yamey's view this would have acquainted accountants with the reversed format and 'offered itself as a convenient representation of the state of affairs of the enterprise' for presentation to the owner (1970, p.74). A final explanation for the wrong way round presentation, which has nothing to do with double entry, is that under the charge and discharge system the accounting statements traditionally started with resources received and then showed how they had been applied.

7

Early Literature

The first books

One of the most important fifteenth-century inventions was movable printing type, first developed in Europe by the German, Johann Gutenberg, in the 1450s. This breakthrough released book production and circulation from the obvious constraints imposed by the need to prepare manuscripts in handwritten form. The first printed text appeared in 1454, the first (Gutenberg) Bible in 1455 and the first printed book on accountancy in 1494. We will see that Gutenberg's invention was fully exploited by writers and publishers of accountancy texts in order to spread the message of double entry.

Pacioli's *Summa* was published in Italy at the height of the Renaissance (revival of learning). It is almost certainly the first *published* text on double entry bookkeeping, but there is some doubt about its originality. Thirty-six years earlier, in 1458, Bendetto Cotrugli authored a manuscript which was eventually published in 1573. The printed version contained a short chapter on double entry. It cannot be confirmed whether this appeared in the 1458 manuscript as the original document has not survived. It is thought there were several other unpublished manuscripts circulating in Italy, in the late fifteenth century, detailing contemporary bookkeeping methods. Pacioli may have drawn on the content of some or any of these works. The bookkeeping section of *Summa* (other sections dealt with arthmetic, algebra, geometry, money and exchange) was separately printed as *De Computis* in 1504.

It has been said that no book has dominated the literature on its subject as much as has *Summa*. Bookkeeping texts published up to 1550 corresponded closely to Pacioli's text, and his influence on early German, Dutch and English writers is clearly evident

(Emmett Taylor, p.182). Even today the main features of the system Pacioli outlined are easily recognisable.

The spread of double entry bookkeeping to other countries is mirrored by the appearance of published texts on the subject. Heinrich Schreiber (Grammateus) was the author of the oldest German text, published in 1518. The first Flemish book (1543) was written by Jan Ympyn Christoffels, an Antwerp merchant who had spent twelve years in Venice. The first book on double entry bookkeeping published in Spain was by Bartoleme Salvador De Solorzano 1590, in Sweden by Hortulanus 1646, in Denmark by Bartholomeus Pedersen 1673, in Scotland by Colinson 1683, in Portugal by Bonavie 1758, in Norway (anonymously) 1775, and in Russia (anonymously) 1783. Few of these texts contained much which was original. Pedersen's book, for instance, is principally a translation of selected material from a book by the Dutchman David Kock (1652), while the Norwegian text is a translation of a book by the Scot, John Mair.

The claim to have discovered the first book written on a particular subject or published in a particular country amounts to a challenge which is often taken up. According to Sheldahl, for example, America's earliest recorded text on double entry bookkeeping, *An Introduction to the Counting House* (1789), was by Sarjeant, an Englishman who taught mathematics in Philadelphia. However, McMickle has made out a case for the fifth edition of the *Young Man's Companion*, author unnamed, published in 1737 as the first American book to contain a section on bookkeeping.

Many early writers on accounting were teachers, like Hugh Oldcastle who wrote the first English text. It was published in 1543, the year Henry VIII married his sixth and last wife. Oldcastle taught arithmetic and bookkeeping in London and, although no copy of his book has ever been found, we know of its existence because Mellis (1588) acknowledges a large debt to Oldcastle in the introduction to his own work. The oldest surviving English text is by James Peele, 1553. Both books drew heavily on Pacioli, but Peele's second book (1569) and John Weddington's book (1567) contain important departures from the Italian system.

One of Weddington's major innovations was to omit the journal and subdivide the memorandum into a number of what, today, we call daybooks, covering such items as inventory, cash receipts, payments, purchases and sales. Weddington's was also the first English text to use arabic numerals throughout, the first to contain compound journal entries, and to distinguish between current and deferred receipts and payments. Peele's text broke new ground by giving the reader detailed instructions about how to balance the accounts when closing the ledger (Yamey, Edey and Thomson, pp.162–66).

We have seen that many publications were translations, either wholly or in part, of earlier texts. Mellis drew from the material in Oldcastle's book and acknowledges this in his preface, but this was not the invariable practice. There are numerous examples of authors copying vast tracts and almost the entire text of an earlier work with no acknowledgement whatsoever. Indeed Mellis's text in many places corresponds very closely to Pacioli. In addition, Mellis seems to have drawn heavily from James Peele, 1553 and 1569, and Peele in turn borrowed from his predecessors, though the degree of correspondence is not so exact as in the case of Mellis (Yamey, 1979, p.210). In a similar vein, the accounting section in the American version of *Young Man's Companion* (1737) was a plagiarism from the fourteenth edition of William Mather's *Young Man's Companion*, 1734, which in turn seems to have been taken from Fisher's *The Instructor: or Young Man's Best Companion* (1727), both published in England (McMickle, pp.44–46).

Double entry under fire in Britain

The rate of publication of bookkeeping texts naturally increased significantly as time went by. Wider coverage of topics and greater diversity in their treatment resulted, but they remained loyal to the main principles of the 'Italian method'. The system became the subject of a determined attack, however, with the appearance, in 1796, of the *English System of Book-keeping by Single or Double-Entry* written by Edward Jones and published in Bristol. This book was intended to replace double entry by combining the simplicity of single entry with comprehensive bookkeeping. It contained some good ideas but failed to achieve its objective.

The first edition listed over 4000 subscribers resident in all parts of England, including the Bank of England and the East India Company which subscribed for five copies each. The author is said to have made £25,000 from his invention. The book is prefaced by a glowing testimony, signed among others by the Governor of the Bank of England and by Robert Peel, MP, father of the nineteenth-century prime minister.

Jones's advertisement for his book contained swingeing criticisms of double entry bookkeeping systems currently in use. He argued that their complexity made fraud and deception easy, and that the process of balancing, although difficult and time consuming, left fraud and error undetected in many cases. Several publications quickly appeared defending double entry against Jones's criticism and exposing the defects of the system he proposed. It was also the subject of satirical comment. James Mill drew attention to the fact that, in Jones's model business 'fabricated purposely to show the excellence of his system, he lost 10 pieces of calico!' Mill then sarcastically journalises the loss as follows (Eldridge, p.51):

> Edward T. Jones (of Bristol) Dr. £15.00
>
> For ten pieces of calico lost by his English system of book-keeping, a loss which at once proves the insufficiency of that system to prevent errors and establishes the superiority of the method of double-entry by which the present error has been detected.

Jones, himself, provided the most conclusive indictment of his system; by 1820 he had abandoned it and, instead, advertised the advantages of double entry. Despite this change, the title was retained throughout all 16 English editions, the most recent in 1882. It was published in America and was also translated into German, French, Italian and Russian.

According to one writer (Jager) 'Jones's significance lies solely in the advertising campaign, novel in its blatancy, which introduced his *system* into commercial circles during the Napoleonic Wars' (quoted in Yamey, 1944, p.408). This is too harsh a judgement. Indeed, Jones made a positive contribution towards the development of accounting technique, although not entirely in the manner he intended. His publication, perhaps mainly because of his outspoken approach, stimulated widespread interest in the subject. The practice of double entry was placed under the microscope and, in numerous cases, found wanting. It became clear that double entry was poorly understood, inadequately taught and unskillfully practised. The result of the reappraisal did not change the fundamentals of double entry, but it undoubtedly improved its practical application. It is equally clear that the short-term success of Jones's publication was due to the dissatisfaction with contemporary bookkeeping practices.

Jones's book was also the first English work on accounting to achieve an international reputation, and his proposals in the field of bookkeeping techniques foreshadowed later developments such as tabular presentation and sectional balancing procedures. It is unlikely that his model was ever widely employed in England.

Teaching methods

Rote learning. Peragallo has said that 'no theory of accounting was devised from the time of Paciolo down to the opening of the nineteenth century' (p.92). If the term 'theory' is taken to include the provision of a rational explanation for the operation of a system of double entry, we will see that Peragallo puts its appearance rather too late. We can agree, however, that for many years after 1494 texts were *essentially* confined to an exposition of the mechanics of double entry. The initial approach was to list a series of specimen transactions (Peele listed 44 according to Jackson, p.289), demonstrate the appropriate journal entry, and instruct readers to memorise their treatment.

An obvious limitation of learning 'by rote' was that the application of the rules was limited to similar transactions. The American economist John B.Canning, writing in 1929, was totally disparaging of early writers on accountancy: 'they made little showing of any systematic thought, though they were sticklers for unswerving adherence to the technical procedure shown. Like many another trade or occupational group, their dicta were amazingly positive and their arguments as amazingly inconsequential' (p.8).

Rote learning was, nevertheless, a teaching method appropriate to the business conditions and accounting procedures extant at the time. Bookkeeping was journal orientated. The journal was the most important record and the one referred to when it was necessary to examine the source and significance of a particular transaction; a procedure which was possible because the number of transactions was small. The ledger was more in the nature of a final resting place for the amounts involved and, indeed, it was often only partially written up or not written up at all.

Littleton and Zimmerman have made the point that, despite double entry's practical origins, there were patterns of thought or theory implicit in the mechanistic procedures employed (p.47). The search, by early writers, for more general rules and explanations led to the personification of accounts. The terms debit, from the Italian *dare* to give, and credit, from *avere* to have (interpreted more loosely to mean to receive), worked well in relation to personal accounts where their use seems to have originated. For example, a debit entry in a customer's personal account recorded the fact that the individual involved was expected to give the proprietor a sum of money at some future date. The extention of the idea of 'giving' and 'receiving' to impersonal accounts was clearly artificial, however, and the justification for this fiction was simply that it helped to explain to students the treatment of non-personal transactions in the accounts.

Some ingenious procedures were used to aid understanding. Oldcastle, for example, taught readers to regard cash as a chest (the word cash is, incidentally, derived from *cassa* meaning a chest) which received and gave money (Coomber, p.212). The accounts used to record revenues and expenses were even more difficult to fit into the new scheme, and use of the terms 'fictitious' or 'imaginary' accounts reflect the contemporary problem of seeking an adequate explanation for their existence (indeed, the term 'nominal' account, now in use, simply means 'in name only'). The system which viewed accounts as giving and receiving was still quite common in the early twentieth century. Personification was an improved scheme of rote learning, but its preoccupation with the mechanics of record keeping, and the lack of attention to reporting, proved to be a fundamental constraint on its long-term usefulness.

Proprietorship theory. Eighteenth-century writers began to attack rote learning. Roger North (1714), for example, said he would not 'labour very hard, or penetrate deep, by exaggerating multitudes of rules and perplexed examples, as most writers on this subject have done' (quoted in Jackson, p.301). A start was instead made to look for the logic underlying accounting procedures; the outcome was the first major contribution of accounting theory to the development of accounting practice.

The proprietorship theory of bookkeeping regards all assets and liabilities as belonging to, and transactions as relating to, the owner. The owner is seen as the central focus for business operations, and the purposes of the records and reports are to keep track of, and measure changes in, his interest in the concern. This line of thought eventually led to the development of the balance sheet equation – Capital = Assets − Liabilities ($C = A - L$) – an increased emphasis on the balance sheet, and a reduction in the amount of attention given to the journal.

Chatfield believes that the origin of the proprietorship theory may be traced, in Britain, to Malcomb (1718) who distinguished transactions which produced a profit, and therefore increased proprietors' capital, from those which did not (p.221). The effect of transactions on assets, liabilities and capital, rather than their personalisation, was further developed by Stephens (1735) and Fulton (1800). The system became fully fledged with Cronhelm's contribution in 1818. He introduced the algebraic approach to transaction analysis, referred to above, with transactions affecting the accounting equation by increasing or decreasing capital, assets and liabilities.

The entity theory. The entity theory began its challenge, in the literature, during the first half of the twentieth century. With hindsight, it seems natural that this theory should have gained ground concurrently with the rapid development of the corporate form. Paton (1922), who was the leading early advocate of the entity concept, adapted the proprietorship theory to the realities of the large corporation (Chatfield, p.224). He made the point that while, in practice, accounting techniques were developed to meet corporate needs, existing theory still assumed that a record of the company's relationship with the proprietor was the main task.

The essential difference between the two theories is as follows: under the proprietorship theory transactions are recorded, assets are valued and accounting statements are prepared from the viewpoint of the proprietor; under the entity theory each of these functions is performed from the viewpoint of the business as a going concern. It is assumed (a fiction in the case of the unincorporated enterprise) that the business owns the assets and owes the liabilities. Reduced to simple formula the entity theory is $A = C + L$, i.e. capital is accorded a less central position in the accounting process than under the proprietorship theory.

The entity theory therefore takes a wider view of the accounting process. Financial statements are seen as a communication device between management and a whole range of user groups. The amount due to the proprietor is looked upon as merely one of a number of liabilities, and the profit figure as the amount owing to the proprietor for services provided. It is the underlying logic of the entity theory that has caused the shareholder oriented profit and loss account to be supplemented, in recent years, by the value added statement, which emphasises the wide range of claims on the revenue generated by a company, and the funds statement, which focuses on the total resource movements during an accounting period.

The entity theory appears particularly appropriate for large companies where the assets do not belong to the shareholders who, in turn, have no personal liability for the firm's debts. The proprietorship view of the firm, on the other hand, continues to apply fairly well to unincorporated enterprises where there is a coincidence between ownership and management. Probably because of its North American origin, the entity theory became established and widely used in US universities much earlier than in Britain.

Much more surprising is the fact that Cronhelm's discoveries, expressed in a clear and concise fashion, remained dormant for over 130 years. It was only in the 1950s that teachers, in this country, began to use the balance sheet approach to explain double entry in terms of the effect of individual transactions on various financial magnitudes.

Theory versus practice

An interesting question, to which there is no definitive answer, is whether the accounting literature has reflected, led or followed accounting practice. The likelihood is that textbooks were well ahead of much existing practice (as is still the case today), but there were some innovative companies coping with new accounting problems not yet dealt with in the literature.

There are a few scattered observations and assertions which shed some light on the relationship between theory and practice. Pacioli made it perfectly clear that he was describing accounting systems in operation and inventing nothing new. What is also clear is that existing systems were, in a number of cases, more complex than the method described by Pacioli. For example, 'the Datini accounts of 1410 include accruals, depreciation, lower of cost or market inventory valuation, and foreign exchange accounts, not one of which was adequately discussed by Pacioli' (Chatfield, p.42). By the end of the fifteenth century, the larger Italian merchants and banking partnerships were using systems which comprised a wide variety of account books, including secret ledgers and cash books as well as other specialised books of original entry used to summarise transactions and reduce the amount of detail in the journal and the ledger.

In seventeenth-century Britain, Dafforne (1635) notes the absence of good bookkeeping texts in the English language, but also refers to the lack of popularity of this method among merchants (Yamey, 1980, p.82). He draws attention to the need for individuals who wish to become acquainted with double entry to go abroad. In general British textbooks at this time are thought to have lagged behind existing practice. Moving on to the nineteenth century, an anonymous article in *McCulloch's Dictionary of Commerce*, 1836, suggests that the larger firms in London and Bristol used rather more sophisticated bookkeeping systems than the one described in Sutcliffe's *Young Man's Best Companion*, 1816 (Etor, p.39). As time went by textbooks no doubt played an increasingly important role in standardising accounting practice and, by the end of the nineteenth century, double entry bookkeeping was in widespread use among the larger British companies.

8

Measuring Profits and Valuing Assets in Britain, 1225–1830

Introduction

It is difficult to generalise about valuation procedures; different sectors of the economy used vastly different methods at the same time. Even firms in the same locality were sometimes decades apart in terms of the sophistication of their accounting methods. The fact that this period saw massive changes in the nature, scale and organisation of business activity was no doubt partly responsible for the degree of variation. In the middle ages, for example, individual traders operated from small premises or on foot; by the end of the Industrial Revolution there were, in certain industries, factories employing hundreds of workers.

Many of the accounting methods, described below, may seem rudimentary judged by present-day standards, but it must be remembered that they were usually satisfactory for contemporary purposes. As time went by, and the preparation of accounting statements became a more common practice, increased attention was devoted to valuation problems.

Profit measurement

Need to measure profit. The original reason for measuring profit was to enable the business manager to decide whether resources were gainfully employed. The nineteenth-century development of the limited company, and the separation of ownership from management, produced two further reasons for measuring profit: first, to identify the balance legally available for the payment of dividends; secondly, as the basis for reporting to creditors and absentee owners.

In earlier times these pressures were evident only in the relatively small number of statutory and chartered companies which raised their capital from the general public.

In the typical pre-industrial organisation profit measurement, even as the basis for management decisions, was rarely a priority. Businesses were run by an owner/manager who was in close touch with all aspects of business activity. He knew whether goods were arriving on time, whether his employees were working hard and whether customers were satisfied with the goods delivered to them. He could also tell, from the amount of cash available, whether his firm was doing well or poorly. Consequently, profit calculations were not needed as the basis for performance assessment and decision making. Nor did the prudent businessman need a formal profit calculation to advise him how much he could afford to spend. He instead based his drawings on the amount of free cash available and adjusted his standard of living accordingly.

The need to measure profit was greater in the case of a partnership, in order to decide how much each partner should receive. Provided cash and goods were withdrawn in an agreed ratio, however, the calculation could be delayed until an existing partner retired or a new partner was admitted and the entire enterprise then revalued.

Early profit calculations. There are examples of *ad hoc* calculations of profit, as the basis for business decisions, stretching back to Roman times. The Roman agricultural writer Columella (*circa* 60 AD) made an estimate of the profits to be derived from vine growing and compared it with the return which could be obtained by instead investing the money at 6 per cent. Columella's analysis has received a great deal of attention and has been criticised on the grounds that many relevant costs were omitted (for example depreciation and the cost of hiring casual labour), but it remains a fairly sophisticated attempt to generate relevant numbers which could be used as the basis for business decisions.

In Britain, an early, surviving, calculation of profit was made by the monks of Christ Church, Canterbury for 1225. Exactly what was meant by profit, however, and the way it was used in this, and other, cases is not altogether clear (Stone, E., p.27). A mid-fourteenth-century treatise, known as the *Gloucester Husbandry,* includes rules for calculating profit which are perhaps indicative of contemporary, best, practice. The exercise starts with the transactions contained in a 'money' charge and discharge statement (see

Chapter 4), 'foreign' (non-recurring) receipts and expenses are then deleted and adjustments made for the values of corn and stock not included in the money-based account. We also know that thirteenth-century profit calculations sometimes even contained an element of accruals accounting. For example, at the Bolton Priory profit included 'hay, *not usually valued,* for the maintenance of sheep' (Noke, p.147). The adjustment of charge and discharge data to provide information for business decisions is also referred to by Yamey:

> Though the charge-and-discharge accounting system was essentially designed to determine the liability of the accounting official, some estates from as early as the time of Edward I [1272–1307] made use of additional records or compilations to give convenient summary views of their financial position or the profitability of their activities (p.13).

The experience at Norwich Cathedral, documented by E.Stone, is a good case study of the development of the profit concept. Prior to 1265 an overall profit figure was calculated using valuations of *all* money and other property entering and leaving the household. After that date profit on arable husbandry and livestock was calculated by deducting, from total manorial profit, those items not directly concerned with farming such as income from 'rents, the manorial court, the mill, [and other] miscellaneous items' (p.31). A 1289 innovation was the introduction of the opportunity cost concept in calculating and evaluating the profits obtained from arable husbandry and livestock.

Clear recognition of the opportunity cost concept is also contained in the literature. For example, an early fourteenth-century edition of the *Seneschaucy* suggests that the auditor should calculate whether there would be more efficient management under a different bailiff or whether it would be more profitable to farm the land out for a fixed rent. A second suggested comparison, albeit in a convoluted manner, was between the current net proceeds from the herd (proceeds of cheese and butter minus the cost of maintaining the cows) with the proceeds if the herd was farmed out (Noke, p.148).

The farm accounts of Robert Loder (1610–20) show 'deep concern with profit maximisation' (Yamey, p.15). They contain quite complex calculations of the profitability of various farming activities; also estimates of what the profit would have been had resources been employed differently. Detailed adjustments include a notional interest charge for capital employed, the identification of the relevant costs of particular schemes, and a depreciation charge for horses used on the farm. The sophistication of the calculations contrasts sharply with the presentation of data in the primitive paragraph form of accounting record.

These are interesting, but isolated, examples. The reason for the slow development of accounting calculations as a basis for decision making no doubt stems from the fact that the provision of accounting data is a dependent variable, and there was simply little demand for such information. This lack of interest was no doubt partly due to the fact that businessmen had limited alternative opportunities. What is also clear is that the structure of society and contemporary business conditions limited their freedom of action.

Macve, for example, has drawn attention to the fact that the medieval landlord's workforce was fixed by the number of villeins and serfs on his estate. Also, at a time when communications were poor, it was important for him to be substantially self-sufficient. It was therefore necessary to undertake a mixture of activities which would, for instance, provide him with fertiliser for his fields, food and clothing for the dependants, and foodstock and water for the animals (pp.247–52). A further constraint on the development of profit measurement procedures may have been an inherent dislike of the profit motive which the landowner considered below his dignity.

Haphazard measuremant procedures. The adoption of double entry techniques as industry developed in the seventeenth and eighteenth centuries did not immediately result in a broad based improvement in profit measurement procedures. Indeed, an examination of the ledgers of British businessmen has produced evidence of woeful ineptitude or lack of interest in profit measurement – probably both (Yamey). The following are the main features.

1. Major assets and liabilities were omitted. We know this because nominal accounts were credited with sums, such as rents received, though no corresponding investment in land or property appeared in the ledger.
2. Profit calculations were haphazard in the sense that some nominal accounts were not closed to the profit and loss account when the latter was balanced.

3. The profit and loss account frequently included personal expenses, capital expenditure, unrealised income and any surplus arising on asset revaluations.
4. The capital account was similarly used to dispose of financial balances no longer considered relevant, sometimes including all the data which should have appeared in the profit and loss account.
5. Pre-payments and accruals were generally ignored.
6. A 'general account' was used for the disposal of items which should have been accounted for in the capital account and the profit and loss account.

The above findings have led to the conclusion that double entry was initially valued as a record keeping device rather than as a means of calculating business profit. It should be borne in mind, however, that the main demand for accounting data came from management concerned with internal resource allocation rather than absentee shareholders keen to assess the overall performance of the enterprise. In the former context, the contribution of double entry was that it provided an efficient framework of ledger accounts which could be used 'to accumulate the expenditures and receipts associated with each particular lot or type of merchandise, investment or trading voyage' (Winjum, p.240). In other words, the manager could sometimes get the required information direct from the ledger.

Innovations. As time went by procedures naturally improved, and a positive accounting development during the Industrial Revolution was the division of business activity into a series of equal accounting periods for reporting purposes. Periodic accounts were of course required by chartered and statutory companies for the purpose of identifying divisible profit, but periodicity went much further. Surviving business records show the preparation of weekly, monthly or other fixed interval reports dealing with such matters as production, consumption of raw materials, and stock levels. Much of this information seems to have been needed by management as a basis for decision making. The quantity of transactions were beyond the capacity of a single brain to absorb, and the absentee owner (e.g. the Guest family controlling the Dowlais Iron Company from London) was a further factor.

A period of economic depression often encourages the businessman to re-examine his business policies and accounting system. This was the case at Josiah Wedgewood's pottery works at Stoke on Trent where, in 1772, sales were falling and stocks increasing. The firm had previously charged customers on the basis of 'what the traffic would bear' but, in the present climate, Wedgewood recognised the need for costing data so that 'we may not fix the prices so high as to prevent sale, nor so low as to leave no proffit upon them' (McKendrick, p.49). His attempts to produce total costings for 31 products included figures for depreciation, administrative and selling costs and interest on capital.

There were some initial problems and, at one stage the industrialist admitted that his calculations were out by a factor of two. Further investigations and refinements caused Wedgewood to reach the following important conclusions, that some expenses 'move like clockwork, & are much the same whether the quantity of goods [produced] be large or small'; others remain 'nearly the same . . . whether we do much or little in the time'; and that in some cases 'we have advanc'd the prices by the inches out of all proportion to the real expence' (ibid., p.52 and p.55). These findings, linked with Wedgewood's conviction that a small reduction in prices would enable his goods to be sold to the 'middling class', caused him to adjust relative prices, marginally reduce overall prices, and expand output. The result was a return to profitability.

Fixed assets

Expenditure on fixed assets increased in the eighteenth century as the result of gradual industrialisation. A number of the most significant innovations occurred in the textile industry, such as Kay's 'Flying Shuttle' in the 1730s, Hargreave's 'Spinning Jenny' (1765), Arkwright's water powered spinning frame (1769), and Cartwright's power loom (1784). These inventions enabled the production of cotton fabric to be the first fully mechanised manufacturing process and paved the way for the replacement of domestic by factory based production.

Much of the machinery required by textile companies and in other pioneering industries, such as iron making, was not particularly expensive, but there were exceptions, e.g. the cost of a water or steam driven mill was approximately £15,000. Also there was the cost of accommodation as the domestic system gave way to factory based production. The natural outcome was that businessmen began to pay more attention to the accounting treatment of capital expenditure. Five methods of accounting for fixed assets and the income derived from them can be distinguished.

Historical cost. The fixed asset was retained in the books at historical cost; depreciation was ignored and revenue was not charged with the cost of fixed assets used up during the course of business operations until a sale took place (even then some companies continued to ignore economic reality and left the asset in the books at its original figure). The omission of a charge was, however, unimportant either where no depreciation had occurred or where the principal objective was to keep track of the asset's existence. Advantages of the method were, and still are, that it is objective and easy to apply.

Net balance method. The fixed asset was reported at original cost plus related expenses, less related receipts. This method, sometimes called the arithmetic balance, produced a conservative measure of profit; the cost of the investment had to be fully recovered before any entry was made in the profit and loss account. The method was considered appropriate where income arose directly from an asset, such as rent from land, dividends from an investment, or minerals from a mine.

Revaluation. The value of the property was appraised periodically; the new value was carried forward and the difference, gain or loss, was transferred to the profit and loss account. This approach treated fixed assets, in effect, as the unsold merchandise of the proprietor undertaking a terminable venture, and was consistent with the proprietorship theory of accounting (see Chapter 7). An advantage of this method was that it was a way, perhaps the only way, of obtaining a figure for fixed assets at a time when business records were incomplete and unreliable. A disadvantage was that it mixed together realised and unrealised profits and losses.

A combination of the net balance method and the revaluation method is described by John Mair, 1768 (reproduced in Littleton, p.225): the cost of the asset (typically a ship or a house) or the value brought forward was debited to the fixed asset account, as were repairs and other related expenses. Credited to the account were profits arising from the use of the asset, such as freight charges and rent. The asset was valued at the end of the period and the difference transferred to the profit and loss account. When the asset was eventually sold the sales proceeds were credited to the account.

Current expense. Expenditure on fixed assets was not separately identified but simply mixed with current expenditure, i.e. no distinction was made between capital and revenue transactions. One explanation for this treatment is that industrial accounting developed out of commercial accounting where fixed assets were of little importance; certainly, in textbooks written for the merchants' counting houses, fixed equipment was commonly ignored. Indeed the term 'stock in trade' originally meant all business assets – 'that part of the trading goods which were used to trade' (Cannan, p.475) – and was attributed this meaning by Colinson writing in 1673 (Parker, 1974, p.360).[1]

Industrial firms were able to account for fixed assets as a current expense, without wiping out reported profit, because of high profit margins and the relatively low ratio of fixed asset costs to total expenditure. For example, even the cost of sinking a pit (admittedly pits were fairly shallow at this time) could sometimes be recovered in just a few months and, where this was not the case, the cost could be comfortably absorbed by revenue generated from pits currently in use.

The method was used mainly by small businesses, where the level of capital expenditure or accounting expertise was low, but also by some very large organisations, e.g. the Dowlais Iron Company which commenced business at the beginning of the Industrial Revolution. By 1842 it was the largest ironworks in the world and, throughout this period of enormous growth, virtually all 'new work' was written off immediately against revenue. As late as 1862 the accountant described capital as 'a great current account of floating assets and liabilities, no additions being made to the assets for improvements of plant or extensions in the works' (Edwards and Baber, p.145). Another example concerns the Dalcoath mine where, in 1872, 1000 workers were employed but the balance sheet figure for invested capital was 'only nominal' because expenditure on new machinery had been treated as a current operating expense (Pollard, p.239).

This ultra-conservative accounting practice probably encouraged businessmen to live within their means, since distributable profits were recognised only after the capital investment had been fully recovered out of revenue. The accounts of course provided very little useful information as the basis for performance assessment and investment decisions, but this was often unimportant because of high margins and the fact that the typical enterprise was organised as a family firm with the managers remaining in close touch with every detail of business operations. Moreover, if relevant data was required to form the basis for business decisions, separate calculations could be made on an *ad hoc* basis.

Cost less depreciation. Perhaps the earliest definition and example of depreciation are provided by the Roman, Vitruvius. He described depreciation as 'the price of the passing of each year', and in valuing a masonry wall argued that 1/80th of its cost should be deducted for each year it had stood (Chatfield, p.96). The purpose of the calculation was to arrive at a valuation for a legal settlement. Early textbook references to depreciation are made by John Mellis (1588) who shows 10 guineas written off for the 'decay' of household implements and by Stephen Monteage (1690) who writes £6 off the opening value of the stock of horses 'for their use and impairing' (Littleton, pp.223–24). Whether the charge is a residual figure, based on periodic appraisal, or a systematic allocation of original cost is not clear. Certainly, the Monteage charge, arrived at by valuing six horses at the beginning of the year at £8 each and at the end of the year at £7 each, suggests the former.

The treatment of depreciation as a systematic allocation of original cost was slow to appear in business records. At the end of the eighteenth century, a charge was not usually made even by joint stock companies. Where it does show up, it is sometimes for tactical reasons. For instance, at Cyfarthfa, William Crawshay (1814) decided that it was 'best to write off and not uphold all accounts of the sort I point out more particularly while there is still Property Tax to pay' (Jones, p.160). Early practical examples of systematic depreciation accounting (all straight line) are at the Carron Ironworks (1769), 8 per cent per annum on buildings, steam engines and machines, and at Boulton and Watt's, Soho Foundry (1790s), 5 per cent on buildings and 8 per cent on steam engines (Pollard, p.244).

The practice of charging depreciation became more common after 1800, particularly in the textile industries where the Industrial Revolution first produced a significant element of capital intensity. For example, at the Charlton (cotton) Mills, Manchester, depreciation was charged at 5 per cent per annum in 1810 (Stone, Williard, p.77). Systematic depreciation accounting becomes more feasible when a company operates a sound system for recording business transactions, and no doubt some small improvement had been made by this time.

It is often difficult to establish, today, the exact nature of items appearing in old business records. As we have seen an entry for depreciation might be the result of periodic appraisal or an allocation of original cost. In addition the sum deducted might take account of such factors as the level of profit, the replacement cost of assets and the rate of technical advance, as well as estimates of the extent of deterioration. A further problem is that the terms wear and tear, more generally used to cover the actual cash cost of repairs, and depreciation were sometimes used interchangably.

On a few, fortunate, occasions the exact nature of an entry is fully explained. For example, Joshua Milne, the Oldham cotton spinner, informed a government committee (1833) that he charged depreciation because of the need to provide for wear and tear, replacement, annual upkeep and fall in value in order to avoid having 'fictitious capital' (Pollard, p.243). R.H.Greg, another cotton spinner, charged depreciation 'not only for actual wear and tear, but also for its deterioration arising out of new inventions' (ibid.). Technical advance did result in some famous eighteenth-century examples of premature obsolescence – the introduction of Heathcoat's patent bobbin net machine reduced the value of hand machines from £1200 to £60. The risk of rapid obsolescence was often countered by applying a high rate of depreciation to textile machinery (ibid.).

It is not possible to assess, accurately, the relative popularity of the accounting methods described in this section. What is clear is that, although some of the methods seem rudimentary, they were often a fairly understandable choice in the circumstances where they were employed. The retention of fixed assets at cost made some sense in the case of durable, general purpose, assets which could easily be transferred to an alternative use. The treatment of fixed assets as a current expense was convenient where the amount involved was immaterial; it was also appropriate where the main reason for measuring profit was to identify the amount which could be prudently withdrawn in cash. Periodic appraisal was consistent with the proprietorship theory, which regarded all assets as part of the merchants' stock in trade. The net balance method had a certain tidiness where revenue was directly generated by a particular asset. The inclusion of a charge for depreciation was rare.

Stock

Early writers not surprisingly fail to agree about how stock should be valued. James Peele (1569) refers to a stock of clothes 'valewed as the cost'; Richard Hayes (1741) tells us that merchants usually value their goods 'at the market price they then go at, at the time of their balancing', though his advice is simply to value stocks at *either* cost or market price. Some writers went on to explain their choice. Alexander Malcolm (1731) favoured cost and put forward a justification for what we today call the realisation concept: 'otherwise you bring in gain or loss into your accounts, which has not yet actually happened, and may, perhaps not happen'. Robert Hamilton (1788) preferred a market price valuation, because 'the gain is in reality obtained so soon as the prices rise, or the loss suffered as soon as they fall' (all from Parker, 1965, pp. 157–58).

De Roover has pointed out that inventory valuation was not all that important in medieval times because, in line with the practice of venture accounting, merchants usually opened a separate account for each batch of goods acquired and left it open until everything was sold (1956, p. 117). With increased industrialisation, characterised by continuous productive activity and the need for management information and *periodic* external reports, the valuation problem had to be tackled. The usual solution was to value stocks at cost, signifying the growing influence of the entity concept, though market price was sometimes used.

The really difficult problem facing pioneer industrialists was how to value manufactured stock. Prime costs could be identified without too much difficulty but overhead costs made the calculation quite complex. For the purpose of preparing periodic accounts: raw materials were valued at cost; work in progress was either estimated or completely omitted on the assumption that the figures at the beginning and end of the year were unlikely to be significantly different; and finished goods were generally valued at either selling price or selling price less an estimated gross profit margin. Where the former procedure was adopted the effect was to recognise profit on the basis of production rather than sales.

Some companies did a bit better. There are examples of valiant efforts being made to compute figures for total cost in industries such as coal, iron and textiles. These costings seem to have been used as the basis for estimating profit margins, but they were rarely integrated with the system of double entry and 'as guides to inventory pricing at the year-end . . . they were much too crude'

(Lee, p.15). One notable exception (no doubt there are others), the Charlton Mills of Manchester, proves that a much more sophisticated accounting system could be operated in practice even at this early stage.

The activities of the mill were divided into cost centres; five carding rooms, eight spinning rooms and the warehouse. Overhead costs, including allowances for depreciation and an imputed return on the owners' capital, were collected in the general expense account and, from this clearing account, re-charged to cost centres at predetermined rates which were adjusted in the light of experience to prevent underabsorption. An intra-company pricing system was devised to value transfers between cost centres. Stock was physically counted and valued on the full cost basis, every two months, to enable the gain or loss of each cost centre to be struck and management accounts to be prepared (Stone, Williard, pp.72–78).

Debtors

Alternative accounting treatments for doubtful debts were to write them off as bad or carry them at book value long after the possibility of recovery had passed. Where the latter course was followed, the use of captions such as 'dubious' or 'desperate' debtors fulfilled both a control function and a valuation objective. It shows a determination to keep a record of the debt 'just in case' the financial position of the debtor improved enabling the amount to be collected. It also reminded the proprietor that the likelihood of collection was low and the value of the asset therefore zero. As Robert Hamilton (1788) put it: 'although it introduces the amount of these debts as an article of your stock at the general balance, no great inconvenience follows, because the title by which they are distinguished must lead you to make a proper estimate' (quoted in Yamey, p.24). Such debts were usually collected together in a single account to avoid wasting room in the ledger.

Scrappy records and business valuation

Pollard has drawn attention to the generally poor quality of accounting records up to and during the Industrial Revolution. His research has shown that, even among some of the most technically advanced, successful, and innovative firms, accounting practices fell far below the standard which we know could be achieved at this time. At the Carron Company, a profit of £10,500 was estimated for 1767 whereas, in fact, a loss of £10,000 had been suffered. The accounts of the Anglesy copper mines, which made major contributions to industrial development, are generally considered to have been 'so badly kept as to be almost useless'. An example of total ignorance concerning a firm's financial position appears in the books of the Walkers of Masbro', which refer to the great surprise on discovering that the assets of the company were worth £82,189 in September 1775. At Boulton and Fothergill, accounts prepared as late as the 1860s showed profits without making provision for doubtful debts which amounted to colossal sums (Pollard, ch.6).

These practices appear to have resulted partly from ignorance, and partly from the lack of attention given to the accounting function. Few clerical staff were employed and even these were expected to perform other duties (ibid., p.231). Interestingly, administrative weaknesses were often not fatal to the enterprise's well being, but sometimes they were. For example, the frequency of bank failures, during the 1820s, is believed to have been partly caused by the scrappy, uncoordinated character of their bookkeeping and the fact that an audit was so rare as to be almost unknown (ibid., p.227).

In the absence of satisfactory records, a common practice was to value the firm *de novo* at the accounting date. Such valuations were unconstrained by the historical cost concept and took account of such variables as the state of the trade. It is therefore not surprising to learn that substantial fluctuations of capital sometimes resulted. For example, Benjamin Gott wrote down the fixed capital of the Bean Ing mill from its long-standing book value of £26,500 to £10,000 in 1817 and £5000 in 1818 because of bad trading conditions (ibid., p.237). Assets were left out of the calculation if they could not easily be valued.[2] An extreme example occurred at the Parys Mine Co. (1816–24) where the increase in capital was found by ignoring even debtors and simply comparing stock in trade valuations at different dates (ibid., p.236).

A second method used to value a firm's capital was earning capacity. According to Thomas Fenwick, 'the famous northern coal-viewer', writing in 1818:

> The mode of valuing coal in Northumberland is according to the system of valuing Annuities – the duration of the colliery being considered the term of the payment of the Annuity – the annual rent of the colliery is considered as the Annuity itself,

> and the percentage is fixed according to the hazard attending the coal property (quoted in Pollard, p.238).

The rate used was usually 8 per cent, but 10 per cent if the investment was risky.

A natural consequence of these approaches to accounts preparation was that, often, no distinction was made between the owner's capital investment and profit earned. Such accounts were eminently suitable for identifying the respective interests of partners when a change of ownership occurred, and as the basis for raising further finance, but they were of little use for performance assessment.

Review

During the seventeenth and eighteenth centuries businessmen adopted double entry bookkeeping mainly as a means of providing a more effective memory aid and mechanism for financial control. Because the calculation of profit was rarely the reason for installing a system of bookkeeping, the numbers generated were often of poor quality. Notable features of contemporary accounting procedures were: profit and loss accounts prepared substantially, if not entirely, on the cash basis; little attention devoted to properly allocating revenues and expenditures to the appropriate accounting period; a lack of consistency in the valuation methods used by businesses for similar assets both in a particular year and over time; a lack of uniformity between businesses in the valuation methods used; the inclusion of unrealised gains; the failure to separate realised and unrealised gains and losses; the failure to distinguish between capital and revenue items; and profit calculated on an irregular basis, perhaps only when there was a change of partners or because the ledgers were full.

The evidence suggests that accountants were rather slow to adapt, for practical use, the theoretical ideas expressed by contemporary classical economists. Adam Smith's *Wealth of Nations* (1776) drew a clear distinction between fixed capital 'employed in the improvement of land, in the purchase of useful machines and instruments of trade, or in such like things as yield revenue or profit without changing masters', and circulating capital 'employed in raising, manufacturing or purchasing goods and selling them again at a profit' (p.112). According to Tucker, early nineteenth-century classical economists developed the distinction between the stock of capital and the flow of income and, when discussing profit calculation, normally assumed that a deduction would be made for depreciation 'by dividing [the asset's] original value by the number of years of its productive life' (p.89). Indeed, economists such as Samuel Read (1829) directed attention to the following important relationship ignored by almost all accountants and businessmen until the twentieth century: the rate of profit 'is always reckoned or estimated by the proportion, or ratio, which it [profit] bears to the stock or capital from which it arises' (quoted in Tucker, p.87).

The growing importance of the partnership, both to provide necessary capital and management skills, increased the need to keep accounting records capable of identifying the profit to be divided between the partners. At the same time, it must be remembered that errors would affect partners in proportion to their right to profits and would be sorted out when a change in the partnership resulted in a revaluation of the business.

The Industrial Revolution provided a huge stimulus for improving accounting procedures. Where goods were traded or subject only to a simple industrial process, revenue was decided by the market and gross margins provided an adequate basis for rudimentary resource allocation decisions. The growth of the factory, with its associated fixed and joint costs and the need to transfer goods from one process to another caused progress to occur, albeit at a slow rate judged by reference to present-day standards. Progress first occurred in the textile industries, and the accounting records of the Charlton Mills, Manchester prove that a highly sophisticated system of costing was possible at the beginning of the nineteenth century. These may be seen as precursors of the techniques which, in Chandler's view, enabled the modern business enterprise to replace Adam Smith's invisible hand of market forces by the visible hand of management as the means of coordinating the activities of the economy and allocating its resources (p.1). The last decades of the Industrial Revolution also took business well into the century when, according to Yamey, 'what had often been incidental [profit measurement], became central' (p.25).

A further aspect of accounting change, brought about by the Industrial Revolution, was the growing use of cost (instead of value) as the basis for reporting fixed assets and stock in the accounts. This signals the start of the entity theory's challenge to the proprietorship theory as the basis for financial report preparation. It was not until the twentieth century, however, that it achieved supremacy. Ironically, at about the same time as the theory *began* to receive explicit recognition in the accounting literature.

9

Joint Stock and Limited Liability

Introduction

The development of the large-scale limited liability company was closely associated with the emergence of the absentee investor and the hierarchical system of professional management. These groups required financial information as the basis for resource allocation decisions (management) and in order to assess the state of their investment (shareholders), but it was completely impracticable to allow all of them direct access to the ledger. Even where access was a possibility, it would not have helped very much. Except for personnel involved in the minute detail of financial control, users are rarely interested in the balance on an individual ledger account; their focus of attention is more likely to be the financial effects of a range of transactions. Summarisation of these transactions in the form of financial statements is an essential first step before an assessment of progress can be made.

The function of accounting statements is, therefore, to fill gaps in knowledge which occur, in large businesses, as the result of physically separating managers from the shop floor and shareholders from the company in which they have invested. It is for these reasons that the growth of the large limited company has been the most important single event transforming accountancy from a discipline concerned principally with classifying and recording business transactions into one where a major preoccupation is the preparation of financial reports. The origins and development of the joint stock company and the concept of limited liability are examined in this chapter.

Corporate personality

Corporate personality means that an organisation is deemed to have an existence separate and distinct from its members. The exact origin of the concept of corporate personality is not known; undoubtedly it developed over time and was certainly in existence well before it was adopted as the basis for the joint stock trading company. For example, the three great institutions of the middle ages, the church, the craft guild and the town, each enjoyed a corporate existence separate from its members. Attributes naturally, though not necessarily, associated with separate corporate personality are perpetual existence (being an artificial person, the corporation does not die), the ownership of property, and the ability to take, or suffer, legal action in the name of the institution.

Corporate personality was invented to meet a need – the separate identification of the organisation's activities. It was not, initially, a legal creation. Many early institutions sought legal recognition, however, in the form of a charter or statute, and often requested the grant of numerous other privileges such as monopoly rights and limited liability.

Origin of joint stock

Business activity in medieval times consisted of a series of small ventures. Traders operated with little or no stock. They purchased items and then looked for a seller, and the sale provided the money to make a new purchase. The level of activity fluctuated and business operations were often discontinuous. Business affairs were frequently intermingled with private affairs and profit, if calculated, was the difference between purchase and selling price, i.e. gross profit.

The link between this, highly individualistic, form of enterprise and the joint stock company was forged by the merchant adventurers of England. Their operations began in the year 1390, and were an extension of the guild principle to encompass overseas trade. These were the so-called 'regulated companies'; a loose organisation rather like a chamber of commerce. It was a mechanism for individuals to join together to conduct a particular branch of overseas trade. Members were admitted on the payment of a fee, but each traded *independently* with his own stock and at his own risk. Indeed, the East India Company initially operated on this basis.

Such activities were entirely consistent with the mercantilist philosophy which saw trade as the means for developing business strength and increasing national wealth. The State therefore encouraged the formation of these 'corporations' by issuing Royal Charters which conferred monopoly rights. The first Royal Charters date from the fourteenth century, but it was with the expansion of trade and settlement overseas, in the sixteenth century, that they became more common.

As overseas trade developed, voyages went further afield and, at a time when piracy was rampant and when there was considerable competition between the leading maritime nations, these adventures involved considerable danger. The expeditions of Frobisher and Drake, in the last quarter of the sixteenth century, sought to make gains at the expense of the Spanish and risked death in battle as well as business failure in search of profit. It was therefore necessary to arm the ships and fortify the trading posts against attack. These developments gave rise to the need for resources beyond the amount which an adventurer, acting on his own, could provide. There was also a need for a skilled managerial class to organise these more complex activities.

Elizabethan merchants therefore transformed the regulated company into organisations which operated on the basis of a *joint* stock. Initially the term described the practice of medieval merchants pooling their stock-in-trade to undertake a particular business activity, for example to purchase and equip a ship for a voyage. By 1600 the term joint stock was in use to describe, instead, the cash advanced to a business, though the investment was not permanent as is the case today.

East India Company

The East India Company was granted a charter by Elizabeth I in 1600. It was not the first chartered company, by any means, but it was the first company to exhibit the main features of the modern joint stock organisation. The year 1600 may therefore be considered the birth date of the English corporation. The company was granted monopoly rights to trade in the seas east of the Cape of Good Hope and west of the Straits of Magellan. As was often the case with chartered companies, it also acted on behalf of the government to help control colonial activities. It carried on a highly profitable trade for its shareholders for over two and a half centuries.

The company mobilised resources by raising capital from a wide range of investors, including earls, dukes, privy councillors, judges, knights, countesses, wealthy widows, merchants and clergymen. It was managed by a Governor and a Court of Committees made up of 24 members. The modern-day equivalent would be the board of directors. The General Court, made up of all the adventurers (shareholders), acted in a supervisory capacity and could overrule a particular recommendation of the Court of Committees. The accounting function was the responsibility of the Accountants General and the accounts were audited by the Auditors General.

During the first sixty years of its existence the East India Company was transformed from a collection of adventurers, making temporary investments, into a modern joint stock enterprise with a permanently invested capital. Between 1600–17 there were 113 distinct voyages, each with a separately subscribed capital. The initial plan was to divide the spoils at the end of each speculation but, because ventures lasted longer than expected, it became common practice to make interim distributions to shareholders as revenue arose. These 'divisions' were based on cash available and made no distinction between capital and revenue.

Non-liquid assets sometimes remained unsold at the end of a venture, making a final division impossible. In such cases the balances, described as 'rests' or 'remains', were carried forward from one adventure to another (Littleton, p.210). In 1630 investors began to subscribe on a time basis rather than a venture basis. The first subscription was for four years, with one quarter paid each year to 'fit out' the ships for new voyages. This marks the transition from adventurers jointly financing a stock of goods to investors holding shares in a company. The change occurred because of the growing number of overlapping ventures; property from five existing voyages was taken over by the new enterprise.

In 1657 the idea of a non-terminable stock became established. Asset based valuations of each £100 of stock, to be made at the end of seven years and then every three years, were arranged to facilitate stock transfers. In 1685 £100 of East India stock was valued at £327 in terms of net assets. The company also began to show some interest in what we now call the separation of capital from revenue for the purpose of identifying distributable profit. The Governor stated, in 1661, that future distributions would be based on profits earned rather than 'divisions' of available cash. We can therefore see that profit measurement became important because of the changed nature of the business organisation.

The idea of a permanent stock was not, however, invented by the East India Company. Earlier chartered enterprises operating on this basis were the Mines Royal (1568), the Mineral and Battery Works (1568), also engaged in mining, and the New River Company (1609), incorporated to bring water to London by conduit (Littleton, p.212). But it is the history of the East India Company which best demonstrates the transition from terminable to permanent investment in a large trading company.

Speculation and risk

During the seventeenth century businessmen began to display a greater awareness of the advantages of forming a 'company' whose activities were financed by the general public. The principal benefit was to release the scale of business operations from the cash constraints imposed by the wealth and financial commitments of the initial promoters. Moreover it provided investment opportunities for a large number of individuals who either did not wish to engage in trade directly or would have been incapable of doing so, perhaps because they possessed insufficient resources and/or lacked the necessary commercial expertise. From the promoters' viewpoint, a further favourable consequence was that it reduced their financial risk by spreading liability for what was often a speculative venture. The use of a joint stock was therefore a natural and spontaneous development to meet business requirements.

Between 1689–95 the number of joint stock companies in England rose from eleven to about 100. Many of these unincorporated enterprises operated on the basis of a joint stock without first obtaining the authority of either a Royal Charter or an Act of Parliament (Davies, p.292). The law at first frowned on these new associations, but their legitimacy, or otherwise, at common law was unclear. They continued to be formed, some large profits were made and, quite naturally, the public's willingness to invest increased. The first two decades of the eighteenth century was a period of considerable speculation with many businesses formed to undertake spectacular ventures. An atmosphere of high optimism, combined with the promise of a large return on a relatively small outlay, caused the general public to advance money without first attempting to confirm either the honesty of the promoters or the soundness of the planned activity. The typical sequence of events was as follows: shares in an unincorporated joint stock company were marketed; money was advanced; the share price rose to a level which was not justified by the underlying business potential; the 'bubble' burst and the share price collapsed.

Clearly the new organisational structure fulfilled a need by mobilising capital. It later became equally clear that the operation of a joint stock company required regulation, but it was initially treated no differently from the sole trader and partnership, i.e. it was left to its own devices. Dishonest promoters, who became aware of the scope provided by anonymity for the fraudulent conversion of shareholders' funds, advertised companies to carry on non-existent trades. Once the money was collected, the promoter disappeared. One rogue did not even bother to go to the trouble of inventing a spurious enterprise; his prospectus merely announced a company 'for an undertaking which shall in time be revealed'. He was as good as his word; 2000 guineas were collected in a single morning and the rascal disappeared in the afternoon (Irish, p.61). This, and other, hair-brained schemes culminated in the infamous South Sea Company scandal.

South Sea Company

The South Sea Company was not a typical 'bubble' company, since it was legitimately established by Act of Parliament (1710) to trade with South American States. It had ambitious schemes but its trading activities never really flourished. It looked elsewhere for business, and its offer, approved by the House of Commons, to take over the national debt for £7.5m caught the public eye. Perhaps because of the close involvement of a number of prominent politicians, the shares were the subject of an immense speculation. The price spiralled and then collapsed; during 1720 the price rose from 130 to over 1000 per cent, including a rise of 340 points during four days in May (Worthington, p.17). The bubble burst (the price fell to 190 by September), thousands of investors were totally ruined and there was a public outcry.

Ministers were implicated and the government was forced to act in order to restore confidence. We can see, with the benefit of hindsight, that the correct response would have been to devise and introduce rules for regulating this new form of business enterprise, since its creation proved that it fulfilled a useful commercial function. An alarmed government instead passed the Royal Exchange and London Assurance Corporation Act (1720), popularly known as the 'Bubble Act'. This limited the number of members of a partnership to six and prohibited the formation of joint stock companies unless authorised by either a Royal Charter or a private Act of Parliament; both were extremely expensive and time consuming processes, and a practical proposition for only the very large enterprise.

Effect of the 'Bubble Act'

The purpose, and probable effect, of the Act was to slow down the development of the joint stock company in Britain, but there is surprisingly little evidence that the absence of a cheap and easy means of achieving corporate status acted as a significant constraint on the rate of economic development. All the evidence is to the contrary. Between 1760–1830 Britain underwent its Industrial Revolution without mobilising capital on a large scale. This was not because money was scarce; the country was extremely rich with many wealthy landlords. Indeed, it has been estimated that, in the mid-eighteenth century, there was sufficient capital available to finance the Industrial Revolution many times over.

The absence of the joint stock mechanism did not hamper economic development, partly because necessary capital expenditure remained at a low level in most industries, and partly because there existed various sources of finance which enabled industry to flourish through the medium of the unincorporated enterprise. These included loans from friends or businessmen who recognised the potential of a new scheme; short-term finance from the rapid expansion of the country banking system;[1] the use of personal savings from an earlier employment; the expansion of an existing business on the basis of retained profits; and the additional resources provided by taking in an extra partner. While it is true that the Bubble Act restricted the number of partners to six (increased to 20 in 1825), this was not a serious constraint on development even in the more capital intensive manufacturing industry. The capacity of individual machines and items of equipment was low, with the result that additional productive units could be added fairly cheaply to existing facilities, i.e. it was possible to develop 'from the ground upwards'.

Where features of the joint stock company were required, businessmen and lawyers demonstrated their ingenuity in obtaining them. The popular mechanism used for this purpose was the deed of settlement company, whereby the proprietors joined together to undertake activities financed by a prescribed joint stock divided into a specified number of shares. The restrictions imposed by the Bubble Act were overcome by vesting property in trustees; sometimes the deed also stipulated that the company might sue and be sued in the names of the trustees, though the legality of this provision was rather doubtful. Shares were often treated as freely transferable despite the prohibition contained in the Act; apparently few companies were proceeded against and the restriction disappeared in 1825. Proprietors even achieved an element of limited liability by expressly writing into contracts a provision to the effect that, if the company defaulted, creditors could claim only against the assets of the company and from any amounts still due from members on their shares.

A curious feature of the philosophy underlying the Bubble Act is that it blamed the corporate form for the potential hazards of joint stock trading. The real problems were the dishonesty of promoters and the gullibility of subscribers, and it was perhaps because the government decided it could not prevent these personality defects from surfacing, in certain cases, that it decided, instead, to outlaw the vehicle for perpetrating fraud. Factors contributing to the government's negative response may have been the absence of adequate accounting procedures to help regulate the new type of organisation, and doubt about the need for a readily available means of incorporation. Adam Smith, writing half a century later (1776), remained convinced that the joint stock mechanism was appropriate only for companies whose 'operations are capable of being reduced to what is called a routine', i.e. banking, fire and marine insurance, canals and water works (p.317). Most of these were adequately served by methods of incorporation already available, i.e the Royal Charter or special Act of Parliament.

The kind of grounds on which charter applications were rejected can be illustrated by reference to the advice given to the government, by the attorney-general, in reponse to an application from the promoters of the Equitable Society (1761): the possible achievement of a monopoly position by driving out unincorporated traders; the ruin caused to thousands when a large corporation was bankrupted; the view that trade thrives better when left open to the 'free speculations of private men'; that the provision of the service by the unincorporated enterprise was perfectly practicable, as proved by the existence of three firms supplying insurance; finally that the grant of incorporation would be unfair to existing businesses (Hunt, p.11).

Statutory and chartered companies

Some early examples of well known chartered companies, in addition to the East India Company, are the Russia Company (1555), the Levant Company (1592) and the Hudson Bay Company (1670). The important privilege often conferred in the charter was a monopoly of trade with a particular geographical area. Early examples of companies incorporated by private Act of Parliament (statutory companies) are the New River Company (1606), which is the oldest company with stock presently listed on the London Stock Exchange, the Bank of England (1694) and London Assurance (1708). The formation of statutory companies, for *trading* purposes, grew out of the canal construction movement which followed James Brindley's success in building the Bridgewater Canal (1760) to carry the Duke of Bridgewater's coals from his Worsley colliery to Manchester. More than one hundred canal acts had received the royal assent by 1800, but it was not until the frenzy of railway construction, in the 1830s and 1840s, that the statutory company really came into its own.

The earliest railway act was passed in 1801 for a construction from Wandsworth to Croydon (Surrey Iron Railway). Carriages were initially horse-drawn, but in 1804 Richard Trevithick built the first steam-powered railway locomotive. These locomotives were used on a number of colliery lines before 1825 when the Stockton and Darlington opened using steam-powered locomotion for the conveyance of goods and passengers. The success of Stephenson's 'Rocket', 1829, and the financial success of the Liverpool and Manchester Railway led to a period of intense activity, during which about one thousand new companies were incorporated. The main stimuli for incorporation were the need to obtain powers for the compulsory purchase of land and to enable capital to be offered to the general public. Incorporation by special Act of Parliament also proved popular among other undertakings of a public nature, such as gas, water and, later, electric lighting companies.

It was not government practice to grant monopoly rights to newly formed domestic companies; indeed, in the nineteenth-century atmosphere of free enterprise, the policy of successive governments was to encourage maximum competition between companies in the same and in related industries, e.g. an acknowledged purpose of the Liverpool and Manchester Railway was to break down the monopoly of the canal companies who maintained 'a strict and illiberal alliance' along the route between those two cities (Clapham, p.396).

Direct attempts were made to prevent monopoly profits by dividend control provisions in the special statutes of many canal companies (e.g. Glamorganshire Canal Company, incorporated in 1790) and in the general statutes applying to gas and water companies (1847). Similar provisions were inserted, by Parliament, in the Liverpool and Manchester Railway's act of incorporation (1826). Subsequent railway acts made no reference to dividend control on the grounds that such a restriction 'would lead to improvidence, or evasion, or both' (Clapham, p.415). The government instead attempted to control railway profits by specifying maximum tolls for different categories of goods and passengers.

Arrival of the registered company

The early decades of the nineteenth century saw an increase in the number of companies engaged in fire and life insurance, and it was from this source that pressure was applied to repeal, in 1825, the restrictive provisions of the Bubble Act. A further statute, passed in the following year, provided for the establishment of joint stock banks without limitation on the number of partners, provided the business was located more than 65 miles from London. These embryo companies were empowered to sue and be sued in the name of the principal officer, but they were not granted limited liability.

The Trading Companies Act of 1834 allowed the Crown to confer, by letters patent, all or any of the privileges of incorporation (except limited liability) without going through the expensive and time consuming process of issuing a charter. Not a great deal of use was made of the Act, partly because of the expense still involved, and partly because of the restrictive rules imposed by the Board of Trade (BOT) regarding the granting of letters patent (Hunt, pp.57–58). An Act of 1837, which introduced certain changes including the removal of liability on the transfer of shares, improved matters a little; between 1837–54, 50 companies received privileges under the Act (Hunt, p.83).

For business in general the position remained unsatisfactory. The repeal of the Bubble Act merely restored the common law position which no one really understood anyway. It seems likely, however, that there was no objection to raising a joint stock at common law, nor to transferring shares, provided fraud did not occur. However, in the absence of regulations, deception and fraud did of course occur, particularly among insurance companies. Many of these were bogus from the outset; the creations of people such as Charles Dickens's Mr Tigg Montague, who promoted the very dubious Anglo-Bengalee Disinterested Loan and Life Assurance Company (*Martin Chuzzlewit*, 1843).

The government's response was to appoint the Gladstone Committee (1841) to discover why joint stock companies were regularly the subject of deception and fraud and to make recommendations. It's radical and farsighted recommendations (1844) were that corporate status should be made more readily available and that the newly created companies should be properly regulated. Specific proposals were that they should register their name, the location of the registered office, the names of directors, the internal rules and regulations, and various other items of information with the newly created office of registrar of companies. The committee believed that companies should also present audited accounts to shareholders attending the annual general meeting, and file this document with the registrar.

JSCA 1844 provided aspiring promoters with a cheap and easy means of incorporation, initially without limited liability, by giving legal effect to these recommendations. This resulted in the establishment of what Robert Lowe, President of the BOT, described as 'little republics' (quoted in Hunt, p. 135). The right to register with limited liability was introduced in 1855 for joint stock companies other than banks and insurance, to which the privilege was extended, respectively, in 1858 and 1862. The limited liability company had at last arrived.

Origin of limited liability

The concept of the par value share was developed by English companies in the seventeenth century. It was designed to provide an element of protection, for shareholders, by placing an effective limit on their obligation to provide capital. The directors could call up the full nominal value of the share, but no more. This provision of course provided no protection for the shareholder against claims from creditors if, and when, the company got into financial difficulties.

The idea of limited liability for business debts seems to have originated in the medieval Italian *en commendite* partnership of the twelfth and thirteenth centuries. Under this scheme the wealthy noble entrusted money to a reliable merchant in exchange for a share of venture profits, and on the understanding that the nobleman's liability was restricted to the amount advanced. This form of organisation flourished, partly because the church's usury laws prevented interest from being charged on loans, and also because the noble had money to invest but believed it was beneath his dignity to engage directly in trade.

The *en commendite* partnership therefore established the principle that, while trading partners were fully liable for partnership debts, a non-participating partner might get a share of profits by risking only the amount of his investment. The use of this scheme spread to other European countries, including France. When, much later (1673), French commercial law was codified by Louis XIV, the formation of *societes en commandite* was specifically authorised (Formoy, p.44).

An element of limited liability was also achieved, at an early stage, in Scotland (Littleton, p.247). That country had always maintained close contact with the continent of Europe. The Scottish Court of Sessions (1532) was modelled upon the law of Paris, and many Scots lawyers were trained in continental law. In eighteenth-century Scotland a doctrine was developed whereby creditors claimed first against the partnership and, only if partnership assets were insufficient, against the partners themselves. 'Silent' partners could not be proceeded against, however, provided care was taken to keep their names out of the firm's name. A similar situation seems to have existed in Ireland from 1782 (Formoy, p.45). England lagged behind, presumably because it was decided that any need for limited liability could be satisfied by Royal Charter or Act of Parliament.

From 1662, beginning with the East India, Guinea and Fishery Companies, it was the occasional practice to include in statutes or charters of incorporation a sentence which had the effect of protecting shareholders against claims by creditors under the bankruptcy acts. Similar clauses were used to benefit the members of the Bank of England (1694) and the South Sea Company (1710). The effectiveness of this provision in achieving limited liability for members is not altogether clear because companies, themselves, had always possessed the power to make calls on shareholders to ensure debts were repaid (e.g. the Royal African Company made such a call in 1705, Davies, p.293). Moreover, creditors could proceed against the corporation to compel the 'general court' to take this course of action. Even here there were uncertainties; it was not altogether clear whether the making of such calls was conditional on the procedure being specifically authorised by the company's charter or act of incorporation, or whether the amount available to be called up was restricted to the authorised capital of the organisation (DuBois, pp.97–100).

Explicit provision for limited liability became more common as time went by. Indeed, during the last four decades of the eighteenth century, it became increasingly recognised as an important motivating force for incorporation; examples include the English Linen Company (1764) and the Warmley Company (1768) (DuBois, pp.95–96). Even among the canal companies of the late eighteenth century, however, the protection of limited liability was by no means always written into statutes of incorporation. Slow development may be put down to the following: sufficient capital could be attracted without the need to offer shareholders this safeguard; limited liability made the acquisition of trade credit and raising loans more difficult; limited liability was considered immoral, in some quarters, because it enabled the entrepreneur to escape the consequences of his actions.

The possibility of granting partnerships limited liability, along continental lines, was examined by a government committee in 1837. The outcome, as mentioned earlier, was to authorise the Crown to confer the privilege of limited liability on shareholders in companies established under the 1834 Act. The introduction of the limited partnership was reconsidered, in the 1850s, by a select committee (1851) and a Royal Commission (1854). Experienced witnesses produced strong arguments which were diametrically opposed to one another (Hunt, pp.125–33). No firm recommendations were made but, in 1855, the government introduced separate bills to establish the limited liability partnership and the limited liability company. The former was lost due to time pressure but the latter became law.

The limited partnership was belatedly created by an Act of 1907. Little use has been made of this organisational structure. Investors requiring protection almost invariably prefer to form a limited company, since this enables the liability of *all* members to be limited and allows them to take part in management without forfeiting this protection.

The limited company and the capital market

Markets for corporate securities may be divided into 'primary' markets, where the company issues shares in exchange for cash, or other assets, and 'secondary' markets which bring together members of the general public who wish to buy and sell shares issued by a company at some earlier date. The role of a secondary market is to reconcile the company's need for long-term finance with the investor's need for liquidity.

The secondary market in company shares originated in London coffee houses, notably Lloyd's Coffee House, in the late seventeenth century. The demand for corporate stocks grew fairly quickly and the early 1690s were years of feverish activity in securities originally issued by the East India, African and the Hudson Bay companies. Indeed, it has been estimated that the equivalent of the whole India company's stock changed hands every two years around this date (Davies, p.292). Dealings in government securities continued to dominate stock exchange activities, however, when, in 1801, the London Stock Exchange was opened to take over the share dealing activities of the coffee houses of Exchange Alley. At the end of the Napoleonic Wars (1815) the National Debt amounted to over £800m. After 1815 dealings in the stocks and shares of canals, railways and other public utilities increased in importance.

The next few decades saw a series of speculative phases, often followed by slump and financial loss. The first of these occurred between 1825–27 when glowing prospectuses were issued by companies which collapsed soon afterwards. Of 624 companies floated during the period, only 127 survived to the end of 1827. Following a period of relative quiet, the mid-1830s was a period of prosperity and speculation in banks, railways and life assurance. The mid-1840s saw the famous railway mania.

The significance of the railways for the development of the formal capital market is demonstrated by the fact that the London Stock Exchange, which has previously dealt principally in government stocks, began to shift its emphasis towards company securities in the mid-1830s. By 1843 railway shares had replaced canal securities as the standard corporate investment. Additional exchanges were created in a number of provincial cities between 1836–45, and these helped to mobilise the large quantities of surplus funds available for investment.

It has been estimated that, at the time JSCA 1844 was passed, there existed just under 1000 statutory and chartered companies. These included 224 gas and water companies, 108 railways, 172 insurance companies, 84 'other public utilities and works', 48 banks and 46 shipping companies (Hunt, p.88). The subsequent creation of the limited company was expected, in some quarters, to result in rapid economic development. The theory was that there were numerous potential shareholders who would now be willing to invest in new projects, and that his would produce more employment, new products and a higher standard of living. These developments did not occur immediately. Many companies incorporated in the 1850s and 1860s, but these were mainly family firms keen to obtain the protection of limited libility.

As capital requirements increased in line with technological developments, the new form of business organisation was increasingly used to fulfil its intended function – namely to raise the large amounts of capital by inviting numerous investors each to advance relatively small sums. The second half of the nineteenth century saw stock market activity extend to other sectors of the economy. The first major surge occurred between 1863–66 when, of the 3500 companies registered, 900 offered shares to the public.

Iron and steel was one of the first manufacturing industries to make use of the joint stock company for this purpose. Many of the leading companies in existence in 1860 had begun as small units and financed their expansion substantially out of retained profits. New discoveries, such as the Bessemer Steel Making Process and the Siemens Open Hearth Process, however, called for the investment of large amounts of money in steel producing plant before production could even commence. There were also the heavy costs associated with mineral exploitation following the advent of the deep pit. Some of the companies incorporated as a result of these developments were well established firms seeking additional finance; others were completely new enterprises promoted to make use of the new technology. By the beginning of the twentieth century, iron and steel was heavily dependent on external finance.

Some statistics help to illustrate the growing popularity of the limited company. It has been estimated that there were 1000 registered companies in 1858 and 2000 in 1864. Official figures show that there were nearly 9000 companies in existence in 1884, over 60,000 at the outbreak of the First World War and over a million today (Parker, p.9). The *Daily Stock and Share List* (renamed the *Stock Exchange Daily Official List,* in 1899) contained 835 securities when first published in 1867. By 1914 there were nearly 4500 securities; today there are over 7000. The Stock Exchange requirement for listed companies to send in a copy of their accounts, introduced in 1881, is further evidence of the growing importance of the large-scale limited company during the last quarter of the nineteenth century.

PART III

CORPORATE FINANCIAL REPORTING PRACTICES

10

Formulating Company Accounting Conventions, 1830–1900

Introduction

The increasing size of the business unit, the separation of ownership from management and the growth of the capital market, during the Victorian era, stimulated the development of financial reporting procedures both within the firm and to outsiders. Indeeed, it has been suggested that many of the conventions on which accounting reports are today based originated during this period (Yamey, p.3).

Laissez-faire was the dominant nineteenth-century political philosophy and a great deal of business activity was allowed to develop, in the hands of private entrepreneurs, free from close regulation. The underlying thesis of this chapter is that, in these circumstances, management was free to choose, and in fact chose, the set of accounting principles and practices that had the highest utility, given the goals the organisation was trying to achieve and the non-regulatory constraints under which it operated. One of these constraints was the requirement for shareholders and creditors to believe the content of published financial statements.

Error, bias and conservatism

What were the main features of financial reporting during this period? There is little agreement. Some authorities believe that nineteenth-century accounts were prepared on a conservative basis whereas others take the opposite view. The fact is that assets and profits were probably both under- and overstated at different times and in different places. This was the result of both error and systematic bias. There is little doubt that some nineteenth-century corporate managers overstated profit in the endeavour to attract capital, and it seems likely that the prudence concept was developed partly to counter this threat. The use of conservative valuation procedures was advocated by influential contemporary authorities such as Dicksee and Garcke and Fells. For example, they recommended cost as the usual basis for valuing stock, with a reduction to market price where this was lower (see Parker, p.161). George O. May confirms that the lower of cost or market rule was well established by the time he entered the profession in 1892 (ibid., p.158). Indeed, the reduction of stock values, below cost, to create a secret reserve was not an unusual occurrence.

The development of the lower of cost or market rule is probably also attributable to the accountant's contemporary preoccupation with liquidations, failures and frauds. The fact that creditors and long-term investors were regarded as the principal users of company accounts, at this time, was also important. Financial stability and long-term, rather than short-term, profit maximisation were their main priorities and, in these circumstances, it was perfectly natural that the accountant should favour asset values and profit figures which were on the low side rather than optimistic, particularly with the threat of litigation in the background. It was also a time when the price level was falling. Some figures are: 1855, 108; 1865, 102; 1875, 102; 1885, 76; 1895, 62 (*Economist*, 1974, p.62). Conservative, sometimes ultra-conservative, accounting practices were therefore a natural product of prevailing circumstances. The problem was that they became firmly entrenched and continued to be applied when environmental conditions had changed drastically.

In an area where the need for subjective judgement was even greater, namely the accounting treatment of fixed assets, there is little doubt that nineteenth-century published financial statements were littered with examples of error and bias. Error no doubt occurred on an even greater scale prior to the nineteenth century, but bias is only likely to have flourished with the need to report to absentee owners. The main causes of error and bias were the failure systematically (a) to distinguish between capital and revenue expenditures and (b) to allocate the original cost of fixed assets to expense. A contemporary assessment of the significance of the latter problem is indicated by Pixley's observation that 'if the construction of the profit and loss account could be carried out without reference to this difficult but interesting subject [depreciation], accountancy might certainly be described as one of the exact sciences' (p.199).

From valuation to matching

The nineteenth century saw a fundamental change in the approach to profit calculation. In earlier times it was a quite common practice first to value assets and liabilities at two dates, secondly to identify net assets at these dates and, finally, to compute profit as the difference between the two figures. During the nineteenth century the calculation of profit became the first stage in the preparation of the final accounts, and only after this was done were the asset and liability balances, which remained, collected together in the balance sheet. The transition is marked by the widespread adoption of the historical cost convention which, when linked with the idea of the going concern, produced asset values on the basis of cost allocations rather than periodic appraisal. Why did this change occur?

One reason was the transition from the proprietorship view of the firm, which treats business assets as personal possessions of the owner, to the entity basis, which regards the assets as an integral part of a permanent business venture (see Chapter 7). This change of view naturally took place during the time period which saw the owner/manager superseded, in certain industries, by the professional manager and the anonymous supplier of capital.

A second reason for the new approach to profit calculation was the use of profits as the basis for dividend declarations. This pointed to the need for some correspondence between profit and liquidity and resulted, for instance, in the exclusion of unrealised profits. Thirdly, the increased emphasis given to historical cost, when measuring profit, resulted in the production of asset figures based on hard facts which could be verified by the newly emerging accountancy profession. Finally, the adoption of the matching concept reduced the scope for management to manipulate profit; with valuations, not only is there the need to make estimates, there is also the need to decide on the appropriate method of valuation from options available which include 'present value', 'selling price' and 'replacement cost'. Dicksee summed up the problem in a nutshell; the valuation approach is 'theoretically perfect but defective in practice' (quoted in Brief, 1983, p.17). A development which facilitated the transition from valuation to matching was the more ready availability of cost figures as the result of improvements in the system of record keeping.

Highlights of nineteenth-century financial reporting developments were, therefore, the rejection of values in favour of cost and choices being made from a range of procedures previously in use.

Identification of capital expenditure

It was the overseas operations of early chartered companies, such as the East India Company, which first resulted in a substantial investment in long-term assets. Indeed, one of the main reasons for obtaining a charter was to enable capital expenditure to be financed by raising funds from the general public. The colourful term sometimes used to describe fixed assets – 'dead stock' – is indicative both of their association with merchanting activities and the fact that they do not directly generate a profit. It was not until the nineteenth century, however, that the need to make a distinction between capital and revenue expenditure became more pressing. This occurred first in the public utilities, later spreading to manufacturing industry where developments in precision engineering towards the end of the century, including the invention of Roberts's measuring machine which was accurate to 1/10,000th of an inch, made possible mechanisation on a vast scale.

The treatment of capital expenditure was examined by the Monteagle Committee (1849) which reported that 'it is impossible to overrate the importance of the strictest adherence to an invariable separation between the capital and income of railway companies' (Third Report, p.viii). It is also clear that the committee understood *why* a proper distinction was important: 'any deviation from [a proper separation] will falsify the account, and deprive the public of the means of measuring the value of the undertaking'. One possible outcome, identified by the committee, was that the investor remains 'in ignorance of the true state of the company's affairs, and is led to give a higher price than the thing is worth, under the belief that the dividends declared come *bona fide* out of profits'. The committee accordingly recommended a 'uniform' (standardised) system of accounts containing sufficient detail to indicate the correct location for capital and revenue items.

Effective government action was delayed until the passage of the Railway Companies Act 1867 (see Chapter 13). This introduced a compulsory audit for railways and insisted that 'no dividend shall be declared by a company until the auditors have certified that the half-yearly accounts proposed to be issued contain a full and true statement of the financial condition of the company, and that the dividend proposed to be declared on any shares is *bona fide* due after charging the revenue of the half-year with all expense' (s.30). The requirement for railway companies to publish standardised accounts was introduced in the following year.

Valuation of fixed assets

There is, today, general agreement that the appropriate method for valuing fixed assets depends upon whether the accounts are prepared for a going concern or for a company about to be wound up. For the going concern, assets are normally reported at their 'value in existing use', which is affected by the following factors: physical deterioration due to usage and/or the passage of time; and technological development which causes an asset to become prematurely obsolete. For the company about to be liquidated, it is the 'value in alternative use' which is relevant, i.e. the market selling price. This is determined by the external forces of supply and demand. In the case of the going concern, the value in alternative use usually becomes relevant only when the asset is at the end of its useful life. It was during the nineteenth century that value in existing use became the popular basis for valuing fixed assets belonging to a continuing venture.

The railways were the first industry to raise massive sums of money from the general public, and railway managers were therefore obliged to tackle the new problem of valuing long-lived capital assets for inclusion in published accounting statements. In reaching their decisions, these pioneers were unable to refer, for guidance, to the literature, the yet unborn accountancy profession or company law. Indeed, it was in an attempt to fill this gap that two authoritative reports on fixed asset valuation (1849 and 1853) were prepared by the general manager of the London and North Western Railway, Captain Mark Huish (reproduced in Edwards, 1986b, pp.199–286). The problem of valuing fixed assets spread to other industries later in the century. In broad terms, the public utilities copied the solutions worked out by the railways (see below), while other industries were influenced by them to a greater or lesser extent.

Not surprisingly, there were substantial differences in the valuation procedures employed both between companies and over time, especially in the early experimental period. Outside the corporate sector accounting practices were probably even more varied. The Dowlais Iron Co., although a partnership, was the largest manufacturing company in the world in the 1840s. It continued to employ accounting procedures better suited, on the face of it, to an earlier, more labour intensive, age; between 1830–90 approximately £1.4m spent on new work was immediately written off against revenue (Edwards and Baber, p.150). Within the corporate sector, the omission from the balance sheet of valuable assets financed by shareholders was not a popular practice, and the methods in common use were the cash flow-based 'repairs and renewals accounting' and 'replacement accounting', and the cost allocation-based depreciation accounting.

Repairs and renewal accounting. Under this method the cost of a fixed asset is capitalised, while maintenance charges and the expense of renewing individual components of assets are charged against revenue. This method gained in popularity because of the nature of the assets used by companies operating in industries where capital investment comprised a significant proportion of total business expenditure. For example, railway tracks, locomotives and blast furnaces are all extremely robust structures, and it is easy to understand how management might believe that, provided there was proper maintenance, such assets possessed a virtually unlimited useful life.

Drawbacks of the method are as follows: even if the asset does not wear out, a stage will eventually be reached where the repair costs are too high to justify the expenditure; the method ignores the fact that technological advance causes all assets to become obsolete in due course; profits are overstated because revenue is not charged with the benefit arising from the use of capital assets; and capital employed is overstated because the fall in value of fixed assets is ignored.

Replacement accounting. Under this method a company capitalises fixed assets acquired at the outset and any subsequent purchases which result in an expansion of productive capacity (e.g. Matheson, pp.2–3). Any fixed assets purchased to replace items which have worn out are written off immediately against revenue. It was argued, by some nineteenth-century writers, that this method worked well enough where companies owned a large number of fixed assets, each with approximately the same value and possessing a relatively short life span, for example a general engineering firm. The system was tolerated, in these circumstances, because the value of assets replaced was approximately equal to the amount which would have been charged if systematic depreciation accounting had been employed.

In the majority of cases, however, the charge against profit is unlikely to bear a close relationship to the value of resources used up during that accounting period. In the early years of a business, and immediately after an expansion has taken place, profit is overstated as no charge is made against revenue to reflect the benefit received from using the new assets. When replacements begin to occur, the amount charged against revenue varies depending on the volume of fixed assets which happen to be replaced during a particular period, rather than the amount of benefit obtained from their use. The experience of the Imperial Continental Gas Association (formed in 1824) was probably fairly common: 'when the periodic renewal of major items of gasworks equipment took place, there were quite serious fluctuations in profit for particular half-years' (Hill, p.384).

A further feature of replacement accounting was that it provided scope for management to influence the level of reported profit by 'timing' the purchase of replacement assets (Litherland, p.479). If the intention was to inflate reported profits, replacement could be delayed; if profits were to be depressed, replacements could be acquired ahead of the date when they were needed. Turning to the balance sheet, fixed assets in use were reported at original cost, with the result that the value of capital employed was overstated unless prices fell fairly dramatically.

There were also difficulties in operating a system of replacement accounting. Fixed assets sometimes wore out and were not replaced and, in these circumstances, the question arose whether they should remain in the balance sheet indefinitely at cost. Even where fixed assets were replaced, it was rarely by an identical item; technical progress normally resulted in an improved version becoming available, and this made it difficult to distinguish between the elements of replacement and enhancement.

A strong argument in favour of each of the above cash flow-based methods is that they resulted in the publication of a balance sheet which reported the actual cost of assets purchased with the capital raised from investors. At a time when the joint stock company was considered a highly speculative investment and the honesty of management was the subject of considerable doubt, a stewardship document of this sort had much to commend it.

Depreciation accounting. The purpose of the depreciation charge, today, is to spread the net cost of a fixed asset (original cost minus sales proceeds) over its estimated useful life. The aim is to ensure that revenue arising during each accounting period bears a fair share of the total costs incurred.

In early accounting texts the term depreciation was often used to describe the difference between fixed asset valuations at two different dates. According to Littleton, it was during the second half of the nineteenth century that writers rejected the valuation approach in favour of cost allocation. For example, W.Inglish's *Bookkeeping* text of 1861 concludes that 'a yearly deduction of 5 and 10 per cent requires to be made from original cost [of buildings and machinery], to allow for deterioration, or wear and tear' (Littleton, p.226).

This transition no doubt reflected changes taking place in contemporary accounting practice, although it is certain that the majority of companies did not account for depreciation in the systematic manner advocated by Inglish. This was partly the result of ignorance, and partly because accounting practices had to be coordinated with management's determination to keep its options open regarding the level of reported profit. It was therefore quite common for depreciation to be accounted for as an appropriation of profit rather than as a charge against profit, and for the amount deducted to vary depending on the desired level of reported profit rather that the degree of benefit arising from use of the asset. Depreciation, when charged, was principally viewed as a means of earmarking, for retention, resources which could be set aside to finance replacement, rather than as a *bona fide* cost of production.

Miscellaneous credit balances, such as share premiums, the balance to the credit of sinking fund accounts, and the proceeds from forfeited shares, were sometimes used to write down the value of fixed assets. Advantages of this practice were that it avoided reducing reported profit while, at the same time, ensuring that the asset was not overstated in the balance sheet; an important priority at a time when the balance sheet was often regarded as a measure of the minimum resources available to meet claims from creditors.

A peculiar feature of the accounting practices of statutory companies using the double account system (see Chapter 13) was to report the accumulated depreciation charge as a source of finance in the general balance sheet. The term 'depreciation fund' was used to describe the balance and replacements were charged against it.

Demand for dividends

Nineteenth-century reporting practices, particularly those employed by railway companies, have been the subject of much criticism (e.g. Brief, 1965, Pollins). The crux of the problem was that, although profitability was sensitive to changing economic conditions, managers believed that their shareholders required a steady dividend. This led some of them to employ valuation procedures designed principally to produce a pattern of reported profit sufficient to cover the planned level of dividend. The aim was profit smoothing on a large scale.

There are numerous examples of railway shareholders vociferous in their demands for higher dividends. Calls of 'give us more money' were heard at the February 1848 general meeting of the Eastern Counties Railway (*Herapath's Journal*, 1848, p.146), while shareholders attending the meeting to approve the London and North Western's June 1841 accounts opposed the maintenance of a reserve fund for rolling stock, with the objective of increasing the dividend from £4.5.0 to £4.10.0 per share (*Railway Times*, 1841, p.842). Railway directors responded to this kind of pressure; according to an editorial in *The Times* (27 August 1866), 'Directors were often tempted to disregard all moral and legal obligations to make things look pleasant to their proprietors'.

Nineteenth-century railway companies were highly capital intensive and, although reported profits were normally fully distributed, dividends remained at a low level. It has been estimated that dividends were 6 per cent on capital up to 1846, 3 per cent in 1850, 3.75 per cent in 1855 and 4.5 per cent in 1870, with major companies paying 5–5.5 per cent at the last date. As indicators of profitability, these figures must be interpreted with caution in view of the general failure to charge depreciation and significant error and bias in allocating items between the capital account and the revenue account (see Chapter 13), particularly in the early years. The problem faced by railway directors attempting to produce a reasonable return for investors is clear enough, however, and is further demonstrated by examining the total asset turnover ratio – it has been estimated that up to 1850 *gross receipts* on all existing railways never reached 8 per cent of capital invested.

It is not altogether clear why profits were low. The indiscriminate sanction of new lines caused over capacity and severe competition. Also, the government imposed lower maximum rates and fares by the Railway Clauses Consolidation Act of 1845. Against this it has been argued that state control of rates and tolls was ineffective because they were still set too high while, beginning in the mid-1840s, amalgamations reduced the degree of competition. Competition remained strong, however, from canals and coastal shipping as well as other railways. Management was therefore compelled to base its pricing policy on what the traffic would bear, and then strive to keep operating costs sufficiently below gross revenue to allow an adequate margin of reported profit.

A further problem was the cost of building the railways which was inflated by the need to obtain legislation to authorise railway construction (the London and Birmingham's statute of incorporation cost over £72,000 and the Great Western's over £88,000) and by the opportunities allowed to landlords and solicitors to extract exorbitant sums for the land which was required. It has been estimated that in 1887 the average cost per mile of railway line in Britain was over £42,000 compared with just over £21,000 in Germany and £11,000 in America.

Throughout the period from the opening of the first line to 1868, investors were able to obtain over 3 per cent on government stocks. It was therefore necessary for the railway companies to pay a significant premium over and above this figure to obtain finance for their more risky investment, although the 7 per cent suggested in the columns of *Herapath's Journal* (1847, p.1429) was rarely achieved. The result was that companies struggled to maintain support from the investing public and, in these circumstances, it is not surprising that the depreciation fund, the need for which was constantly in dispute, should ultimately have failed to find favour with railway management. Many companies could afford to make no charge whatsoever. Even leading companies like the London and North Western and the Midland, who made *nominal* deductions in the 1840s and early 1850s, soon found these were wholly insufficient to meet the cost of renewals and replacements and abandoned the pretence.

It is, therefore, no doubt correct to view the temporary abandonment of depreciation accounting principally as a casualty of the demand for dividends, but other important influences conspired to help produce this outcome. The lack of a consensus view among the leading railway companies was an important factor blurring the issue.

The reports prepared by Captain Mark Huish contained two basic recommendations: rolling stock should be maintained out of revenue, and a depreciation fund should be built up to meet the anticipated cost of replacing the permanent way. Huish explained these apparently conflicting proposals on the grounds that, whereas rolling stock could be systematically renewed by current repairs or gradual replacement, the railway track deteriorated more slowly producing a sudden cost burden. Huish's report proved instrumental in settling a long-standing controversy on the valuation and maintenance of rolling stock, and a number of companies initially followed the London and North Western's lead in setting up a fund for the replacement of the permanent way, although the experiment was short lived. At the other leading railway company, the Great Western, Isambard Brunel, who was appointed engineer in 1833 and established his professional reputation building the Great Western line, rejected the need for a fund for the track because 'we have no sufficient experience to form a tolerably approximate estimate of the amount required' (*Railway Times*, 1851, p.161).

Finally, it seems likely that prevailing income tax regulations exerted some influence on the choice of accounting method. The tax was reintroduced in 1842, after a lapse of 26 years, at the rate of 7d in the £. A deduction was allowed for the actual cost of 'repairs or alterations' to fixed assets, but nothing for depreciation until 1879. This provided no encouragement for the railway companies early flirtation with depreciation accounting; on the contrary, revenue law provided obvious support for cash flow-based methods, particularly as some income tax commissioners interpreted the phrase 'repairs or alterations' to cover expenditure on 'renewals' and even 'replacements' (Edwards, 1986a, p.258)

Inconsistency and bias

The following three case studies illustrate the variety of accounting practices employed between 1830–1900, and the scope available for management to devise 'creative' accounting procedures in an unregulated environment.

Northampton Gas Light Company. The company was incorporated in 1823 and began to supply gas in the following year. The accounting treatment of capital expenditure changed dramatically over the years (Roberts, pp.347–52). The company used depreciation accounting, from 1854 to 1857, but most of the accumulated charge was written back to the profit and loss account in 1858. The company's special Act of that year incorporated the Gas Works Clauses Act of 1847 which placed restrictions and controls on the prices, profits and dividends of gas companies. The write back enabled a large dividend to be paid before the new regulations came into effect. Depreciation accounting was abandoned for all assets other than gas meters in 1864, and also for gas meters in 1872. Afterwards the company used replacement accounting to deal with capital expenditure in its accounts.

Wigan Coal and Iron Co. Ltd. The company was formed in 1865 and, during the early years of its existence, it was one of the largest manufacturing companies with an issued capital of over £2m (Edwards and Webb, 1982, pp.264–69). The auditors' report on the company's first set of published accounts recommended that an annual sum of at least £25,000 be charged for depreciation. The proposal was put into effect immediately but discontinued in 1868. No explanation for the change was given. However, the Regulation of Railway Act, which received the royal assent a few months before the accounts were published, contained an implied approval for the omission of depreciation provided fixed assets were properly maintained. Evidence which supports the idea that the company's directors were influenced by this statute is contained in the directors' report which refers to the fact that 'the whole of the works have been kept in good and efficient working order'; an assertion which closely resembles the engineers certificates that railway companies were required to publish from 1868.

The appointment of a practising accountant as auditor in 1870 (the previous auditors had been shareholders) resulted in the reintroduction of a depreciation charge. The directors reported that 'depreciation is inseparable from mining operations . . . [and we are] . . . convinced that an adequate provision should be made'. The company depreciated items of moveable plant at percentages determined by each asset's expected useful life, while extractions of minerals were costed at rates per ton based on estimates of available reserves.

Between 1870–93 a large amount of money (£355,000), earmarked for retention in the business as the result of charging depreciation, was needed to finance neither replacements nor expansion. Reasons for this were that the level of activity was fairly stable, assets were long lasting and prices were falling. A possible solution to over-capitalisation is a capital reduction scheme (legalised by the Companies Act 1877), but this was for some reason considered inappropriate. To avoid further accumulations, the directors simply reduced the depreciation charge to 25 per cent of its previous figure in order to increase reported profit and enable higher dividends to be declared. A systematic depreciation charge was re-introduced in 1904.

Shelton Iron Steel and Coal Co. Ltd. This company was incorporated in 1889 and, like Wigan, was quoted on the London Stock Exchange. No consistent method of accounting for capital expenditure was employed between 1889 and 1920, when it was acquired by John Summers & Sons Ltd and converted to the status of a private company (Edwards, 1980, pp.245–57). The failure to charge depreciation on a systematic basis – nominal, lump-sum deductions were made on just six occasions – was not evidence of ignorant self-deception; a consultant's report of 1892 stressed the need for a charge and provided calculations of the amounts which should be deducted. The evidence suggests that a more likely explanation is that the accounts, which received a clean audit certificate, were designed to achieve external reporting objectives now examined.

Finance for business activity may be classified into cash generated by the firm and cash raised from outsiders. In an unregulated environment management is free to select the accounting method which best supports its chosen strategies. For example, if the aim is to finance activity from internal sources, the capital accounting procedure which produces the lowest total for reported profit, i.e. the immediate write off of capital expenditure against revenue, is likely to be favoured. In such circumstances claims for higher wages and dividends and more tax, which might have been made if the true facts were known, are avoided. If management instead decides to emphasise external financing, the objective will be to report profits and declare dividends which provoke a favourable response among the investing public. This results in 'window dressing' and, perhaps, the publication of fraudulent accounts. If such a strategy is chosen, write offs must be kept to a minimum and the system of repairs and renewals accounting has obvious attractions.

Events at Shelton were consistent with the above hypothesis. The company was formed to take over an existing business and, immediately following flotation, it was clear that a period of reasonable prosperity was at an end. The previous owners had got out at the right time and, despite the optimism expressed in successive chairman's reports, trading was unlikely to be highly remunerative. The management structure was poorly organised and the company was still heavily committed to the manufacture of iron for which demand was declining. In addition the company was under-capitalised from the outset.

Cash was needed and, during the first 16 years of the company's existence, £0.5m worth of debentures were issued. To stimulate demand for these securities the directors endeavoured to present the company's trading results in the most favourable light. Deductions for depreciation were made from time to time, but the decision to make a deduction was based on external reporting objectives rather than the reality of depreciation, while the amount of the deduction depended on the level of profits rather than the extent of the wear and tear. For instance, the prospectus publicising the 1898 issue of debentures contained profit figures for 1896 and 1897 described as 'after providing for depreciation'. The aggregate depreciation charged up to that date was in fact £7000, representing an average rate of 0.2 per cent per annum, on cost, since incorporation. If the company had used the depreciation rates suggested by the consulting engineer, or those laid down by Matheson in *The Depreciation of Factories*, (p.41) the company would have reported far worse results and been unable to declare a dividend.

The fact that the 1898 prospectus gave the intended, albeit misleading, impression to the outside world is demonstrated by an extract from the newspaper *Finance* which referred to the capital expenditure balance having been arrived at after 'writing-off the proper amount for depreciation'. In the directors' report for 1893 the direcors justified the failure to make a charge on the grounds that 'the company's plant and works have been fully maintained out of revenue', i.e. repairs and renewals accounting was employed.

Beginning in 1904, a series of successful business decisions together with the favourable conditions for iron and steel making created by the First World War saw the company out of its difficult beginnings and into a period of sustained prosperity. The upturn in trading fortunes produced a change in the company's capital accounting procedures; during the second decade of the twentieth century, a variety of undisclosed deductions were made from profits to cover improvements, extentions and new work. It was also during this period that the company's chairman began to extol the virtues of conservatism in financial matters. His report on the 1915 accounts refers to the fact that 'every figure in the whole balance sheet is on a thoroughly sound and conservative basis'. This claim could certainly not have been made during the first 20 years of the company's existence. Clearly the directors had decided to shift the emphasis from external to internal finance and were using financial reporting procedures best suited to achieve the new objective.

Depreciation accounting comes of age

There were three aspects to the nineteenth-century depreciation debate: whether depreciation occurred; whether it was necessary to make a charge for depreciation; and, if so, how much? Initially, the popular answer to the first question was 'No', eliminating the need even to consider the second and third questions. There existed a widespread presumption that, provided the fixed assets were properly looked after, they possessed an unlimited physical life or, at least, that the replacement date was sufficiently remote to be ignored. Where this view prevailed, companies used the repairs and renewals basis. Other companies, which recognised the fact that fixed assets did eventually wear out, combined repairs and renewals accounting with the practice of debiting replacements either to revenue or against the balance on a depreciation fund account.

In practice, the distinction between different methods of accounting for capital expenditure was often blurred. Nineteenth-century company directors rarely provided a clear statement of how they had treated fixed assets. This made it easier to switch between accounting methods depending on which best suited the following, sometimes conflicting, managerial objectives: the need to report a profit figure sufficient to cover an adequate dividend and the need to include a charge which fairly measured the rate at which fixed assets were used up.

By the turn of the century writers such as Dicksee (p.2), Dickinson (p.176), and Garcke and Fells (p.94) were making it perfectly clear that they considered a charge essential, but management continued to devise arguments to justify its omission. According to Dicksee management sometimes argued that 'under the particular circumstances there obtaining, a direct charge for depreciation is unnecessary, because such provision as might under normal circumstances be proper in this connection is in that particular instance provided by other means'.

In an attempt to encourage businessmen to charge depreciation, some writers argued that its omission was an important cause of business failure (Montgomery, p.313). Their line of argument was that the failure to make a charge meant that resources were not available to acquire new machinery and this, in turn, resulted in profits falling. In the specific case of the Imperial Continental Gas Association, Hill believed that 'serious financial stringency was experienced at times because down to 1850 the Association used to distribute in dividend almost all its profits and had no fund of retained profit with which to finance capital expenditure' (p.384). This was by no means the inevitable outcome; the Shelton case study shows that the absence of a charge, and even the absence of profit over a significant period, need have no disastrous repercussions provided steps are taken to ensure cash inflows exceed cash outflows.

An important event leading to the widespread adoption of depreciation accounting was the experience of the railway companies. At the beginning of the twentieth century certain railway companies began voluntarily to make provision for depreciation. The reason for this change was that it became evident, from experience, that no amount of maintenance could prolong indefinitely the economic life of fixed assets.[1] An article in *The Accountant* drew attention to the fact that 'railways *in toto* are a comparatively modern industry; and just because the system of accounting imposed by statute some thirty five years ago[2] seems to have worked well up to a point, it must not therefore be considered that the system has stood the test of time and may therefore be regarded as for all purposes efficient' (1902, p.899). It was felt that the convenience of the system had 'too long blinded many to its inherent defects'.

The inherent defects were as follows: inflated profits were reported and excessive dividends paid; it was often necessary to finance the replacement of fixed assets out of a new capital issue because funds generated from current operations were insufficient to cover their cost; capital employed was overstated because useless assets were carried permanently at cost in the balance sheet. The practice of charging depreciation gained in popularity; in 1905 *The Accountant* reported that railway companies 'are voluntarily making large provisions for depreciation in addition to charging all repairs and renewals against revenue' (p.189, see also Chapter 13). Directors nevertheless continued to resist the *strict* application of the accruals concept to fixed assets. They preferred to retain a significant element of discretion concerning the amount of the charge, particularly when profits were low.

Review

Financial reporting at the beginning of the nineteenth century was characterised by the odd scrappy profit calculation and balance sheets which contained assets valued in a wide variety of different ways. The use of systematic depreciation accounting was extremely rare. The emergence of the professional manager and absentee investor created a strong demand for financial information. Management's response was to experiment with new methods of asset valuation, and by the end of the century significant changes had occurred. The four fundamental concepts specified in Statement of

Standard Accounting Practice (SSAP) 2 (1971) – accruals, going concern, consistency and prudence – were already well established.

The application of the accruals concept to credit transactions was quite common even at the beginning of the century but, by 1900, it was the general rule within the private sector. The widespread adoption of the going concern (and historical cost) concept reflected the transition from the proprietor to the entity as the main focus for financial statements, while the selection of particular valuation procedures from the variety available inevitably led to a larger measure of consistency between consecutive accounting periods. We have seen that the concept of conservatism was a product of the late nineteenth-century environmental conditions. The adoption of depreciation accounting, in some quarters, completed a basic framework for financial reporting which remains in use today.

It must be recognised, however, that the absence of *general* agreement about which profit measurement and asset valuation procedures should be used provided ample scope for nineteenth-century corporate managers to prepare reports designed to meet particular managerial objectives rather than to portray fairly the underlying economic facts. We have seen that these these opportunities were fully exploited in some quarters.

11

Changing Patterns of Disclosure, 1900–40[1]

Progress; voluntary or prescriptive

An assumption made in this chapter and, indeed, throughout this book, is that the choice of accounting procedure is important. Accounting reports are a commodity supplied by management to satisfy a demand for financial information from shareholders and other interested parties. The priorities of the producers and consumers of accounting reports do not, however, always coincide. For instance, management, when planning to raise further capital, aims to publish accounts which are a favourable advertisement of the company's achievements and potential. Investors, on the other hand, usually prefer objective data on which to base their decisions. If managerial bias is allowed to intrude, investors may well be misled and a suboptimal allocation of resources is likely to result.

To what extent should the form and content of company accounts therefore be regulated? There are marked differences of opinion on this matter. Some argue that the form and content of company accounts, and even the valuation bases followed, should be prescribed in minute detail. Resulting advantages accruing to user groups include reduced scope for manipulation, improved comparability and widespread compliance with procedures considered to represent best practice. Opponents claim that close regulation is likely to inhibit the invention of new procedures and arrest progress in accountancy; therefore they argue that the maximum amount of discretion should be allowed to management acting in conjunction with its financial advisors.

At the beginning of the twentieth century the published accounts of most limited companies were almost totally free from regulation, whereas today they are closely controlled. In terms of the degree of control, the century can be conveniently split into the periods before and after 1940. Prior to 1940, there were few legal regulations (see next section). Traditional arguments against increasing statutory requirements, presented for example to the Greene Committee by the ICAEW, were that shareholders enjoyed other valuable protections; they could ask the directors for information at the annual general meeting (AGM) and rely on the auditor to protect their interests (*Minutes*, p.lxviii).

It became evident, during the period 1900–40, that the effectiveness of these safeguards depended rather too much on the goodwill of the management and the efficiency of the auditors. Requests for more information did not always elicit the required response from management. The shareholders of the Rio de Janeiro Flour Mills & Granaries Co. Ltd, for example, deduced the existence of an undisclosed contingency reserve from the wording of the profit and loss account for 1928. They asked the chairman to explain why the fund should not appear in the accounts so they might know what was available to be drawn upon in future lean years. The chairman merely replied that it would be inexpedient to disclose their actual amount (*Accountant*, 26 January 1926, p.126). In 1931 the Royal Mail case (see Chapter 12) demonstrated that accounts, which strictly complied with prevailing legal requirements, could be framed in a manner designed to mislead shareholders and creditors. The criticism aroused by this revelation probably had a greater impact on the quality of published data than all the Companies Acts passed up to that date.

In an atmosphere of soul searching, within both the accountancy profession and the business community in general, De Paula of the Dunlop Rubber Co. Ltd led the way in voluntarily devising improved financial reporting procedures. De Paula was one of the most progressive accountants of the inter-war period. In 1926 he succeeded Dicksee as part-time professor of accounting at the LSE (he was also senior partner of De Paula, Turner, Lake & Co.). On 1 January 1930 he resigned these positions to become chief accountant of the Dunlop Rubber Co. Ltd; soon afterwards he was appointed controller of finance. This gave him a splendid opportunity to put into effect his full disclosure philosophy. The 1929 accounts were much improved and attracted favourable press comment, but it was the 1933 accounts which received the acclamation of the business world. Features of the Dunlop accounts were the inclusion of a consolidated balance sheet and profit and loss account, both audited, the disclosure of all reserves, the inclusion of comparative figures and a detailed classification of balance sheet items.

Since 1940 far more extensive requirements have been prescribed by statute, the accountancy profession and the London Stock Exchange. These developments are examined in Chapter 19.

Published range of financial reports[2]

Between 1900–40 legal obligations were imposed on registered companies both to present audited accounts to their members (shareholders' accounts) and to file certain specified financial data with the registrar of companies (registrar's accounts).

> *1900–1907*. Companies were legally obliged to present an audited balance sheet to shareholders attending the AGM. There was no filing requirement.
>
> *1907–28*. Non-private companies were *also* required to file a statement 'in the form of a balance sheet' with the registrar. Disclosure requirements differed; the registrar's balance sheet did not have to contain a statement of profit or loss, but it did have to state how fixed assets had been valued.
>
> *1928–47*. Companies were obliged to present shareholders with a directors' report, and it was made clear that this document, together with the shareholders' balance sheet and the audit report should be filed with the registrar. The profit and loss account, which directors were for the first time required to present to individuals attending the AGM, did not have to be filed.

The directors often made no attempt to take advantage of these differential legal requirements, and the shareholders' accounts were filed unamended with the registrar. This possibly indicates a general willingness to make available information in excess of prevailing legal requirements. More likely, management believed that, at a time when disclosure requirements attaching to the shareholders' accounts were fairly meagre, little would be gained in terms of confidentiality by preparing separate accounts for the registrar. There were exceptions. The 1919 balance sheet filed by Richard Thomas & Co. Ltd, for example, contained the single heading 'depreciation, reserves, suspense and profit and loss accounts £1,202,725' instead of the following details which appeared in the shareholders' accounts:

	£
Reserve account	439,345
Depreciation account	167,036
Stock suspense accounts	57,858
AB&C suspense accounts	300,763
Profit and loss account	237,723
Total	1,202,725

The published range of financial reports often exceeded legal requirements. For example, the presentation of a profit and loss account to shareholders became universal practice only when the provisions of the Companies Act (CA) 1928 took effect but it was by no means unknown prior to that date. When presented to shareholders, a profit and loss account was often also circulated and filed with the registrar.

From the beginning of the twentieth century quoted companies complied with a stock exchange requirement to make a directors' report available to shareholders. Not all quoted companies filed this document with the registrar, probably because it often contained profit and loss data which was considered to be more sensitive. Annual accounts, at this time, frequently consisted of a single sheet of paper with the directors' report printed on one side and the balance sheet and audit report on the other. To conceal information contained in the directors' report from the general public, a popular device was to paste the printed accounts on to the annual return so that only the side containing the balance sheet and audit report remained visible. Another way of achieving the same objective was to abstract the balance sheet and audit report data, from the shareholders' accounts, and file them in typed or manuscript form.

Methods of presentation

Despite the absence of statutory requirements governing their format, accounts published during this period exhibited many common features. Balance sheets were presented in the horizontal format, indicating that the vertical presentation, now in widespread use, is an essentially post-war development. An intriguing exception to the traditional British 'wrong way round' format (outlawed for registered companies by CA 1981) is contained in the 1903 and 1904 balance sheets of Head Wrightson & Co. Ltd which displayed assets in the left-hand column and liabilities on the right.

Profit and loss accounts usually followed the ledger account presentation, though the columnar format was often adopted where profit and loss data appeared in the directors' report. The undistributed balance of profit invariably appeared at the foot of the balance sheet, either as a liability or as an asset depending on whether it was a credit or a debit. This presentation was in line with the 1862 model balance sheet (see Figure 15.1). It emphasises the idea of undistributed profit as the excess of assets compared with capital plus liabilities, and contains no implication that profit represents a quantity of resources over which the proprietors possess any particular lien. An alternative explanation for its location is that it reflects a mechanical approach to accounts construction, being inserted as the final entry to check arithmetic accuracy.

There was considerable variation in the treatment of published items of income, expenditure and appropriations of profit. A common practice, prior to 1928, was to show certain deductions from profit on the face of the balance sheet though, in the absence of clear agreement concerning the difference between charges against profit and appropriations of profit, the items disclosed usually comprised a mixture of the two categories. The accounting significance of the terms 'provision' and 'reserve' was not given an authoritative definition until Recommendation on Accounting Principles (Recommendation) 6 was issued by the ICAEW in 1943. The wide range of profit and loss account data, *sometimes* disclosed on the face of the balance sheet, is illustrated by reference to the accounts of the South Durham Steel & Iron Co. Ltd for 1908 (Figure 11.1).

When, after 1928, it became a statutory requirement to publish a profit and loss account, less information appeared in the retained profit section of the balance sheet. Moreover, the range of items reported in the profit and loss account was often no more than could be previously gleaned from an examination of the balance sheet in conjunction with the directors' report. Throughout the period 1900–40, the profit and loss data disclosed usually exceeded the 1928 requirement for directors to report 'the amount, if any, which they recommend should be paid out by way of dividend, and the amount, if any, which they propose to carry to the reserve fund, general reserve or reserve account shown specifically on the balance sheet' (s.39).

The order of presentation of liabilities and assets in the balance sheet usually followed a fairly common pattern. Liabilities were listed in order of decreasing permanence, except that the profit and loss account and reserve balances appeared at the foot of the list; assets were arranged in order of increasing liquidity. An example of a different presentation may be found in the accounts of Richard Thomas & Co. Ltd, during the late 1930s, where liabilities were listed in the approximate order they would rank for repayment in the event of liquidation, and assets were listed in terms of decreasing liquidity.

Figure 11.1
Balance Sheet extract
South Durham Steel & Iron Co. Ltd, 30th September, 1908

Profit and Loss Account.			
		£	£
Amount at 30th September, 1907, as per last Account			39,421
Less:	Provision for Dividend on Preference Shares accrued and paid to 30th September, 1907	4,500	
	Dividend on Ordinary Shares to 30th September, 1907, paid 28th November, 1907	17,500	22,000
			17,421
Add:	Profit for year to 30th September, 1908		55,164
	Amount transferred from Reserve Account		25,000
			97,585
Deduct:	Interest on Debenture Stock to 30th September, 1908	13,500	
	Dividend on Cumulative Preference Shares paid to 30th June, 1908	13,500	
	Income Tax	1,324	
	Directors' Fees	1,250	
	Trustees for Debenture Stockholders' Remuneration	315	
	Depreciation	30,000	59,889
			37,696

CA 1928 introduced an obligation 'to distinguish between the amounts respectively of the fixed assets and of the floating assets' (s.40). The ICAEW's natural concern with the extent of the professional accountant's legal responsibilities is shown by its decision to seek counsel's opinion on the significance of this provision. Counsel advised that it was unnecessary to label the assets in groups as fixed or floating; it was quite sufficient merely to describe balance sheet items in a manner which enabled users to identify their appropriate location. The statutory provision was therefore aimed at the odd company which, up to 1928, published a single balance sheet entry covering most, or all, of its assets. Nevertheless, it became fairly common practice to classify assets under subheadings and/or give subtotals. As alternatives to the term floating assets, the subheadings current assets and, less often, liquid assets were sometimes used.

The most intriguing balance sheet presentation which has come to the writer's attention is that for the Wigan Coal, Iron & Steel Co. Ltd which, between 1870–1928, was presented in a format almost identical to that recommended in Table A of CA 1862. The fact that it compares well with the balance sheets presented by many other companies, even at the end of that period, suggests a lack of technical development in company reporting over a period of 66 years.

Fixed assets and depreciation

Valuation. Today valuation procedures are fairly closely regulated by SSAPs and the Companies Act. Between 1900–40, the sole requirement, introduced for the registrar's accounts in 1907 and extended to the shareholders' accounts in 1928, was to show how the values of fixed assets had been computed. The examination of published accounts suggests that the systematic depreciation of fixed assets did not become a widespread practice until after 1940. The total omission of a depreciation charge was not uncommon and, when a deduction was made, it was often as a lump sum, related to the level of profit, and accounted for as an appropriation of profits. Indeed, as late as the 1930s, the chairman of John Summers & Sons Ltd, in private correspondence, referred to the fact that 'few steel concerns have written off any depreciation for many years' (quoted in Edwards, 1981, p.22).

The directors sometimes attempted to justify the omission of a charge by indicating the use of alternative procedures to account for capital expenditure. The continued use of 'repairs and renewals accounting' (see Chapter 10) is indicated by comments to the effect that 'the works and plant have been efficiently maintained out of revenue'. A contrasting practice, also common in earlier times, was to write off capital expenditure immediately it was incurred. A most striking example occurred at GKN where, throughout the period 1900–20, fixed assets were reported unchanged at their value, on incorporation, of £2,821,200. This is also an exceptional example of the stability of accounting procedures within companies over time; the Dowlais Iron Co., forerunner of GKN, used this procedure throughout the nineteenth century.

A method of accounting for fixed assets used by local government during the twentieth century was also sometimes employed in the private sector. The approach, which has been called 'modified accruals accounting', involves writing off fixed assets financed by loans at the same rate as the loan is repaid (where the loan is repaid as a single sum, an advance provision must be built up, Jones, p.146). At the Shelton Iron, Steel and Coal Co. Ltd, this method was used between 1890–1928 when debentures totalling £0.5m were raised and repaid (Edwards, 1980, p.251). An advantage of this approach is that it avoids the need to estimate depreciation; an obvious drawback is the lack of any close connection between the extent of depreciation and the amount of money repaid, especially where no attempt has been made to match the period of the loan with the life of the asset.

Where the directors failed to charge depreciation it was quite usual for the auditors to refer to this omission, but unusual for them to qualify their report. Auditors rarely made any reference to the adequacy of the charge, even where there was no obvious explanation for substantial fluctuations, from year to year, other than the fact that profits had also risen or fallen. The more demanding auditor met with a dusty response. The chairman's report to the shareholders of the South Durham Steel & Iron Co. Ltd (1918) countered the auditors' criticism of the failure to make a provision by arguing that 'as we have always dealt so liberally with this item, especially in recent years, your directors consider that it is unnecessary to set aside any sum for this purpose on the present occasion' (Edwards, 1981, p.24).

Today the acknowledged reason for charging depreciation is to produce a profit figure which takes full account of the cost of resources used up during the course of business activity. Often this was not the objective during the period 1900–40. Failure to make a regular and systematic charge, the fact that fixed assets were written down by making use of a wide range of extraneous balances (e.g. balances on share premium accounts, provisions surplus to requirements, and gains from the sales of investments), and the numerous occasions on which the directors commented on the condition of a company's fixed assets, are findings which suggest that management continued to accept a larger measure of responsibility for the financial position displayed in the balance sheet than for the reported profit figure.

The failure to charge adequate depreciation, reduce reported profit and restrict dividends accordingly, may have been one of the reasons why a number of iron and steel companies were forced to make substantial capital reorganisations during the inter-war period. For example, the Barrow Haematite Steel Co. Ltd, which entered into a scheme of arrangement in 1932, had not charged depreciation since 1916.

Disclosure. A single omnibus heading was generally used to cover all fixed assets reported in the balance sheet until CA 1928 came into effect on 1 November 1929, and to cover all tangible fixed assets reported thereafter. Sometimes the caption also encompassed investments, as in the accounts of John Brown for each year up to 31 March 1929 when the balance sheet contained the following entry to describe nearly 90 per cent of the company's assets:

> Freehold and leasehold land, buildings and steel works; shipyard and engineering works; collieries and investments in other companies and properties, 6,799,339

Best practice usually involved reporting the following amounts in respect of fixed assets: the balance brought forward; additions during the year; the proceeds arising from any disposals; and the depreciation charge for the year (the last two items appeared as deductions). The use of sales proceeds, rather than the book value of items sold or scrapped, suggests that, either fixed asset registers were not kept, or that they were in too poor a state to allow identification of the latter figure. Probably it was also for this reason that the division of fixed assets into their major classifications was an exceptional practice, and a figure for accumulated depreciation was rarely provided.

The 1928 Act's requirement for the separate statement of goodwill, patents and trademarks brought about a significant improvement in the accounts of certain companies. For example, in Bovril's accounts for the year to 31 December 1928, £3m of the company's £6m assets was covered by the description 'goodwill, trademarks, freehold and leasehold properties and interest in associated companies, government stock, etc.'. The 1929 balance sheet was more illuminating:

Goodwill and trademarks	£2,414,323
Freehold, leasehold properties,	£241,508
Plant, motors and office furniture	£40,755
Debts due from subsidiaries	£204,552

The fact that over 80 per cent of the 1928 omnibus item comprised intangibles was revealed (Edwards, 1976, p.296)

Companies often reported that their fixed assets were valued 'at cost less depreciation' but, in the absence of separate figures for cost and aggregate depreciation (not required by statute until 1947), it was difficult to assess the adequacy of the charge. Where a shortfall was suspected, action was sometimes taken. For example, in 1929 the shareholders of Cheshire United Salt Co. Ltd referred the accounts back to the directors so that a proper charge might be made and the accounts redrafted to comply with the new Act. The amended version included a depreciation charge which reduced reported profit by 20 per cent and also revealed that, out of total fixed assets previously reported at £120,153, £79,966 consisted of goodwill. (*Accountant*, 9 November, 1929).

The Economist, one of the few persistent critics of accounting practices in the 1920s, was particularly scathing of the financial reporting procedures employed by the P & O Steam Navigation Co. Ltd whose chairman, Lord Inchcape, was a self-confessed advocate of secrecy. The 1923 accounts, for example, were pilloried because they showed a net profit after providing an unstated amount for depreciation. According to *The Economist*: 'As we have protested many times in the past, the presentation of a profit and loss account of this nature is of little value, and entirely fails to give the shareholder a true idea of his company's position' (quoted in Kitchen, p.124).

The introduction to the fourth edition of Leake's *Depreciation of Wasting Assets* (1923) drew attention to the generally chaotic treatment of capital expenditure. By way of contrast, the fifth edition (1948) tells us that, *recently*, considerable progress had been made in developing suitable systems for recording capital expenditure and computing depreciation in a methodical manner (p.xiii). It is possible that a great deal of the improvement referred to by Leake occurred in response to Recommendation 9 (issued by the ICAEW in 1945) which advised directors to make an annual charge.

Investments

Iron and steel was one of the first industries to make use of share acquisitions as a means of achieving close trading links with suppliers and consumers (vertical integration). Trade investments therefore featured prominently in their accounts and the method of valuation was usually given. Terms commonly used were 'at cost', 'at cost less amount written off', 'at or under cost', and 'at cost less depreciation'. Valuation bases were not always as conservative as these terms suggest, particularly in view of the fact that the 1920s and early 1930s were periods of falling prices. For example, the 1930 balance sheet of John Brown & Co. Ltd reported investments 'at or under cost', but a reconstruction scheme undertaken later that year required £2m to be written off. A revealing contemporary comment on the valuation practices of iron and steel companies is again contained in the personal correspondence of Henry Summers:

> Most of the steel Co's balance sheets show that a large part of their capital is in associated companies, Guest Keen have 16.5 millions. They show reserves at 3.5 millions, this would be wiped out twice over if their subsidiary concerns were written down to their true value. Baldwins have 2 millions in subsidiary concerns which we know are of little value (quoted in Edwards, 1981, p.32).

CA 1928 introduced requirements for the separate disclosure of shares in, amounts due to, and amounts due from subsidiaries. This resulted in many companies reporting previously unidentified balances. The legislature's failure to go further and require holding companies to publish group accounts was, however, soon the subject of criticism (see Chapter 18).

Stock

Re Kingston Cotton Mill Co. Ltd (1896) decided that it was not the auditor's duty to take stock, and that he was not guilty of negligence if he accepted the certificate of a responsible official where there were no suspicious circumstances. This did not release the auditor from all responsibility for stock valuation; his right to rely on certificates was constrained by *re Westminster Road Construction and Engineering Co. Ltd* (1932) which decided that an auditor had failed in his duty where an over-valuation of work in progress remained undetected in circumstances where there was ample evidence available. It was, nevertheless, common practice throughout the period 1900–40 to include, either on the face of the balance sheet or, failing that, in the auditors' report, a statement drawing attention to the fact that stock had been valued and/or certified by the company's officials or an independent third party.

Information about how the stock had been valued was often provided. The directors of John Summers (1920–37), where stock was valued at 'cost or market price, whichever is the lower', stated that they used a valuation basis considered to represent best practice. Other, far less common, methods used were 'market value' at the Round Oak Works Ltd (1926–28) and the inclusion of 'a proportion of estimated profit on work-in-progress' at Head Wrightson and Co. Ltd (1903–11).

The not uncommon practice of valuing stock well below cost, to create a secret reserve (see next section), came under attack from the government just after the First World War. A document was issued, for the guidance of Inland Revenue tax officers, which insisted on stock being valued at cost price or market price, whichever was the lower. The balance sheet of the South Durham Steel & Iron Co. Ltd, for 1919, shows an addition to reserves of £270,783, described as 'increase placed on the value of the stock-in-trade to meet the requirements of the Inland Revenue for taxation purposes'. A disappointed chairman commented that this would have the effect 'not only of preventing traders making provision during good years for the lean years which must follow, but also of aggravating the loss in bad years' (quoted in Edwards, 1981, p.33).

Secret reserves

There has always been support for the policy of building up reserves on the grounds that it reflects a prudent financial policy which is likely to improve long-term financial stability. Profits set aside in good years can be drawn upon when trading conditions become more difficult. The controversy associated with such transfers was whether or not they should be disclosed.

The classic method of creating a secret reserve was to make an undisclosed transfer to an account which did not appear on the face of the balance sheet. This might be because it was submerged under a vague heading such as 'sundry creditors' or because the reserve together with an equivalent amount of cash was simply omitted from the balance sheet.[3] Other ways of creating the same effect were to overstate a liability, to understate fixed assets by making excessive depreciation charges, or to reduce stock well below cost.

Up to the 1920s the widespread popularity of secret reserves may be attributed to the fact that their existence guaranteed a balance sheet which understated the financial strength of the concern. This state of affairs was considered satisfactory from the viewpoint of both the creditor and the long-term investor. The position of the short-term speculator was less well served, but it was felt that he could be left to look after himself.

During the inter-war years, however, the profit and loss account replaced the balance sheet as the principal statement used to assess the progress and prospects of a firm. The significance of secret reserves for profit and loss account data is quite different from its impact upon reported balance sheet values. In the balance sheet the creation and utilisation of secret reserves merely affects the extent to which values are understated. In the profit and loss account, depending on the direction of the transfer, their occurs either an *under*statement or an *over*statement of reported profits in relation to actual trading results. In these circumstances, there is a considerable risk that external users will be misled, although a counter argument is that to publish the 'true' profit figure, for a single accounting period, is itself misleading where trade is of a cyclical nature.

The existence of secret reserves could sometimes be deduced, or suspected, by the careful reader of company accounts. For example, one imprecise caption sometimes used to satisfy the auditor's insistence on technical accuracy but, at the same time, to conceal the existence of a 'free' reserve from the layman, was 'sundry creditors and credit balances'. Where the existence of a free reserve was indicated on the face of the balance sheet, omnibus headings were sometimes used to conceal the actual amount set aside. The 1928 balance sheet of the Imperial Tabacco Co. Ltd, for example, included the item

> Creditors, provisions for taxation and bonus to customers, estimated capital liability under dividend guarantees; *amounts set aside for contingencies* and to meet fluctuations in the value of leaf tobacco stocks, employers' liability, marine and other funds (my emphasis)

Similarly, the accounts of J.Lyons for the year to 31 March 1929 included the figure £2,352,877 described as 'Trade and other creditors, bills payable, credit balances and reserves' (Edwards, 1976, p.294)

Sometimes the maintenance of a secret reserve was explicitly sanctioned by a company's articles, e.g. those registered by GKN in

1900 authorised the directors to make transfers to an 'internal reserve fund'. Use of secret reserves was discontinued in 1919. The decision to 'come clean', and show the reserve of nearly £1m on the face of the balance sheet, might well have been motivated by the knowledge that a bid was planned for John Lysaght Ltd, with shares in GKN issued as consideration.

Public reappraisal of secret reserves was a product of the uses and abuses to which they were put during the difficult economic conditions of the 1920s. There had been an immediate post-war boom, mainly due to the large volume of liquid assets in the hands of the banks and the general public and the demand for consumer goods which had been unavailable during the war. Production proved incapable of meeting demand, however, and prices spiralled. In an attempt to take the heat out of the economy the government raised the bank rate to 7 per cent and reduced public expenditure. This overreaction helped bring about a collapse of the economy. 1921 was a particularly bad year and unemployment exceeded 1.5 million. Government policy, in particular a determination to maintain a balanced budget, made matters worse rather than better. Unemployment peaked at over 2.5 million (one in five of the working population) between 1931–33, and it was not until the second half of the 1930s that recovery was stimulated by a general improvement in world trade, rearmament, cheap money and the government's willingness to accept budget deficits.

During this difficult period companies made widespread use of secret reserves to help conceal their financial problems and maintain credibility with providers of finance. We can be fairly sure that there were plenty of instances where no reference whatsoever was made to the fact that a secret reserve had been drawn upon to boost reported profit. Where a transfer was disclosed, presentation took one of the following forms.

1. Transfers from a secret reserve with the amount transferred given.

   Examples:

   'Amount transferred from reserve for contingency £75,000'
   Richard Thomas, 1925

   'Transfer of balance of amount standing to the credit of Account 'Reserve for taxation and contingency £57,861'
   Richard Thomas, 1931

   'Reserve not now required £3,944'
   Samuel Fox, 1932

2. Transfers from a secret reserve with the amount transferred left unstated.

Examples:

'Profit to 30 September 1923, including transfer from reserve for taxation no longer required £182,109'
South Durham, 1923

'Profit including divs. and int. received, and transfers from contingency accounts, and after charging maintenance, repairs, depreciation, income tax, salaries of man. directors, bad debts and other expenses £106,753'
Rylands & Sons Ltd, 1930

'Credit balance for the year ended 30 April 1931, including transfers from reserves £15,456'
Head Wrightson, 1931

The wording used by the directors of the Royal Mail Steam Packet Co. Ltd, to describe the profit figure which was at the centre of the well-known prosecution of that company's auditor and chairman in 1931 (Chapter 12), came into the second category. It is often said that the creation of secret reserves continued after 1931, but that revelations in the Royal Mail case put an end to their undisclosed utilisation. This is not so.

The internal records of John Summers, for example, show that secret reserves were maintained, and added to, well into the 1930s. Undisclosed transfers to the credit of the profit and loss account were also made in each of the years 1931–33, albeit in an indirect manner. The amount transferred (£50,000) comprised two-thirds of the £75,000 depreciation charge reported for each of those years. And this was the reporting practice of a financially cautious company! The chairman commented, privately,

> we have used our subsidiaries to hide profits but the public think otherwise hence our shares are much lower than they ought to be . . . I have no desire to conceal anything if its disclosure would make the appearance worse. The important thing for the shareholders is that there are no undisclosed liabilities.

In the following year (1934) an internal memorandum claimed that 'unlike most steel firms we put only a small part of our goods in the window and whilst others use magnifying glass our windows are opaque' (quoted in Edwards, 1981, p.39). The maintenance of secret reserves was discontinued in 1938 when £200,000 to the credit of the 'special reserve No. 1 account' was disclosed in the balance sheet. None of these events were commented on by the auditors.

Review

The case for a full disclosure of accounting policies was recognised, in some quarters, at a very early stage. The following observation was contained in the *Morning Chronicle* of 17 May 1845:

> This, at least, will be generally agreed to, that the principle adopted by any company . . . is of comparatively minor importance, provided that the system pursued be distinctly avowed and understood by the shareholders. It is the deception practised upon unwary proprietors by avowing one rule and clandestinely acting upon another, that has brought so much discredit and disaster (quoted in Irish, p.71).

This chapter shows that, even during the period 1900–40, companies had by no means given effect to the principle of full disclosure. 'The Englishman's home is his Castle' mentality extended to business affairs and, while it is fair to say that the demand for financial information was often not particularly strong, where it surfaced, it was often resisted by company chairmen as an unwarranted invasion of privacy. Prominent critics of contemporary financial reporting procedures, whose advice was ignored, included the former Prime Minister, Andrew Bonar Law. In a speech delivered on 29 November 1923 he observed that 'none of us would be the worse for a breath of fresh air, easier access to information with regard to wages and prices and profits in our great industries, and perhaps also with regard to stocks and orders' (quoted in Dickinson, p.486).

The principal enactment between 1900–40, CA 1928, appears, with the benefit of hindsight, to have been an unduly tentative measure. Its failure to impose precise obligations on management allowed some companies to continue their practice of publishing reports which were meaningless and even misleading. Important areas of neglect were secret reserves, depreciation, and group accounts. Where the Act placed a specific obligation on directors, it was complied with; where no such obligation was imposed, a wide variety of disclosure practices continued to be employed. It was in connection with the disclosure of information on the asset side of the balance sheet that the Act was most specific.

In general, differences in accounting practice between firms were more marked than changes over time. Overall there was a *gradual* trend towards increased disclosure, but there are numerous examples of directors ceasing to publish certain items of information and even accounting reports, especially in the first quarter of the twentieth century, e.g. the Cunard Company ceased to publish a profit and loss account in 1922. This was not unusual judging from Dickinson's address (1924) to the Royal Statistical Society: 'the practice in [Britain and the US] has been in the past, and appears to be still more so in the present, to reduce rather than to increase the very inadequate information which is given with regard to earnings and costs' (p.477). When substantial improvements were made to the reporting practices of the more secretive companies, in the 1930s, often the publicised motive was that it enabled shareholders to be better informed (Edwards, 1981, p.34).

The valuation practices employed between 1900–40 were, in the main, unacceptable compared with present-day standards. In mitigation, it should be pointed out that directors increasingly provided some indication of how the balances had been arrived at, which should have helped users to make their own assessment of reported figures on the basis of their knowledge of contemporary practices.

Throughout the period companies published a great deal more financial information than the law required. If we accept agency theory, which views financial reports as a commodity supplied to meet a demand, these improvements may be attributed to the growing pressure for information exerted by user groups, in particular shareholders, during the first 40 years of the present century. Managers, for their part, responded and supplied the required data on the assumption that the willingness of investors to finance industrial and commercial activity would otherwise decline.

As regulations were weak, it is not surprising that companies supplied more information than was required by law. What is more difficult to explain is the extent of the inter-company differences in reporting practices. Possible explanations are that there were significant variations in the extent to which users demanded financial information, in the way in which business activity was financed, and in the amount directors were willing to pay for capital.

12

Falsification of Accounts

Introduction

Accounting history is littered with examples of financial information used as a means of deception. The immediate reactions of the business community and investing public are outrage and the demand for more strict controls. Such behaviour is not always met with sympathy. According to Mr Justice Eve, in evidence given to the Greene Committee, 'these demands, originating in a distrustfulness almost approaching panic, not infrequently emerge finally as undigested attempts on the part of those who make them to shift on to the community at large, or the State, as they prefer to call it, responsibilities resting on their own shoulders' (*Minutes*, p.lxxvi).

An early example of accountancy used as a means of deception is contained in Pacioli's *Summa*. He tells us that Venetian traders kept two sets of books, one to show customers and the other to show suppliers. The position has since developed further. It is sometimes said that, today, Italian businessmen keep three sets of books; one copy each for shareholders, the tax authorities and management. The absence of reliable information has, on a number of occasions in the past, been the cause of intense speculation in corporate securities followed by dramatic failure. A number of these scandals are discussed elsewhere in this book.

The South Sea bubble fiasco (see Chapter 9), for example, provoked sufficient public outrage to cause Parliament to appoint a committee of enquiry which engaged Charles Snell, accountant, to investigate the affairs of the firm, Sawbridge & Co., belonging to a director of the South Sea Company. It is the first recorded example of an investigating accountant's report, but it is not a particularly impressive document, resembling a piece of special pleading rather than an independent enquiry (reproduced in Worthington, p.108). A period of intense speculation in railway shares (called the 'railway mania'), which played a major role in the general financial crisis of 1847, was followed by a series of investigations which revealed numerous 'fabrications' of accounts, the most notable of which is detailed in Quilter, Ball & Co.'s report on the Eastern Counties Railway (see Chapter 13).

The common purposes of these deceptions were to conceal financial problems, maintain business confidence and raise cash. A cynical justification for such action, which ranges from window dressing to outright fraud, is that the proof of honesty is the ability to pay debts when they fall due. However, the argument that great profits would have been made if only the company had survived a little longer has been dismissed by Avory L.J. as 'nothing more or less than the threadbare plea of every clerk or servant who robs his master and says that he hoped to repay the money, before his crime was discovered, by backing a winner' (*Accountant*, 1 February 1930, p.160). In this chapter the events surrounding the collapse of two major companies are examined as illustrations of the 'shock effect' of financial disasters on accounting practices and regulatory requirements.

City of Glasgow Bank (1878)

Prior to 1878 the accounts of banks were not usually audited; in Scotland, the only exception was the Bank of Scotland and, even there, the accounts were merely inspected by two shareholders. The absence of an audit was justified on the grounds that such an investigation was incompatible with the bank's obligation to keep confidential the financial affairs of its customers. The collapse of the City of Glasgow Bank in 1878 caused a reappraisal of this idea (see Forbes, French, and Tyson for full details).

Formed in 1839, the Glasgow bank was a relative newcomer to banking circles. It adopted an aggressive, expansionist, policy, and by 1878 had the largest network of branches in Scotland. Cash was in plentiful supply and the bank found it easy to attract deposits; the problem was to secure their profitable investment. In the 1870s the British economy suffered a severe period of depression and interest rates were generally low. Banks in general and the Glasgow bank, in particular, looked abroad for a better return on their money. The established overseas outlet for funds was the East India trade but, by the 1870s, various developments, including competition from American cotton producers, made this trade far less attractive.

The bank also looked to the developing countries of Australasia and to North American Railway building where there were good long-term prospects. A major problem with these investments, however, was that such a commitment conflicted with a banking company's normal priority for solvency. In the endeavour to find a profitable outlet for investible funds, a further fundamental precept of sound banking was totally disregarded; instead of maintaining a broad portfolio of customers, most of the bank's cash was recklessly advanced to just four 'adventurers' and their associates. When the Glasgow bank collapsed these 'deadly accounts' comprised £6m or 70 per cent of its total advances.

The deception. The balances on the deadly accounts had grown quickly during the late 1860s and early 1870s, when good money was thrown after bad in the endeavour to help extricate the adventurers from their financial difficulties. Information about the accounts was confined to two or three key officials who made up the 'committee on head office accounts'. It was not until 1875, when a new manager was appointed, that the board of directors was fully informed of the seriousness of the bank's situation and the £4.25m then outstanding on the deadly accounts.

Throughout the 1870s the bank was heavily dependent, for survival, on the willingness of the London discount market to accept the ever increasing volume of bills issued by the company. To help maintain confidence, the bank supported its quotation by buying its own shares and publishing 'imaginary' balance sheets. The deception began in 1873 when the bank's liabilities were reduced by £0.75m – a figure literally 'plucked from the air' (Forbes, p.47). The last balance sheet, published as at at 5 June 1878, understated liabilities by £2.3m and overstated assets by approximately £4m. In addition, the earnings for the year were inflated by £125,000. These machinations enabled the company to report handsome profits and declare dividends in line with the market rate. The issue of fake accounts was a successful ploy; despite suspicion and rumour, the bank remained free from serious criticism until its financial difficulties were of a magnitude impossible to suppress.

Disquiet with the bank's financial affairs gained momentum in autumn 1878 when the *Glasgow News* published a report indicating 'Metropolitan concern regarding a Scottish Bank unspecified'. This was a reference to the high rate of interest demanded by brokers accepting the bank's bills on the London discount market. The bank turned to other Scottish banks for assistance, and they appointed a professional accountant to examine the books. Its financial problems must have been massively evident because, on the basis of a report prepared within twenty-four hours, the consortium declined to assist. Kerr, Andersons, Muir & Main, chartered accountants, were then engaged to make a full investigation. Their report informed an astonished public that there were assets of only £6m available to meet liabilities of £12m.

Tyson believes that publication of the bank's true financial position would probably have resulted in closure in 1873 and, although losses would then have been incurred, they would have been of a far lower magnitude (p.130).

Unlimited liability. The unlimited liability of bank shareholders, for their company's debts, was still the normal position in 1878; the only exceptions were the Bank of Scotland, the Royal Bank of Scotland and the British Linen Bank (Forbes, p.42). Shareholders in the Glasgow bank comprised a wide cross-section of the community, including spinsters, tradesmen, teachers, lawyers, insurance agents, farmers, and bank agents. These people not only lost their whole investment, they were also liable to meet debts in the region of £6m. At the date of closure there were 8465 shares in issue; the average liability was, therefore, approximately £700 per share (equivalent to about £20,000 per share at 1988 prices). Many of the shareholders were people of modest means and had invested all their savings in the bank. These were bankrupted by the first call of £500 per share to meet the claims from creditors. To meet the shortfall, it was then necessary to make an enormous second, and final, call of £2250 per share. This left most of the remaining shareholders in financial ruin; of 1819 shareholders at the date of liquidation, only about 250 remained solvent.

Unlimited liability meant that the creditors claims were met in full, but at an enormous price. Private homes were sold and men, women and children were driven into the workhouse. The directors were charged with falsifying the bank's balance sheets; their prison sentences, ranging from 8 months to 18 months, were considered totally inadequate by an vengeful public and press.

The bank's failure demonstrated the unsuitability of unlimited liability for the modern, large scale, business organisation. It alerted shareholders to the risk of investing in banks, and they probably concluded that other business investments left them even more exposed. Their natural response was to demand the protection of limited liability (which had been legally available for banks since 1858) as a precondition for investment, believing that the risk of massive financial loss otherwise outweighed the prospect of relatively modest gains. The effect of the bank's collapse was, therefore, finally to destroy the nineteenth-century commercial concept that those who benefited from the profits of business activity should also bear all the losses.

Statutory Audit of Banks. Legislation was demanded to restore confidence among the investing public and help prevent a recurrence of these abuses. A number of private members' bills were immediately presented to Parliament containing requirements for a statutory audit and the publication of standardised accounts by banks and other joint stock companies. These bills were unsuccessful, but the provisions, so far as they related to banks, were included in a government bill which became CA 1879. Some of the clauses of the draft bill, e.g. provision for a prescribed form of balance sheet for banks, did not survive the Parliamentary process, but the Act introduced two important innovations. First, provision was made for a 'reserve capital', i.e. shares to be issued, as partly paid, with the balance available to be called up, if needed, on liquidation. The power to have a reserve capital was permissive but was adopted by most banks. Secondly, provision was made for the publication of an audited balance sheet.

The audit requirement was criticised because of the failure to instruct the auditor to compare the accounts with the underlying vouchers, or to authorise the auditor to examine the directors. The mere obligation to compare the accounts with the books was thought, in some quarters, to imply the need for only a 'mechanical' audit. Certainly this seems to have been the intention of the Chancellor of the Exchequer who, when introducing the bill, observed that the auditor's duty was to issue

> [a] report certifying whether the accounts are given correctly, and disclose a true and fair statement of the accounts of the bank as shown by the books. It is impossible for an auditor to go into the books and say from them whether this is a good bill, or that is a good security. That is not only impossible to effect, but to attempt it would be delusive and dangerous (quoted in Tyson, p.131).

Further criticisms of the Act were that it contained no penalties for failure to comply with its audit provisions and did not require the auditor to be a practising accountant. The threat of a fiasco similar to that suffered by the Glasgow bank, however, encouraged other banks to engage professional accountants to do this work. The Act did not tackle the question of a limited company buying its own shares, but this practice was declared illegal in *Trevor* v *Whitworth* (1887).

Royal Mail case (1931)

Secret reserves legitimised. A major financial reporting issue during the first half of the twentieth century was the legitimacy and financial probity of secret reserves. Their use was given judicial approval in *Newton* v *Birmingham Small Arms Co. Ltd* (1906). The defendant company had passed a special resolution which empowered the directors to do the following: to make undisclosed transfers from the profit and loss account to an 'internal reserve fund' which did not appear on the face of the balance sheet; to apply the reserve fund for any purpose which they believed would protect or advance the interests or value of the company; to disclose movements on the reserve fund to the company's auditors who were, however, barred from reporting these transactions to the shareholders.

Newton, a shareholder, applied for an injunction to restrain the directors from acting on this special resolution. The action was successful. Auditors had an obligation to report to shareholders under CA 1900, and the court concluded that the resolution prevented them from fully doing their job. Buckley J. made it clear, however, that the court did not necessarily object to the maintenance of secret reserves. Indeed, he observed that assets were often prudently stated at less than their probable real value, that the published balance sheet often understated a company's financial position and should certainly not overstate it, that there were legitimate reasons for approving a certain element of secrecy, and that undue publicity might be harmful to the company's business.

The contemporary interpretation of the decision was that secret reserves were perfectly in order provided the directors acted honestly and so long as the auditors were allowed to comment on them if they considered it appropriate. The case, which has since been described as the 'charter for the creators of secret reserves' (Samuel, p.278), was partly responsible for secrecy, obscurity, excessive summarisation and distortion becoming common features of financial reporting for the next quarter of a century.

Dicksee believed that *Newton* v *BSA* was interpreted too widely by auditors who failed to draw attention to an excessive use of secret reserves so as to undermine the accounts as a measure of a company's financial position (p.40). This was not a popular view. The chairman of Lever Brothers Ltd, Francis D'Arcy Cooper (a prominent chartered accountant), believed that empirical evidence had proved the worth of secret reserves. He told the Greene Committee that, without them, 'you would not have had a company in England which was solvent' following the financial crisis of 1921 (*Minutes*, no.3852). As late as 1929 William Cash, a past president of the ICAEW, informed the Bristol Society of Chartered Accountants that 'the strength of a commercial undertaking lies in the hidden reserves' (*Accountant*, 6 July 1929, p.20).

These beliefs and practices were the subject of a complete reappraisal following the prosecution of the chairman, Lord Kylsant, and the auditor of the Royal Mail Steam Packet Co. Ltd in 1931.

Expansion and financial instability. Owen Crosby Phillips (later Lord Kylsant) was appointed managing director of the, then, ailing shipping company in 1903. He was an expansionist and achieved considerable success for many years. His policies resulted in a high ratio of loan capital to equity within the long-term capital structure of the group but, in the absence of a requirement to publish consolidated accounts, the extent of the gearing was successfully concealed by an intricate scheme of cross-shareholdings between the various group companies.

The financial stability of the group was put to the test when, in the immediate post-war period, Phillips made two tactical errors. He placed orders to replace ships lost during the war but, as most shipping companies were doing the same, prices spiralled up to four times the figures asked for similar vessels built a couple of years later. In addition, he purchased a large proportion of the merchant ships owned by the British Government, ostensibly to eliminate potential competition. These events were followed by an almost immediate down-turn in shipping transportation activity and Phillips was left with a considerably over-valued fleet which, at prevailing rates of freight, could not pay its way. On a personal level events were more encouraging; in 1923 he was created Lord Kylsant, first Baron of Carmarthen.

The prudent solution to this predicament would have been the implementation of a scheme for the reduction of capital. Kylsant rejected this option on the grounds that heavy reliance on debt capital would restrict his freedom of action and prejudice further development and expansion of the group. He instead chose to wait for the upturn in trading conditions which, he believed, would rectify the financial imbalance. Meanwhile, public confidence had to be retained, and this caused Kylsant to extend his financial ingenuity to the development of dangerous and misleading reporting practices.

The deception. The Royal Mail Company made large profits during the First World War, and these were the subject of an excess profits duty levied by the Government to help finance military expenditure. The tax was complicated and, at the outset, ultimate liability could not be calculated with any degree of accuracy. The company therefore adopted the prudent policy of making generous provisions. In due course, tax was paid and there remained a provision, surplus to requirements, of over £1.8m. Between 1921–29 the apparent profitability of the holding company was exaggerated by using this undisclosed surplus, and various other credit balances, to boost reported profits (Samuel, Appendix B). In addition, the results reported by individual companies were inflated by intra-group dividend transfers. This chicanery enabled healthy profits to be reported during a period when the group was actually suffering heavy losses. Dividend payments, outside the group, were financed using bank overdrafts, and cash from the sale of surplus properties, tax refunds, and other extraneous sources.

The Royal Mail Company had enjoyed a reputation for publishing informative accounts in the early years of the century but, in common with other hard-pressed firms, the accounts gradually revealed less and less. Reporting standards were compromised as Kylsant sank deeper into the deception of the investing public, and it appears that he was successful in pursuing this objective; as late as 1928 his company was recommended by *Fairplay* as a sound investment. Kylsant's justification for the deception was that the shipping industry saw periods of slump and boom and, provided he could overcome the short-term problems, an up-turn in trading fortunes would fully vindicate his policies. In the event, improvement in the shipping trade did occur, but not until the early 1930s – a little too late.

The financial difficulties of the company surfaced when loans from the Treasury could not be repaid. An enquiry revealed the group's poor financial state and full details of the deception. Kylsant's bargaining position was strengthened, however, by the Government's reluctance to make matters public. The Royal Mail Company was the 'flagship' of the British shipping industry and its failure would result in the loss of many jobs, particularly at Harland and Wolff in Northern Ireland. There ensued a battle of wills between Government officials and their advisers on one side and the stubborn Kylsant on the other. Kylsant over played his hand; he totally refused to accept any curtailment of his business activities, government support was withdrawn and the group collapsed.

The Prosecution. On 20 July 1931 Lord Kylsant and Harold Morland (the auditor) stood in the dock at the Old Bailey charged with publishing a balance sheet which was false and fraudulent. The essence of the prosecution, in *Rex* v *Lord Kylsant and another* (more popularly known as the Royal Mail case), was that the balance sheet for 1926 was intentionally misleading; it showed a trading profit for the year of approximately £439,000 whereas, in reality, the company had suffered a trading loss of about £300,000. The transformation was achieved by an undisclosed transfer, from reserves, of nearly £750,000. The case turned on the wording used to describe profit for the year. It was as follows:

> Balance for the year, including dividends on shares in allied and other companies, adjustment of taxation reserves, *less* depreciation of fleet, etc. £439,213.

The case for the defence was that the phrase 'adjustment of taxation reserves' was inserted, at the auditor's insistence, to render the caption technically correct. The prosecution contended that the wording was grossly misleading, since it implied that the company was thriving, and had earned a substantial profit, subject to some modest adjustment to taxation reserves. An important factor in obtaining the defendants' acquittal was the evidence given by Lord Plender, an expert witness and the leading professional figure of the inter-war period (see biographical sketch by Edwards, 1985).

Plender found himself in an uncomfortable position. He was chairman of the Government's advisory committee responsibile for monitoring treasury guaranteed loans to the Royal Mail group. Research has shown that he was slow to grasp the extent of the group's financial problems (Green and Moss, p.107), so that firm action was delayed while matters got worse; an outcome which might have been avoided if Morland had acquainted the committee, of which he was also a member, with the real position of the group. It is known that Plender was also 'saddened' by Morland's failure to ensure that the shareholders were not better informed. However, secret reserves were in widespread use during the 1920s and, under cross-examination, Plender confirmed that the wording used to describe the transfer was technically correct and in accordance with best accounting practice. In defence counsel's view, it was this piece of evidence which secured the acquittal of Kylsant and Morland.

The Royal Mail case proved that, although CA 1929 improved the informative value of the balance sheet (see Chapter 11), it remained legal to use secret reserves to distort totally the true trend of trading results.[1] However, the fact that the attorney-general had considered it appropriate to bring the action was deemed significant, and Mr Justice Wright's charge to the jury contained the following express criticism of the reporting practices of the Royal Mail Company and an implied criticism of the external audit function (Brooks, p.224).

> It is a little astounding, and one cannot help wondering whether those who manage big companies do not forget sometimes that the body of directors of a company are the agents and trustees of the shareholders, that they owe them full information, subject to proper and reasonable commercial necessity, and it is their interests that they have to study.

The defendants had escaped on a technicality and the judge took the opportunity to warn professional accountants that, if a similar situation recurred, they were unlikely to be treated so leniently.

Legal versus moral responsibility. The accountancy profession had, in the past, maintained that the content of the accounts was not all-important, and that more fundamental protections were provided by the external audit and the shareholders' right to cross-examine the directors at the AGM. The Royal Mail saga demonstrated the feebleness of these claims. The case proved that a properly carried out audit was an inadequate protection; it also came to light that Kylsant had categorically refused to give information for which he was specifically asked at the 1930 AGM. Action was needed to improve the informative value of company accounts but, in organising its response, a shocked accountancy profession was hampered by a lack of consensus between the two leading professional bodies.

The Society of Incorporated Accountants and Auditors (SIAA), under the leadership of Henry Morgan, believed it was unreasonable and impracticable to expect the auditor to impose, on business, accounting obligations in excess of minimum legal requirements. In its view a new Companies Act was a precondition for an improvement in the standards of financial reporting. The ICAEW, on the other hand, did not regard detailed legislative prescription as either a desirable or a feasible proposition. It's ideal was an accountancy profession which experimented with new methods and procedures and, as a result, achieved an improvement in the overall standard of financial reporting. Within this scenario, the role of the legislature was relegated to one of providing statutory support for procedures which had already achieved widespread acceptance. Perhaps the main difference between the two bodies was that the SIAA regarded accounting procedures as already being sufficiently developed to enable a statutory choice to be made, whereas the ICAEW did not.

Accountants and institutions lined up behind either the SIAA or the ICAEW. *The Accountant* provided the focal point for an active debate. A leading article in that journal argued that the first lesson to learn from the Royal Mail case was the need to reappraise the implicit assumption 'that secrecy is a necessary adjunct of commercial success' (29 August 1931, p.314). The practice of publishing obscure accounting reports, based on the hazards of disclosing information to competitors, was rejected, as was the paternalistic conception of management's role. It was deemed preferable to alarm shareholders with a frank disclosure of a company's financial position than to keep them in a fool's paradise until it was too late to take remedial action.

In one of a series of speeches the president of the ICAEW urged 'the disclosure of such information in regard to [companies'] affairs as will restore in the public and investors such confidence in the commercial world as will secure their support and respect' (*Accountant*, 12 December 1931, p.774). The presidential address to the ICAEW's 1932 AGM, normally set aside for an assessment of purely domestic matters, was instead devoted to an examination of the implications of the Royal Mail case. Legislation was opposed, not only because a professional initiative was favoured, but also because 'auditors will be reduced to mere automata, to obey audit programmes laid down by statutes' (*Accountant*, 7 May 1932, p.629). Speeches delivered by a small number of other prominent chartered accountants emphasised these points and also stressed the importance of earning capacity in assessing the viability of a commercial enterprise. This was a significant step forward, marking a change in emphasis from the balance sheet to the profit and loss account.

The ICAEW's decision to encourage accountants to work for an improvement in reporting standards, but provide no explicit guidelines concerning what should actually be done, was met with alarm and disgust from the rank and file members. Many practicioners, although opposed to further legislation, would have welcomed a technical release which set out their responsibilities and objectives when preparing accounting reports. The ICAEW was fully aware of the desire for guidance, and appointed a special committee to examine the problem, and counsel's opinion was taken. The ICAEW's conclusion was that, whereas a general pronouncement would be of little value and could easily be circumvented or misapplied, a detailed pronouncement was impracticable in view of the diversity of business situations and ways in which secret reserves arose.

Progress and regulation

Public response to the findings in the Royal Mail Case, together with persistent pressure from the media and MP's, encouraged the BOT to monitor closely accounting practices and business attitudes during the 1930s (Bircher, pp.108–16). A wide-ranging internal review of the operation of CA 1929, undertaken between 1931–32, gave consideration to the possibility of making changes in the following areas: to prescribe a statutory form for the profit and loss account and balance sheet; to prevent the use of omnibus headings and secret reserves; to oblige holding companies to publish consolidated balance sheets; and to require the auditor's report to cover the profit and loss account (as well as the balance sheet).

The findings were reviewed by Sir Charles Hipwood, second secretary at the BOT, who decided (March 1932) against action on the grounds that opinion was divided on many issues, that there were no defects of 'such cardinal importance that it requires immediate action', and that it would be best to give the new code at least ten years before undertaking a comprehensive revision (Bircher, p.109). These conclusions remained the basic BOT response to further agitation for reform in the 1930s.

The internal records of the BOT show that a great deal of weight was attached to the views expressed publicly by Plender (president of the ICAEW 1910–12 and 1929–30), who believed that matters of account were best left to the now well-established professional accountancy bodies.[2] That this was likely to result in gradual, rather than radical, change is indicated by Plender's continued conviction that 'so long as they [secret reserves] are made honestly and prudently there may be advantages and often considerable justification for their existence' (*Financial News*, 26 April 1932). By way of contrast, the persistent campaign for legal reform mounted by Henry Morgan (president of the SIAA 1929–32) left the BOT unconvinced of the need for change.

In retrospect the correct choice was probably made; legislation without careful thought and experiment might have firmly entrenched ineffective procedures and done more harm than good. The failure of the professional bodies to take a stronger initiative cannot be explained in these terms, but they had no history of providing written guidance for members and were not yet ready to accept this obligation. A general raising of financial reporting standards during the 1930s (see Chapter 11) was, therefore, a voluntary response to the abuses revealed by the Royal Mail case. It was a period which saw the replacement of legalism by realism in financial reporting.

Following further press criticism in the early 1940s, the ICAEW at last assumed a measure of direct responsibility for financial reporting procedures (see Chapter 19). The Taxation and Financial Relations Committee, established in 1942, issued a series of Recommendations which helped to raise the general standard of published accounts. These included Recommendation 6 (1943) which encouraged the full disclosure of transfers to and from reserves. The need also to amend company law attracted the attention of the Labour President of the BOT, Hugh Dalton (Bircher, p. 117). His determination to achieve more radical changes than in the past is indicated by the decision to appoint an accountant from the 'younger school' to the Cohen Committee, rather than an elder statesman such as Plender. A review of possible candidates eventually resulted in the choice of Kettle of Deloitte, Plender & Griffiths ahead of Howitt of Peat, Marwick, Mitchell, Barton of Barton Mayhew, Benson of Cooper Brothers, Robson of Price Waterhouse, and Dowling of Thomson McLintock. The work of that committee, which recommended that secret reserves be outlawed (legislated upon in CA 1947) is examined in Chapter 16.

PART IV

RULES AND REGULATIONS

13

Statutory Companies and the Double Account System

Private statutes

The affairs of public utility companies (canal, railway, gas, electricity and water) were usually regulated by private Acts of Parliament. This was because special powers were required to compulsorily purchase land and, particularly in the case of the railways, to raise finance from the general public. The years up to 1845 saw a continuous and rapid increase in the number and complexity of the provisions contained in these private Acts of Parliament. The Surrey Iron Railway's Act, 1801, contained just 95 sections whereas the Act for the Lancaster and Carlisle Railway, passed in 1844, ran to 381 sections.

Private acts gradually incorporated more extensive accounting provisions. Up to the third decade of the nineteenth century they usually required accounting records to be kept, but rarely made any provision for the publication or audit of financial statements. The Northampton Gas Light Company's 1823 Act of incorporation, for example, merely empowered the shareholders, at general meetings, to 'call for and examine and settle the accounts of the said company' (s.30). By way of contrast, statutes passed in the early 1840s contained fairly extensive accounting provisions; the Newcastle and Darlington Railway's Act of 1842, for example, included provisions very similar to those contained in the Companies Clauses Consolidation Act passed three years later. This change was presumably in response to shareholders demanding more stringent accounting regulations and promoters recognising that, by providing them, capital availability was likely to increase.

Public Statutes

General. The Companies Clauses Consolidation Act, 1845, was passed to avoid the need for companies to repeat the numerous standard provisions usually contained in private Acts of Parliament. It set out model clauses covering the following matters: the manner in which the company's capital should be raised, and further capital borrowed; the rights of the shareholders; the powers and duties of directors; the declaration and payment of dividends; the keeping and auditing of accounts, and, generally, the mode in which the company's affairs should be conducted in relation to the shareholders and creditors of the company.

The provisions of the 'clauses' Act were incorporated, by reference, in the private statutes of public utility companies formed after 1845, or returning to Parliament after that date to obtain authority to extend operations and/or raise additional finance.[1] This simplified and cheapened the process of statutory incorporation. It of course remained open for Parliament to amend or dispense with particular provisions of the general Act wherever such a course was considered desirable.

The accounting provisions contained in the 1845 Act were rather more extensive than those introduced for registered companies by the Joint Stock Companies Act of the previous year. The 1845 Act, for example, included the requirement that

> an exact balance sheet shall be made up, which shall exhibit a true statement of the capital stock, credits, and property of every description belonging to the company, and the debts due by the company at the date of making such balance sheet, and a distinct view of the profit or loss which shall have arisen on the transactions of the company in the course of the preceding half year (s.116).

Accounting regulations for particular categories of statutory company are summarised below.

Railways. The affairs of British railway companies were subject to much closer regulation than those of most other companies. Even so, their development was basically left to private enterprise, and it was only at a fairly late stage, compared with other European countries, that the government began to impose detailed accounting regulations in respect of form and content. Prior to 1867 the only accounting requirement relating specifically to railway companies was for an annual account to be filed with the clerk of the peace where it should be open to public inspection. The account to show 'the total receipts and expenditure of all funds levied by virtue of this or the special Act for the year . . . with a statement of the balance of such account, duly audited and certified by the directors' (Railway Clauses Consolidation Act 1845, s. 107).

Requirements for a statutory audit (1867) and for the preparation of standardised accounts (1868) to be supplied, on application, to shareholders and filed with the BOT were imposed when the railway network was substantially complete. These accounts were in the form, described later in this chapter, which became known as the double account system.

Gas. Standard clauses for inclusion in the private Acts of statutory gas companies were contained in the Gas Works Clauses Act 1847, and an interesting feature was the provision made for a reduction in the rates charged to customers where profits exceeded a certain percentage of paid-up capital. The Act also required an annual account to be transmitted to the clerk of the peace where it remained available for public inspection. In 1860 the Government turned its attention to gas companies operating in the London Metropolis and made provision for the Home Secretary to issue a prescribed form of accounts to be filled in, returned to him, and laid before Parliament each year. The Gas Works Clauses Act 1871 applied to all companies; under it a standard form of accounts was to be submitted annually to the local authority and made available at a price not exceeding one shilling to any applicant. The form of accounts laid down in the Act followed the same basic scheme as had been introduced three years earlier for railways.

Electricity. A BOT prescribed form of accounts, conforming to the double account system, was introduced for electric lighting companies in 1882. The accounts were to be made available to applicants at a price not exceeding one shilling per copy. A 'clauses' Act, which included an audit requirement, was introduced for this category of company in 1899.

Water. The Water Works Clauses Act 1847 contained provisions similar to those imposed for gas companies by the Gas Works Clauses Act 1847; each Act received the royal assent on 23 April and resulted from bills which had the same sponsors. The Metropolis

Water Act 1871 made provision for annual accounts, conforming also to a double account format prescribed by the BOT, to be audited and returned to the Board, the town clerk of the City of London and other parties. There was also a requirement for copies to be supplied, on application, to members of the general public. This Act was repealed in 1902 when a Water Board was established to take over the Metropolitan Water Companies and to manage the supply of water within London and certain adjoining districts. The accounts of the Water Board were to be made up in the same manner 'as the accounts of county councils' (s.19), i.e. public sector accounting requirements applied.

No statutory accounting requirements were ever imposed for water companies generally, though the system prescribed for the metropolis naturally became popular. The double account system was also adopted voluntarily in other sectors of the economy where the pattern of expenditure possessed similar characteristics, i.e. where a large initial investment was required to establish the infrastructure of the concern, followed subsequently by the need to finance only current operations, e.g. dock companies and companies working wasting assets such as mines and quarries. Most companies required by law to use the double account system disappeared in the spate of nationalisation following the Second World War and, to the best of my knowledge, no British company continues to employ this presentation.

Evolution of the double account system

A large number of statutory companies were incorporated to help establish and develop the British framework of public utilities. Their formation increased the demand for accounting information from absentee investors wishing to know how their money had been spent. A further consequence was the need for businessmen and accountants to devote more attention to the problem of valuing highly expensive, long-lived assets, owned by these companies, for inclusion in the accounts. The double account system was an attempt to devise financial reporting procedures appropriate to meet these challenges. It is therefore a good illustration of the utilitarian nature of the accounting process. The distinguishing charateristic of the system is the subdivision of the conventional balance sheet into the following two accounting statements:

1. The capital account which sets out the capital raised from issuing shares and debentures and the amounts spent on the acquisition of fixed (i.e. capital) assets.
2. The general balance sheet which lists the balance unspent (or overspent) on capital account, the undistributed balance on revenue account, and the assets and liabilities that are in a continuous state of change as the result of trading transactions.

An illustrative presentation of these statements, in summarised form, is given in Figure 13.1.

Figure 13.1
The Double Account Balance Sheet

Capital Account

Expenditure:	£	Receipts:	£
Fixed assets	xxx	Shares	xxx
Balance carried to general balance sheet	xxx	Debentures	xxx
	xxx		xxx

General Balance Sheet

	£		£
Balance from capital account	xxx	Stock	xxx
Balance from revenue account	xxx	Debtors	xxx
Creditors	xxx	Cash	xxx
	xxx		xxx

Note.The ledger account presentation is reversed in the general balance sheet, though this was not always the case in statutory companies which employed the double account system at an early stage.

Capital account. The development of the double account system is mainly associated with the railways, but there were earlier, important, events. For our purposes the story starts with the canal companies of the late eighteenth century which, in many ways, pioneered the path subsequently followed by the railways. Large sums of money were raised from investors at the outset, and spent establishing the infrastructure of the concern. The building stage often took a number of years and, as the canal was the only tangible evidence of how capital raised had been applied, it was *natural* that a statement, called the 'capital account', should be used to report these transactions. The account was, therefore, a stewardship document designed to provide a history of all the past dealings with capital raised under statutory authority; it was not intended to display, and did not display, the present economic value of the business.

The preparation of the capital account also received a degree of *legal* recognition in statutes which contained provisions designed to prevent monopoly profits. The Glamorganshire Canal Company's Act of incorporation (1790), for example, provided that

> the clear profits to be received by the said company of proprietors from the said navigation shall never exceed the sum of eight pounds per centum per annum upon all such money as shall be actually laid out and expended in making and completing the said navigation, and the several works relating thereto, and in defraying the charges and expenses of obtaining and passing this Act (s.46).

To give effect to this limitation, the company was required to file a statement of the amount initially invested in the canal and then, annually, a statement of profits. A capital account was filed for this purpose. If the average profit, over a three-year period, exceeded 8 per cent, the Justices were authorised to reduce prices to ensure the maximum was no longer exceeded.

On completion of the canal the capital account was closed and no longer reported. At agreed intervals, half-yearly or yearly, an operating statement was prepared by canal managers and presented to shareholders. This document was needed as the basis for dividend declarations, although it no doubt also helped users make a modest assessment of performance, for example by disclosing receipts from traffic. Some assets and liabilities, considered of interest to report users, were also occasionally listed separately in the published accounts. These procedures were embraced and developed by the managers of railway companies.

Closure of the capital account proved impossible for railway companies because, unlike canal companies, they continued to incur significant amounts of capital expenditure after the initial infrastructure had been established. Whereas the canal companies owned only the waterway, the railway companies also acted as the carriers of goods. This obliged them to acquire additional locomotives and carriages as traffic increased. In addition, the initial route was often extended into branch lines. The result was that the capital account continued to be published, in tandem with the revenue account, to show the up-to-date position.

General balance sheet. Early examples of the general balance sheet can be found in the accounts of canal companies. For instance, in the accounts of the Glamorganshire Canal Company for 1815, where it is called 'The Account of Debits and Credits', and in the accounts of the Kennet and Avon Canal Company for 1817, where it is called the 'General Account'. The earliest example of the double account system, known to this writer, containing both a capital account and a general balance sheet, appears in the published accounts of the London and Birmingham Railway for the half year to 31 December 1838 (reproduced in Edwards, 1985, p.32). Indeed, the London and Birmingham Railway appears to have played a major role in formulating the system, in the sense that it assembled a single coherent package comprising a variety of accounting statements scattered among the reporting practices of canal companies.

Cash accounting and partial accruals accounting. In the early 1840s most railway companies continued to use either pure cash accounting methods or, more commonly, what might be described as 'partial accruals accounting'. The latter term is used to cover the situation where companies made some, but not full, adjustment to take account of credit transactions and the depreciation of fixed assets (the extent of the adjustments naturally varied from company to company). The failure of railway companies to make fuller use of what we today call accruals accounting is a little surprising in view of the fact that the procedures were well known, in certain quarters, even at this time, and railway companies, which were often vast concerns, might have been expected to use the most up to date accounting techniques.

Part of the explanation for the continued popularity of cash accounting and partial accruals accounting is that these methods provided considerable scope for the manipulation of published reports. According to the accountant George Bott, writing in 1843, 'a railway company may be in debt to a very considerable amount, and still present to the proprietors a respectable balance of cash in hand on revenue account'. He goes on to demonstrate numerically 'how a railway in almost bankrupt condition, may represent itself as a fair remunerative concern' by following the popular practice of preparing accounts on the cash basis (*Railway Times*, 1843, p.350).

The importance of publishing the general balance sheet was stressed in a letter to *Herapath's Journal* from Hewitt Davies, a shareholder in the London, Brighton and South Coast Railway. In his view, its value 'to the shareholders cannot be sufficiently appreciated, unless shareholders are aware of the borrowing and lending, the advances to forward other schemes, and the abuses which may be made of a trusteeship which gives no account of its assets and debts' (1850, p.361). He concluded that the document was often withheld because of the abuses it would reveal.

In the endeavour to improve matters, pressure was placed on management to close the capital account. The temptation provided by an open capital account was expressed succinctly in evidence presented to the Monteagle Committee by the Stock Exchange's railway statistician, Mihill Slaughter.

> So long as you have a capital account open, you have two sources of receipts, one [capital] a much larger source of receipt than the other [revenue]; and I am afraid that with the best intentions, even on the part of such a Board as the London and North-Western, they can hardly avoid occasionally a little tripping' (*Minutes*, no.1110).

For the reasons given above, however, closure of the capital account proved impracticable.

Shareholder demand for better information concerning the progress of their existing investment, and as a basis for future investment decisions, or demands by the press, politicians and others on behalf of shareholders, coupled with examples of better practices in use by competitors, are major factors bringing about improvements in external financial reporting procedures. Management, realising that the cost of external finance may otherwise rise, perhaps to an unserviceable level, responds to these demands and makes available the information required. This happened, in the case of railway companies, in the second half of the 1840s.

During the railway construction stage it was regarded as a legitimate practice to charge the return paid to shareholders (called 'interest') to the capital account. The justification for this treatment was that finance costs would have been part of the price charged if the work had been contracted out. The provision of an adequate return for shareholders became far more difficult once the line was open. The essential problem was that it took time to build up traffic and revenue receipts, out of which dividends had now to be paid, usually remained at a relatively low level for a number of years.

The prudent course would have been to forego the dividend, but generous returns had been forecast in company prospectuses and were eagerly awaited by investors and speculators. Moreover, the directors recognised that additional capital requirements would be more easily raised if adequate dividends were currently being paid on earlier advances. The response of some managers was to overstate profits by omitting liabilities, crediting a range of capital receipts to revenue and debiting revenue expenses to capital. It appears that the main body of railway shareholders were easily deluded by favourable reports when in what George Glyn, chairman of the London and North Western Railway (LNWR), described (1849) as 'that calm and dreamy state which, while they are getting large dividends, they are so apt to fall into' (*Railway Times*, p.834).

The true financial facts could not be suppressed indefinitely. Dividends suffered and, as one prominent railway historian put it, investors 'awoke one day from dreams of boundless wealth to the reality of general ruin' (quoted in Edwards, 1985, p.34). Disappointed shareholders set up committees of inquiry which, in turn, engaged professional accountants to help with the investigation. The result of their findings was, in many cases, confirmation of the suspicion that the accounts had indeed been 'cooked'. The most famous revelations are contained in Quilter Ball & Co.'s report on the Eastern Counties Railway (see Monteagle Committee, pp.409–14), whose chairman was George Hudson, the 'Railway King'. Their report showed that £318,144 was wrongly omitted from the debit of the revenue account (made up of revenue items debited to capital, £233,925, debts owing for expenditure incurred, £61,013, and bad debts not written off, £23,206); £35,315 was wrongly credited to the revenue account; and interest charged to capital instead of revenue amounted to £84,591. Confidence disappeared and, between 1845–48, the average fall in the prices of shares in twelve leading railway companies was 64 per cent.

The Monteagle Committee. The public outcry, which usually occurs when 'fingers are burned' caused the Government to appoint the Monteagle Committee to consider 'whether the railway Acts do not require amendment with a view of providing for a more effectual audit of accounts'. Recommendations were made for the publication of standardised accounts, for auditors to be given wide powers of enquiry, for government auditors to be appointed to act in conjunction with the company's own auditors, and for the government auditors' views to be published where they differed from those of the other auditors. Between 1849–51 three bills were presented to Parliament embodying these recommendations. Each failed, partly because of opposition from the 'railway interest' in Parliament which, at this time, comprised about 80 MPs who were either railway directors or sponsored by railway companies. A more general explanation for the failure of attempts to pass what *The Economist* (1849, p.795) dismissed as 'interfering and meddling' legislation is that the proposals were too far out of line with the *laissez-faire* ideal.

The perceived need for government action was also reduced by railway companies taking steps to put their own house in order. The threat of government interference encouraged companies to re-examine their accounting practices and the LNWR, which did not come under attack, provided leadership in devising improved means of financial communication. In a bid to allay unease and suspicion, the directors took the unprecedented step of circulating to shareholders (October 1848) a statement of liabilities, estimated future expenditure and how it was to be financed. This practice was copied by other railway companies including the Great Western which used it as a model. The LNWR's further decision to issue more comprehensive accounts, from December 1848, was followed by other companies who also began to apply the accruals concept fully to credit transactions and publish a general balance sheet.[2] The effect of greater disclosure was to restore confidence in particular lines; in other cases it confirmed the general public's worst suspicions. In general, however, the move was successful and the value of shares rose following publication of more detailed accounts.

The spread of more effective accounting, in the form of the double account system, was no doubt partly due to the growing employment of professional accountants to assist committees of investigation, advise on the design of accounting systems and audit railway company accounts. The large number of financial journals published is evidence of a heavy demand for accounting information and for investment analysis. These journals also helped to improve standards by drawing attention to unsatisfactory procedures.

The Regulation of Railways Act 1868

The lack of Government interest in regulating the railways for some years after 1851 has been attributed to voluntary improvements in financial reporting and auditing procedures and to the fact that the industry returned to relative normality following the financial crisis of 1847. Between 1847 and 1850 few new railway companies were formed and building was at a low level whereas, between 1850–70, 8000 miles of track were laid, including a boom period between 1852–56. The major financial crisis of 1866, particularly the failure of Watson Overend & Co. (a firm of railway contractors which had placed a lot of railway paper on the market) revived Government interest in the financial reporting procedures employed by railway companies. The 1867 Royal Commission on Railways emphasised the importance of having a uniform system of accounts and there was general agreement that action was needed.

The Regulation of Railways Bill was introduced to the House of Lords on 9 March 1868. The first draft contained a clause setting out the general requirement for uniform accounts, but the schedule intended to contain the standardised forms was left blank. This was because the government had not yet decided what the precise form should be and were consulting 'some most eminent accountants' on the matter. The aim was to design a system which facilitated comparability and provided shareholders with a means to 'see at a glance what was the exact financial position of each company' (*Hansard*, vol.190, col.1955).

The prescribed forms were drawn up with the railway companies' 'consent and approval' (Cole Committee 1910, *Minutes*, no.10169), which is not surprising in view of the fact that, by the mid-1860s, the railway interest amounted to over 200 Members of Parliament, of which 60 – what Alderman describes as the 'efficent interest' (p.26) – were the directors of large national railways. This powerful lobby was able to ensure that legislation did not differ significantly from existing practices. The forms prescribed were closely in line with the procedures employed by the LNWR and other leading companies, but their effect was to extend observed best practice to the more secretive companies – a device which was to become the traditional British way of achieving accounting reform.

Criticism of the double account system

The Act did, to some extent, achieve its objectives, but it also attracted a great deal of criticism, not all of which was with the benefit of hindsight. Attention was soon drawn to the fact that, although the Act indicated which figures should be reported, it provided no explicit instructions concerning how these figures should be computed. As a leading article in *The Economist* put it, 'The prescription of a uniform set of accounts is very good, but the distrust of the public has hitherto related to the substance of the accounts, and changing the form will not mend matters much' (29 August 1868, p.992).

The specific failure to include a requirement to charge depreciation was also the subject of much debate. While it was pointed out that the difference between the double account system and the conventional presentation was only of form, it was admitted that the presentation did give rise to a different attitude towards depreciation. The perceived problem was that the separation of the balance sheet into two parts implied that the value of fixed assets, reported at cost in the capital account, could be ignored for the purpose of computing the profit figure reported in the general balance sheet. Where a company was determined to make a charge, there remained the technical problem of accounting for the adjustment. The general view was that depreciation should not be deducted from fixed assets, reported in the capital account, since the function of this document was to provide a stewardship record of capital receipts and expenditures. These observations led some people to the following conclusions: that the overall impression conveyed by the double account system was that a charge was not required and that the system affected actual practice.

These conclusions attribute too much significance to the Act. It is clear that the double account system did not, of itself, prevent a charge from being made. There are numerous examples of railway companies depreciating rolling stock in the 1840s and permanent way in the 1850s (see Chapter 10); indeed it seems likely that this was a quite common accounting practice for short periods of time. In many cases these companies were already using the double account system and they solved the problem of finding a location for the accumulated charge by reporting it as a source of finance in the general balance sheet. Whether or not one believes that the Act implied the lack of any need to charge depreciation, railway companies had anyway abandoned the use of depreciation accounting in favour of replacement or repairs and renewals accounting long before 1868 and, in the mid-1860s, railway officials rejected as impracticable a proposal to re-introduce depreciation in their companies' accounts (*Accountant*, 27 June 1885, p.14). Contemporary accounting practices determined the content of the 1868 Act, rather than the other way around, and the absence of any reference to depreciation merely allowed railway managers to continue to use the preferred procedures.

It was not until the beginning of the twentieth century that the need to replace assets, which remained in the books at cost, and in respect of which no adequate 'depreciation reserves' had been created, convinced railway managers of the merits of depreciation accounting. The voluntary inclusion of a charge received legislative recognition in 1911 (see Chapter 10).[3] In succeeding years depreciation was accounted for in the following broad manner under the double account system. The debit entry to the revenue account was matched by a credit entry to a depreciation fund account or renewal fund account in the general balance sheet, against which was charged the cost of renewals and replacements when they occurred. In practice the amount credited to this fund rarely equalled the amount of accumulated depreciation to date, but it was usually sufficient to cover the cost of renewals and replacements currently falling due. Where this was not the case, additional charges were made direct to revenue. Considerable reliance continued to be placed on the assumption that public utility companies adopting the double account system kept their fixed assets in an effective state of repair (Cutforth, 1931, p.57).

Review

The operation of public utilities, based on the activities of statutory companies, lasted for nearly two centuries. It began with the incorporation of the canal companies in the 1760s and ended with the labour government's nationalisation programme just after the Second World War. The basic nature of these companies' activities remained unchanged throughout this period, but accounting methods underwent significant transition in an attempt to satisfy user demands for better information. There were four broad stages.[4] During the first stage (1760–1840) a capital account was prepared to report the construction of the works; it was then 'closed' and an operating statement used to identify divisible profits. These accounts were prepared mainly on the cash basis, but adjustments were sometimes made for credit transactions overlapping the end of the accounting period, and also unused stock. Some assets and liabilities were occasionally listed as a memorandum note to the accounts. The second stage (1840–1855) saw companies applying the accruals concept more vigorously to credit transactions and unused stock, and also experimenting with the more difficult valuation problems associated with long lived assets. Depreciation accounting was employed in certain quarters. A further feature of this period was the widespread adoption of the double account system, epitomised by the publication of the general balance sheet. The third stage (1855–1900) saw public utility companies making full use of accruals accounting, except for the failure to depreciate fixed assets which were instead accounted for on the repairs and renewals basis or on the replacement basis. The final stage (post-1900) saw the public utilities fall into line with the practice, in other industries, of employing 'full' accruals accounting.[5]

14

Profits, Dividends and Capital Maintenance

Limited liability and creditor protection

The creation of the limited liability company shifted a great deal of business risk to creditors. Whereas, previously, a shortage of business assets on liquidation resulted in claims against the personal possessions of the owner, losses were now borne by the supplier of goods and loan finance. In a sense the position of the investor also became more risky. The development of the large scale limited company created a new species of shareholder which needed protection. This absentee investor had no direct involvement in management, and relied on the directors to behave in a trustworthy manner and use the capital efficiently. It was, however, the creditor's increased exposure to risk which attracted more attention from company lawyers.

Certain safeguards were already available when, in 1855, limited liability was introduced for most registered companies. For example, loans could be secured against a company's assets, and creditors could seek personal guarantees from directors in respect of contracts to supply goods or advance money to the company. In addition, registered companies were obliged to publish an audited balance sheet, although this requirement was repealed just a year after limited liability was introduced, and it was not reinstated until 1900. The reasons for repeal, and the safeguards provided by regulations contained in a company's own articles of association, are discussed in Chapter 15.

Ultra Vires rule

During the second half of the nineteenth century the courts developed certain schemes for the protection of creditors and, to a lesser extent, shareholders. One of these was the *ultra vires* rule.

The 'objects' clause, contained in a company's memorandum of association, sets out the planned activities of the company. In *Ashbury Railway Carriage Co.* v *Riche* (1875) the doctrine of *ultra vires* was applied to show that it was an illegal act, beyond the powers of the company, to use funds for purposes other than those set out in the memorandum. For instance, if the company's object is to mine gold in North Wales, money invested for this purpose should not be used to acquire a chain of hotels in the Cotswolds. Any debt arising from an *ultra vires* transaction is unenforceable against the company.

The effectiveness of the rule was soon eroded by promoters taking steps to ensure that the objects clause was drawn up sufficiently widely to cover not only transactions expected to be undertaken at the outset, but all incidental operations and areas of business activity into which the company might conceivably wish to expand at some future date.

Reserve capital

A company may issue shares at par value or at a premium, but it is not obliged to call up the full amount immediately. In such circumstances the shareholder remains potentially liable for the balance not yet called up, and the amount involved serves as a 'safety net' for the payment of debts due to creditors should the company get into financial difficulties. To ensure the safety net remains in place, a company may resolve that the uncalled capital is to be collected only in the event of a winding-up. The amount is then designated 'reserve capital'. The adoption of this provision, introduced in 1879 following the collapse of the City of Glasgow Bank (see Chapter 12), results in a type of organisation which falls somewhere between a limited and an unlimited company. In retrospect it is not surprising that the device did not prove popular with shareholders, and its use tended to be confined to banks and insurance companies. It has now virtually fallen into disuse.

Capital maintenance rules

The basic safeguard devised for the protection of creditors is embodied in the capital maintenance rules. The starting point for applying these rules, in practice, was the court decision that share capital could only be treated as paid up to the extent that resources were actually received by the company either in cash or in kind. In addition, the courts insisted that share capital, once raised, could not be returned to the members; the intention being that these resources would remain in the business and, in the absence of unlimited liability, act as a substitute protection for creditors. Weaknesses in these rules, which became apparent over the years, were the reluctance of the court to investigate the adequacy of consideration received in a form other than cash, the failure of the legislature to specify a minimum share capital for companies (there was an example of a company formed with a share capital of ½d divided into 2 shares of 1 farthing each), and the fact that nothing could be done to prevent the erosion of capital by a succession of trading losses.

The nature and purpose of the capital maintenance rule was clearly set out in *Trevor* v *Whitworth* (1887) which decided that it was illegal for a company to purchase its own shares, even when authorised to do so by an express provision in its memorandum. During the course of delivering his judgement, Lord Herschell laid down the principle that creditors 'have a right to rely and were intended by the legislature to have a right to rely, on the capital remaining undiminished . . . by the return of any part of it to the shareholders'.

This did not mean that capital could never be returned to the shareholders. The legislature had already reached the conclusion that such a provision would be unduly restrictive. CA 1867 permitted the return of capital where it could be demonstrated that available cash was surplus to business requirements. In such circumstances, clearly nothing is gained by forcing a company to retain cash it does not need.

CA 1877 made further provision for capital reduction by allowing companies to write off any amount no longer represented by available assets. Again the provision made a great deal of sense. Consider the case of a company which owns four ships and one ship is destroyed at sea. Approximately one-quarter of the capital is lost, but the company remains viable with three ships continuing to generate profits. A capital reduction, in these circumstances, enables the loss of the ship to be recognised and the balance sheet to report the true economic facts. The company is then able to pay dividends to shareholders out of the profits generated by the remainder of the fleet, i.e. the loss of capital does not have to be first made good. Safeguards were of course needed to ensure that the creditors' position was not weakened by the capital reduction; these remain in operation today. In particular, a reduction must be confirmed by the court and, if a creditor objects to the scheme, the court may direct either that payment of the debt is secured or that an agreed amount is set aside to meet it.

In more recent years provisions have been introduced which enable a company to reorganise its share capital to meet changing business circumstances without recourse to the court. CA 1948 authorised companies to issue redeemable preference shares, and CA 1981 extended this power to cover ordinary shares. The same statute empowered companies to purchase their shares on the open market. Safeguards have again been established in an attempt to ensure that the capital maintenance doctrine is not destroyed. In the case of public companies, the rules require the redemption or purchase to be made either out of a fresh issue of shares or out of profits otherwise available for distribution. In the former case one type of capital is replaced by another; in the latter case an amount equivalent to the nominal value of shares redeemed is transferred from distributable (divisible) profit to a non-distributable 'capital redemption reserve'. The intention in both cases is to maintain intact the permanent capital of the company.

The same rules apply to private companies but, in addition, the 1981 Act introduced a provision which enables them to make redemptions and purchases out of *capital*, i.e. the permanent capital of a private company may actually be reduced. In these circumstances protection for creditors is achieved by stringent legal requirements. The directors must make a statutory declaration that, after the capital reduction, the company can pay its debts and that the business will continue as a going concern for at least one year. The company's auditors have to report whether the directors' opinions are, in the circumstances, reasonable. Publicity must be given to the intention to reduce capital and creditors can apply to the court to stop the planned reduction. If subsequent events prove that the declaration was ill-founded, past shareholders are liable to contribute up to the amount of the capital returned to them. A director who did not have reasonable grounds for making the declaration can also be made to contribute in these circumstances.

Attention, so far, has focused on the significance of statute law for the operation of the capital maintenance rules. We now turn our attention to a series of court decisions which allowed directors a great deal of latitude when calculating distributable profits. Their effect was to erode the protection which the capital maintenance rules were intended to provide, by permitting the return to shareholders of capital masquerading as the payment of a dividend.

The dividend cases

Preliminary issues. Provisions stating either that dividends must not be paid out of capital or that dividends may be paid only out of clear profits were included in statutes and charters at an early stage. The charter of the Bank of Ireland (1721), for example, provided for dividends to be paid 'only out of the interest, profit and produce' (DuBois, p.412). For companies in general there was no *overall* statutory authority for these kinds of restrictions until 1980, although their usefulness was acknowledged by the Companies Clauses Act 1845 (s.121) and by CA 1862, Table A (art.116).

Soon after the creation of the registered company there began a series of cases concerned with establishing whether profit had been properly measured, principally for the purpose of discovering whether a legitimate dividend had been paid. The reason for the cluster of 'dividend cases' was to help clarify profit measurement procedures at a time when there were no statutory regulations or generally accepted accounting procedures in the modern sense of the term. Although heavily criticised in some quarters, most of the decisions did not differ significantly from commonly accepted commercial practice of the time.

The court's basic approach was to allow the directors to decide whether a company could afford to pay a dividend. It interfered only where, due to the inadequacy of profits, a dividend had been improperly paid. In these circumstances intervention was considered justified to provide an element of protection for creditors or particular classes of shareholders. The typical sequence of events was as follows. A dispute arose between, perhaps, management and preference shareholders, where the latter believed that profit was overstated and a dividend had been improperly paid to the ordinary shareholders. The matter was brought before a court of law which was obliged to rule on the question of whether legitimate profit measurement procedures had been employed.

One of the best known early cases is Flitcroft's case (1882) which established beyond doubt the directors' obligation to do all that was within their powers to maintain capital intact. An action was brought against the directors for paying a dividend out of 'fictitious' profits, computed without deducting debts which were *known* to be bad. According to Jessel, M.R.,

> the creditor . . . gives credit to the company on the faith of the implied representation that the capital shall be applied only for the purposes of the business, and he has therefore a right to say that the corporation shall keep its capital and not return it to the shareholders.

The plaintiff was successful and the directors were obliged to reimburse the company as their action amounted to an unauthorised reduction of capital.

A whole range of other accounting issues came under the judicial microscope (Reid 1987), including the treatment of doubtful debts, interest accrued on investments, preliminary expenses, interest paid on capital during the construction of public utilities, depreciation, foreign currency rate fluctuations, risk, the realisation of profits, and the allocation of revenues and expenditures between capital and income (aspects of these are discussed below). The cases resulted in a sophisticated discussion of financial reporting procedures well before they became the subject of textbook comment by such authorities as Dicksee, Pixley and so on. No doubt the findings had a significant effect on the development of accounting practices and conventions.

Uncertainty. From an early stage, the court demonstrated an awareness of accountancy's achilles heel – uncertainty. The mere fact that information contained in an accounting statement might be invalidated by future events was never considered a sufficient reason to intervene. But views differed about the degree of care expected from management. The essential questions were whether, in the absence of fraud, directors should be free to employ whatever accounting procedures suited them, whether they should be expected to adopt what accountants then considered appropriate reporting procedures, or whether something in between was acceptable. There are plenty of signals in each of these directions.

In general the court expected some estimate to be made of future developments when reaching dividend distribution decisions, but they did not always expect their financial effect to be estimated for the purpose of the accounts. In *Burnes* v *Pennell* (1849), a cash based accounting statement was prepared and, in response to the complaint that no provision had been made for risk, Lord Campbell replied that 'no estimate could be made for losses thereafter to occur, unless the directors had been endowed with the faculty of second sight, and could have discovered the shadows of coming shipwrecks and captures'.

Stringer's case (1869) dealt both with the question of uncertainty and the question of when profit might be considered 'realised'[1] for the purpose of a dividend declaration. The Mercantile Trading Co. Ltd was formed to run the blockade established by the federal against the confederate states. Its function was to supply the confederate government with such articles as they required, bringing back cotton in return. Clearly it was a business of an extremely hazardous nature. After eight months of operation accounts were prepared for the period to February 1864. A profit was reported, but this was arrived at after taking credit for a debt due of £62,000 from the confederate government and valuing stocks of cotton still in the confederate states at £17,000. Each of these assets was subsequently lost. The court was required to decide whether the dividend was properly paid. The initial, negative, decision paid particular attention to the fact that insufficient weight was given to the realisability of the assets and that the profit was not 'profit in hand'.

This conclusion was rejected on appeal on the grounds that an honest, albeit 'sanguine', attempt was made to value the assets for inclusion in the balance sheet. Attention was focused on the fact that transactions were fully described in the balance sheet. The court was unconcerned that the profits had not been received in cash. According to Selwyn, L.J. 'there are very few dividends indeed which would not be open to more or less question if such a rule as that were laid down'.

Depreciation. The apparent simplicity of the *general* rule, laid down in Flitcroft's case, that a dividend should not be paid if the effect was to reduce the value of the net assets below paid-up share capital, was totally illusory. The unanswered question was: 'How should assets be valued for the purpose of determining whether capital has been maintained intact?' No consensus existed and procedures in common use (see Chapter 10) produced vastly different balances for net assets, leading to a variety of possible conclusions about whether capital remained intact.

One important question was whether fixed assets should be depreciated when measuring profit; some early cases indicated that a charge should be made. In *re Ebbw Vale Steel, Iron & Coal Co. Ltd*

(1877) the company's property had suffered a considerable decline in value and the directors sought counsel's opinion about whether a dividend could be paid without taking account of this loss. Counsel advised that the assets should be written down, prompting the directors to apply to the court for the loss to be written off against capital. The court decided that this was was not permissible under the Companies Acts then in force.

Later in the year, CA 1877 authorised companies to write off capital no longer represented by available assets provided certain conditions were met. The company successfully returned to the court where Jessel, M.R., presiding, pointed out that the Act was useful in enabling the resumption of dividend payments. The clear implication was that, unless a company applied for a reduction, losses of capital needed to be made good out of revenue before a dividend could be paid. Two years later, in *Davison* v *Gillies*, the court decided that depreciation must be charged where required by a company's articles of association. In *Glasier* v *Rolls* (1889) the court expressed the opinion that profits should be calculated as a prudent man of business would calculate them.

Lee v *Neuchatel Asphalte Co.* (1889) directed the court's attention, for the first time, specifically to the question of whether company law required depreciation to be charged when calculating distributable profit. The company was formed to work a quarry, and the question was whether it needed to amortise its principal asset. The decision reached, at court of appeal, was that no such provision needed to be made. In other words the quarry might be valued at original cost for the purpose of deciding whether capital had been maintained intact.

In previous cases, judges had taken the view that the overall impression conveyed by the Companies Act was that a dividend could not be paid out of capital. Lindley's approach was quite different. He drew attention to the fact that the Companies Act made no express statement about how profit should be calculated, nor was there any requirement that a loss of capital should be made good before paying a dividend. In Lindley's sanguine view 'If it is said that such a course involves payment of dividends out of capital, the answer is that the Act nowhere forbids such a payment as is here supposed'.

A second major contribution to the development of accounting thought, made by Lindley in this case, resulted from his assertion that profit measurement was a matter for businessmen and not a proper subject for an Act of Parliament. He believed that to prevent directors from paying dividends out of capital, in circumstances similar to the 'Lee' case, might have the effect of prohibiting honest business and paralysing the trade of the country, presumably because such a course would make it difficult for companies to raise finance.

There is little doubt that nineteenth-century judges such as Lindley (also Jessel and Buckley) exerted an enormous influence on the development of company law in general, and accounting practices in particular. A leading column in *The Accountant* (19 May 1900) to mark the retirement of Lindley from his position as Master of the Rolls contained the following comments:

> There is no department of law that forms so sure and searching a touchstone of judicial power. On the one hand the framework which the legislature has devised for the protection of the shareholders and of the public has to be steadfastly maintained. On the other hand, the pedantic interpretation of the Companies Acts which would fetter business in bands of iron and ignore new developments of our commercial life has to be avoided. How admirably the ex Master of the Rolls has achieved this two-fold object! (p.476).

The article goes on to point out that not all Lindley's decisions were welcomed by accountants and certainly the Lee decision was met with strong disapproval from the fledgling accountancy profession. *The Accountant* was the medium for a heated debate. A leading article claimed that the decision was contrary to normal accounting practice. This was not true. Although *best* accounting practice may have required a charge to be made, many businesses calculated profit without making any deduction whatsoever for depreciation in 1889 and much later. In assessing the significance of the Lee decision, there were two basic questions to be answered. Did the failure to impose a requirement to charge depreciation matter all that much in the case of companies, such as the Neuchatel Asphalte Co., organised as terminable ventures? Did the decision apply to all companies, or only terminable ventures working wasting assets? These matters are now discussed.

The Neuchatel Asphalte Co. was formed to work a quarry and then liquidate. In such circumstances there is certainly no need to charge depreciation in order to maintain intact productive capacity. The payment of a dividend which includes a capital element does no more than accelerate the return to members of the capital which, in a profitable concern, they would anyway receive on liquidation.

The objection lies elsewhere. The failure to charge depreciation produces a figure for profit which requires interpretation and adjustment before it can be used as the basis for performance assessment. Again, however, there is little likelihood of the shareholder suffering any harm provided he is fully acquainted with the facts. The position of the creditor is of course much more exposed. Failure to charge depreciation may mean that he loses some, at least, of the protection which the capital maintenance doctrine was intended to provide. This did not worry Lindley who believed that creditors were adequately protected by the directors' obligation to satisfy themselves that creditors could be paid, in due course, before declaring a dividend: 'so long as they pay their creditors, there is no reason why they should not go on and divide profits so far as I can see, although every shilling of the capital may be lost'. If a company was insolvent, or if the declaration of a dividend might produce acute financial embarrassment, the courts would declare the payment illegal but, provided the company was currently 'in funds', the court was unwilling to place any restriction on businessmen's freedom of action to allocate resources to what was considered their most productive use.

One obvious problem with what has been described as 'The Solvency Test' (French, p.319) is that failure to charge depreciation has long-term rather than short-term financial repercussions. The omission is unlikely to be of much significance early in the life of an asset, when the loss is unrealised, but the time eventually comes when the asset is worn out and must be replaced. Where insufficient funds have been retained to maintain capital intact, the likelihood of the company being able to continue at its existing level of operations is reduced. Indeed, in the long-term, such a course of action can lead to the need to reconstruct capital or liquidate. In these circumstances shareholders and creditors are quite likely to suffer severe financial loss.

Turning now to the second question: Did the decision apply to all companies, or only terminable ventures working wasting assets? Some enlightenment was provided by the decision in *Verner* v *General and Commercial Investment Trust Ltd* (1894); a friendly action brought to clarify matters. This case involved an investment company whose fixed assets consisted of its portfolio of shares. During the accounting period, in dispute, the trust had an excess of income over current expenditure, but the surplus was less than the fall in the market value of the portfolio. The court's decision was that a dividend could be paid out of the operating surplus and Lindley, who again presided, re-emphasised the points he had made in the Lee case. In addition, he drew attention to the need to distinguish between capital invested in fixed assets and capital invested in circulating (current) assets. He made it clear that losses of only the latter needed to be made good when calculating distributable profit.

The case again involved a specialist form of business organisation, however, and it was still not clear whether the decision had general application. Moreover, the capital asset had changed in value due to external market forces of supply and demand; an event which would, even today, often be ignored when measuring profit. The position was clarified by Vaughan Williams, J. who, in *re Kingston Cotton Mills* (1896), expressed the opinion that all business concerns could ignore an *unrealised* loss in the value of a fixed asset. *Cox* v *Edinburgh and District Tramway Co. Ltd* (1898), which decided that obsolete assets need not be removed from the capital account before paying a dividend out of current revenue, indicated that *realised* capital losses could also be safely disregarded.

Realised and unrealised profits. In view of the court's willingness to ignore a fall in the value of a fixed asset when calculating distributable profit, one might reasonably have expected increases in the value of fixed assets to be treated in a similar manner. This did not happen. *Lubbock* v *British Bank of South America* (1892) decided that a realised capital profit could be used as the basis for a dividend payment provided the company's articles permitted such a distribution. *Foster* v *New Trinidad Lake Asphalte Co. Ltd* (1901) confirmed this decision, but added the proviso that a distribution was in order only if a capital surplus remained after revaluing the company's remaining fixed assets.

As a result of these two decisions *realised* profits on the sale of fixed assets could be included as part of distributable profit and, although reference might be made to their existence, the amount involved was rarely specified in company accounts until CA 1948 took effect.[2] This provided obvious scope for management to boost reported profit and increase cash available for dividends by selling fixed assets when operating results were poor.

An unreported nineteenth-century case, *re Midland Land and Investment Corporation, Ltd* (1886), approved the payment of dividends out of an *unrealised* capital profit. Their divisibility was also the subject of more recent, and better known, court decisions. In *Westburn Sugar Refineries Ltd* v *IRC* (1960), a Scottish case, it was decided that such profits were non-distributable. However, the English case *Dimbula Valley (Ceylon) Tea Co. Ltd* v *Laurie* (1961) reached the opposite conclusion. The English decision ran contrary to one of the basic concepts of accountancy, namely that profit must be realised before it may be regarded as available for distribution. Although some might doubt the need to delay recognising profit on readily saleable stocks, a strict application of the realisation concept does seem to make more sense in the case of fixed assets. By their very nature, there is no intention to sell in the normal course of business and, by the date of disposal, market price may well have fluctuated downwards. The simple answer to this line of argument, given by Buckley J in the Dimbula Valley case, was that the valuation problems associated with stocks and fixed assets involved

> a difference of degree but not of principle. Moreover, if a company has fluid assets available for the payment of a dividend, I can see nothing wrong in using these assets for payment of a dividend and at the same time as a matter of account treating that dividend as paid out of [an unrealised] capital surplus.

Periodic or accumulated profits. A further important question considered by the courts was whether dividend distributions should be based on the results of an individual accounting period or the accumulated position since the company was incorporated. The decision reached in *Ammonia Soda Co. Ltd* v *Chamberlain* (1918) demonstrates the court's determination to allow businessmen the maximum latitude when calculating distributable profit. In this case it was decided that accumulated losses of circulating capital need not be made good before paying a dividend out of profits reported for the current year, i.e. each accounting period might be considered in isolation for the purpose of identifying distributable profit.[3] A practical justification for the decision was that it avoided the need for a company to arrange a formal capital reduction, to wipe the slate clean, before distributing the current year's profit.

Distributable profit versus reported profit

The pre-1980 legal position may be summarised as follows:

1. company could pay a dividend out of realised and (in England and Wales, but not Scotland) unrealised capital profits, but need

make provision for neither realised nor unrealised capital losses.

2. Directors could choose to base a dividend distribution on either accumulated profits to date or profits for the current accounting period whichever produced the higher figure.

An argument in favour of these court decisions is that they allowed directors a large measure of freedom to allocate resources in the most productive manner to either internal or external use. For example, a rigid requirement to charge depreciation means that resources, equal to the amount of capital invested at the outset, are locked in to a business until steps are taken either to obtain court approval for a capital reduction or to liquidate the company. The dividend decisions removed the need for directors to comply with these formalities. At the same time the decisions caused difficulties because businessmen failed to draw a careful distinction between distributable profit and reported profit. Following the Lee case (1889), the *literature* began to make a differentiation which, in theory, paved the way for directors to charge depreciation in the published accounts but base their distribution decision on funds generated from operations (profit + depreciation).

In practice this simply did not happen; the same figure was used for both purposes. Possible reasons for this include: the desire to avoid the confusion which could result from the publication of two different profit figures; a natural reluctance to report a profit figure which was not in accordance with legal regulations relating to distributable profit; and the fact that directors and most accountants did not perceive the need for a distinction to be made. With the growing separation of ownership from management, the performance of the firm was judged mainly in terms of the amount of the dividend paid, i.e. dividends were the performance indicator and it was therefore logical to report, as profit, the amount legally available for this purpose.

The failure to draw a distinction between the two versions of profit meant that the calculation of reported profit was influenced by two conflicting objectives – on the one hand, a desire to produce a figure which was useful as the basis for corporate assessment, and on the other hand, a determination to ensure that the reported figure covered the planned dividend payment. The desire to educate users of accounting information conflicted with the need to retain confidence in the business and, for a long while, the latter influence proved stronger. Where directors wished to increase the dividend, a common ploy was to reduce or altogether omit the depreciation charge when calculating reported profit, thereby publishing a figure which *The Accountant* described as 'absolutely false, misleading and mischievous' (23 March, 1889, p.149)

The use of published accounts to report a profit figure adequate to cover the desired level of dividend, rather than portray 'actual' results, i.e. as measured by good accounting practice, was quite common over the next thirty-odd years. Businessmen were able to use suboptimal measurement procedures for the following reasons: the accountancy profession was young; there were no generally accepted accounting procedures in the present sense of the term; and managers could cite legal decisions in support of procedures they preferred to employ. Fortunately, however, the legal decisions were permissive rather than mandatory, e.g. directors *could* omit a depreciation charge but they were not *obliged* to do so. Gradually financial reporting practices improved but, even today, company directors can employ a variety of schemes to influence the level of reported profit. The classification of non-recurring transactions as exceptional or extraordinary, for example, may be based more on the desire to inflate or depress reported profit than on a keen assessment of the nature of the item involved. The objective, no doubt, often remains the same as in earlier times – to report the smooth, upward, trend of profits favoured by the stock market.

Statutory definition of distributable profit

CA 1980 (now CA 1985) belatedly, some would think, defined distributable profit as accumulated realised profits minus accumulated realised losses. Provisos are that the realised profits have not already been distributed or capitalised, and that realised losses have not been previously written off in either a reduction or reorganisation of capital. Profits or losses may be either capital or revenue in their origin.

CA 1985 contains some helpful guidance regarding the treatment of particular items in the accounts for the purpose of calculating distributable profit. For example, fixed assets which have a limited useful life must be reported at purchase price or construction cost less depreciation; intangibles may only be shown as assets if acquired for valuable consideration (e.g. non-purchased goodwill cannot appear in the accounts); current assets should be reported at the 'lower of cost or net realisable value'; stock valuation may use FIFO, LIFO or similar method; research costs, preliminary expenses and expenses on the issue of securities must not be capitalised; and purchased goodwill (where capitalised) must be written off over its useful life (this does not apply to goodwill on consolidation). A further helpful rule, which avoids possible confusion, is the statement that provisions, as defined by the Companies Act, are to be treated as *realised* losses, e.g. any provision made for bad debts or depreciation. Where a company has revalued fixed assets for the purpose of the accounts, any additional depreciation charged as the result of the revaluation may be added back for the purpose of computing distributable profits. The Act also makes it clear that any items not specifically dealt with by statute are to be decided in the light of accepted accounting practice.[4]

The effect of CA's 1980–81 on the rules, previously in force, for calculating distributable profits may be summarised, in approximate terms, as follows:

1. The Lee and Verner decisions overruled; depreciation must be charged when computing distributable profits.
2. *Lubbock* v *British Bank of South America* confirmed; dividends may be paid out of realised capital profits.
3. *Foster* v *New Trinidad Lake Asphalte Co. Ltd* confirmed; before a realised capital profit may be distributed, provision must be made for any excess of unrealised losses over unrealised profits resulting from a revaluation of the company's remaining assets.
4. *Dimbula Valley (Ceylon) Tea Co. Ltd* v *Laurie* overruled and *Westburn Sugar Refineries Ltd* v *IRC* confirmed; dividends may not be paid out of unrealised capital profits.
5. *Ammonia Soda Co. Ltd* v *Chamberlain* overruled; the profit and loss account to be regarded as continuous.

The overall effect is to give specific legal emphasis to the realisation and accruals concepts and general statutory support for the, more rigid, profit measurement procedures traditionally favoured by accountants.

15

Self Regulation in a *Laissez-Faire* Environment

Laissez-faire

Adam Smith's brilliant invective (1776) against government interference in economic matters massively influenced late eighteenth-century and nineteenth-century politicians. Smith provided them with an academic cloak of respectability with which to justify their policy aims and ideas, in particular the desire for unbridled industrialisation. William Pitt the younger, who moved government policies a little in this direction at the end of the eighteenth century, summed up the theories as follows: 'trade, industry and barter would always find their own level, and be impeded by regulations which violated their natural operation' (quoted in Alderman, p.54). British trade nevertheless remained sluggish following the end of the Napoleonic Wars (1815). This prompted prominent statesmen, such as William Huskisson, Sir Robert Peel and W.E.Gladstone to implement, more vigorously, Smith's *laissez-faire* philosophy. The culmination of this activity was the repeal of the corn laws (1846), paving the way for Britain to become the 'workshop of the world'.

It was accepted, however, that the *laissez-faire* ideal required some modification where there were weak groups in need of protection. This concession was made in response to the Benthamite, utilitarian, argument that regulation was justified to help achieve the greatest happiness for the greatest number. An early example of intervention, on social grounds, was the Mines and Collieries Act (1842) which prohibited the employment underground of all females and boys under 10 years of age. A second example was the (textile) Factory Act (1844) which limited the working hours of adult women and young persons under 18 years of age to 12 hours a day, and prohibited factory employment of all children under 8.

State intervention, in order to implement the government's economic policy, was also considered desirable in certain cases. For example, it was initially intended that railway companies should provide a 'rail road' and make money by charging tolls to all those who wanted to run their waggons and locomotives along the line. In other words the railway would operate in broadly the same way as a canal or turnpike company. This proved impracticable because of the speed at which trains run, the primitive signalling arrangements, and the fact that trains cannot pass one another on a single line going in either the same or opposite directions. Each railway company therefore became the sole carrier of goods and passengers along the line it had laid. Regulations were therefore deemed desirable to protect the public against this state created monopoly.

The Railway Regulation Act (1844) required companies to provide one covered carriage train per day in each direction, with a third class fare not exceeding 1d per mile. The Act was also, potentially, the first nationalisation measure since it gave the government the power (never exercised) to purchase a railway, on certain terms, after the expiration of 21 years. An Act of 1846 obliged railway companies to pay compensation if passengers were killed or injured in railway accidents. Chapter 13 gives details of the accounting regulations imposed on railways beginning in 1845. Too much government interference was guarded against, however, by the 'railway interest' in Parliament.

To regulate or not to regulate?

Peel's Tory government (1841–46) was also active in creating the registered company to which limited liability was extended by Palmerston's Whig administration (1855–58). It has been argued that the creation of the limited liability company was in a sense emancipatory because it removed restrictions on the mobility of capital. At the same time it was clearly interventionalist because it accorded companies privileges denied to the individual entrepreneur (Taylor, p.12). On the matter of accounting regulation, we will see that the government could not, initially, make up its mind whether to interfere or leave well alone.

JSCA 1844 introduced facilities for the easy formation of joint stock companies, but required compliance with certain minimum formalities including an obligation to file, with the newly created registrar of companies, a deed of settlement setting out rules and regulations for the conduct of the company's affairs. The first of the modern companies acts was enacted in 1856, and this replaced the deed of settlement by two documents; the memorandum and articles of association. The company's internal regulations were, and still are, the subject of the latter document, and promoters could choose either to file specially prepared articles or to use the model regulations contained in Table B attached to the 1856 Act. It was not necessary to adopt Table B expressly, either in whole or in part, since its provisions applied to the extent that special articles failed either to deal with or explicitly to exclude matters contained therein.

Under JSCA 1844 the directors had been obliged to arrange for the appointment of auditors, for the balance sheet to be presented to shareholders at the general meeting, and for the balance sheet and audit report to be filed with the registrar of companies where it was available for public inspection. These regulations were repealed in 1856, though rather more elaborate provisions were listed for voluntary adoption in Table B. The *laissez-faire* philosophy has been cited to explain Parliament's decision to abandon regulations which could have been construed as an unnecessary interference in a matter for private negotiation between shareholders and management. A specific objection to compulsory accounting and audit measures was that they could easily be evaded by unscrupulous directors but, at the same time, cause investors to relax their vigilance. The *laissez-faire* explanation is not entirely convincing, however, because, although it is consistent with the change made in 1856, it does not explain why provisions, more restrictive in principle, were given full statutory force eleven years earlier.

One alternative explanation is that the accounting provisions of the 1844 Act simply did not work well. An ability on the part of companies to prepare a balance sheet, and the appointment of accountants possessing the necessary expertise to discharge the duties, specified in the 1844 Act, were both assumed; often neither of these conditions was satisfied in practice. The result was an audit which one witness giving evidence before the Monteagle Committee (1849) described as 'moonshine, as against dishonest directors' (*Minutes*, no.2548) and another as 'the greatest farce possible' (*Minutes*, no.2761).

Part of the problem was the common practice of appointing, as auditors, shareholders who made only a cursory examination of the accounts, but the position was no doubt exacerbated by the small number of professional accountants in practice at this time (see Chapter 20). The result was that accounts filed by companies between 1844–56, now deposited with the Public Records Office, were often a jumbled collection of unrelated financial facts. For example, the Dunstan Iron Ore Co. published a document, called a 'Balance Sheet from September 1854 to the 8th November 1855', listing the following: as debits, amounts received from the issue of shares and the sale of goods, debtors for goods, calls in arrears, cash and bills in hand, estimated values for plant and stock; and, as credits, expenditure, amounts owed and a balancing figure.

The 1856 decision to make the accounts and audit provisions voluntary might also have been prompted by the fact that registered companies, in which there was a separation between ownership and management, at this time accounted for a relatively small proportion of total economic activity. The majority of company registrations prior to 1880 were made solely to obtain the protection of limited liability for the existing owner/managers, and these proprietorship companies did not need the kinds of safeguards which statutory accounting requirements were intended to provide. The accounts and audit provisions contained in Table B were repeated, with some amendment, in CA 1862, Table A. The most significant difference is that the latter omitted the requirement for the accounts to be kept 'upon the principle of double entry, in a cash book, journal and ledger' (Table B, art.69). Again, the reason might be that the regulation proved too ambitious.

The separation of ownership and management, as companies increasingly looked to the general public to provide the funds needed to help finance expansion, became a noticeable feature in a number of industries after about 1880. This development produced a perceived need for more accountability from management, but the official response was slow. During the last three decades of the nineteenth century a number of bills were presented to Parliament designed to make company directors more accountable (they were, of course, already accountable in equity in the same manner as trustees) to shareholders for resources entrusted to them. These were unsuccessful, though statutory obligations, sometimes extensive, were imposed on the officials of particular categories of company. The Railway Acts of 1867–68, for example, were passed just about the time that strong *laissez-faire* convictions began to wane.

The accountability required from the directors of registered companies remained free from statutory control until the requirement for an external audit was reintroduced in 1900. It was a further half century before extensive accounting regulations were imposed on this type of company.

Articles of association

Model articles. The main accounts and audit provisions contained in articles 78–94 of Table A attached to CA 1862 may be summarised as follows. The accounting requirements obliged the directors: to maintain a record of business transactions, and to make them available for inspection by the members (78); to present an income and expenditure account to the AGM, distinguishing between sources of income and categories of expenditure (79–80); to present a balance sheet to the meeting conforming to a presribed format (see Figure 15.1) 'or as near thereto as circumstances admit' (81); to circulate a copy of the balance sheet to members seven days before the meeting (82). The audit clauses made provision for: an annual audit (83); the appointment of the auditor by the members (84); the appointment as auditor of a person who might be a member but should not be a director (86); fixing the remuneration of auditors (88); the auditor to have a right of access to the books and to interview directors (93–94); the auditor to have a duty to examine and report on whether the balance sheet is 'full and fair' and gives a 'true and correct view of the state of the company's affairs (92, 94).

CA 1862 empowered the BOT to alter Table A and, upon publication in the *London Gazette,* the revised regulations might be adopted by companies subsequently registered. It was not until 1906 that the government took advantage of this provision;[1] the revised Table A was subsequently incorporated, without amendment, when company law was next consolidated in 1908.

Contemporary practices. Books, articles and government reports published during the last quarter of the nineteenth century and the early years of the twentieth century contain conflicting views regarding the extent to which Table A was adopted, without amendment, and the perceived suitability of individual clauses where special articles were filed. In 1887 the Manchester Accountants Students' Society was told that 'there are a very large number [of companies] registered without articles, and so entirely governed by Table A' (*Accountant,* 16 April, p.219), but this assessment must be contrasted with the view of ICAEW president, Frederick

Figure 15.1
Form of Balance Sheet referred to in Table A

Dr. BALANCE SHEET of the Co. made up to 18 Cr.

CAPITAL AND LIABILITIES

			£.s.d.	£.s.d.
I CAPITAL		Showing:		
	1.	The Number of Shares		
	2.	The Amount paid per Share		
	3.	If any arrears of Calls, the Nature of the Arrear, and the Names of the Defaulters		
	4.	The Particulars of any forfeited Shares		
II. DEBTS AND LIABILITIES of the Company.		Showing:		
	5.	The Amount of Loans on Mortgages or Debenture Bonds.		
	6.	The Amount of Debts owing by the Company, distinguishing (a.) Debts for which Acceptances have been given (b.) Debts to Tradesmen for Supplies of Stock in Trade or other Articles. (c.) Debts for Law Expenses. (d.) Debts for Interest on Debentures or other loans (e.) Unclaimed Dividends (f.) Debts not enumerated above.		
VI. RESERVE FUND		Showing: The Amount set aside from Profits to meet Contingencies.		
VII PROFIT AND LOSS		Showing: The disposable Balance for Payment of Dividend, &c.		
CONTINGENT LIABILITIES.		Claims against the Company not acknowledged as Debts. Monies for which the Company is contingently liable		

PROPERTY AND ASSETS

			£.s.d.	£.s.d.
III PROPERTY held by Company		Showing:		
	7.	Immovable Property, distinguishing (a.) Freehold Land (b.) Freehold Buildings (c.) Leasehold Buildings		
	8.	Movable Property, distinguishing (d.) Stock in Trade (e.) Plant The cost to be stated with Deductions for Deterioration in Value as charged to the Reserve Fund or Profit and Loss.		
IV. DEBTS owing to the Company.		Showing:		
	9.	Debts considered good for which the Company hold Bills or other Securities.		
	10.	Debts considered good for which the Company hold no Security		
	11.	Debts considered doubtful and bad Any Debt due from a Director or other Officer of the Company to be separately stated.		
V. CASH AND INVESTMENTS.		Showing:		
	12.	The Nature of Investment and Rate of Interest.		
	13.	The Amount of Cash, where lodged, and if bearing Interest.		

Whinney, that very few companies adopted Table A (*Accountant*, 27 October 1888, p.695), and David Chadwick MP's assertion that 'not one per cent. of the companies established [under CA 1862] have adopted Schedule A' (Lowe Committee, *Minutes*, no.1947)

Part of the explanation for this discrepancy may be that Whinney had in mind the practice of large companies which found a need to prepare special articles to meet their particular requirements, whereas small companies found more use for Table A as a means of cheapening the process of incorporation. Also, there may have been an element of exaggeration in Chadwick's comments designed to elicit statutory support for the set of standardised accounts which he presented to the Lowe Committee, 1877 (see Chapter 17).

An assessment of the views expressed regarding the adoption of Table A, *in toto*, ought also to take account of the fact that its model provisions became less applicable as time went by. The effect of changing business requirements was that, by 1890, the model provisions were being described as 'somewhat antiquated' and 'cumbersome and almost obsolete' (*Acccountant*, 6 December, p.669). The Davey Committee (1895) believed that Table A should be redrafted 'to make it conform more closely to modern practice and business requirements' (para.61). Similar sentiments were expressed in evidence submitted to the Loreburn Committee (1906) which helped draft the revised Table A that was soon afterwards given statutory effect by the BOT.

Turning to the practice of filing articles which incorporated *some* of the clauses contained in Table A, there is fairly widespread agreement that the specimen provisions were generally used as a model and the exact wording of many clauses often adopted. The result was, according to two witnesses giving evidence to the Loreburn Committee, 'a convenient uniformity in the general outline of the articles of most companies' (p.352).

The accounting provisions of Table A were modified to a far greater extent than those relating to audit. This was in line with contemporary reporting practices which tended to keep published accounting information to a minimum, based on the argument that company accounts might get into the hands of competitors, and that shareholders were adequately protected by an effective audit and their right to attend and ask questions at the AGM.

Departures from Table A in specially prepared articles of association, with respect to the 'accounts' provisions, restricted both the quantity of published material and the access allowed to members. Clauses dealing with the publication and content of the income and expenditure account were frequently omitted, or else considerably modified. In particular, companies' articles left out the requirement to distinguish the several sources from which income was derived and, even where this provision was retained, published accounts normally distinguished only gross profits on trading from transfer fees. The subsequent omission of this provision from the 1906 revised Table A is an example of British company law's tendency to reflect business practice. Probably it is also evidence of the general consensus in favour of financial confidentiality, and even secrecy, which remained free from serious challenge for a further twenty-five years. Indeed it was not until 1981 that companies were legally required to publish a profit and loss account containing the level of detail implied by the general requirements contained in article 80 of Table A.

The standard provisions dealing with the content of the balance sheet were often modified or omitted, and the internal regulations usually empowered the directors simply to draw up the statement 'in such form as they . . . shall from time to time determine' (*Accountant*, 10 January 1885, p.11). The prescribed form of balance sheet proved unpopular, perhaps because it was considered unsuitable or, more likely, because it contained rather more detail than management wished to disclose. Certainly the Table A balance sheet was more elaborate than those generally published by companies during the nineteenth century, and well into the twentieth century. The specimen balance sheet was omitted from the 1906 revised articles, and a statutorily prescribed format was not introduced until 1981.

The requirement for books to be open to shareholders for inspection was usually omitted, allegedly because of the danger of competitors purchasing shares in order to obtain access to this information. A further popular restriction was to replace the requirement to print and circulate a balance sheet to shareholders by an obligation to make the document available for inspection at the company's registered office for an extremely limited time period.

The fairly common requirement for the directors' report to deal with 'the state and condition of the company' was a significant exception to the general practice of registering special articles that called for the publication of less information than did the model articles. The probable explanation is that Table A (art.36) assumed that the directors would make a report to shareholders, and it was therefore necessary to decide on its content. Information about the state and condition of a company is of a qualitative nature and, in freely providing this material, directors probably perceived similar benefits to those which are thought to accrue today as the result of voluntarily publishing information in the chairman's review. In some cases it is seen as an opportunity for management to say some comforting words to shareholders, free from the scrutiny of the auditors and the need to substantiate its opinions with hard financial facts.[2]

Few large companies registered audit articles identical to those contained in Table A. Companies invariably made provision for an annual audit, but articles often omitted the requirement 'to examine [the balance sheet] with the accounts and vouchers' (art.92). This omission is significant since it suggests that nineteenth-century company promoters neither expected nor, perhaps, wanted the auditor to do a thorough job. Some of the contemporary literature does suggest that many auditors merely carried out a 'mechanical' audit, comprising a simple comparison of balance sheet figures with the totals appearing in the company's books. Certainly, the small amount of time (7 days) allowed the auditor, by the articles of some companies, would have enabled them to undertake no more than a superficial examination of balance sheet figures. The fairly common certification 'audited and found correct' further supports the idea that the nineteenth-century audit was often a fairly routine affair which ignored the difficult problems of valuation that are principal features of the auditors' duties today.

The standard provision barring directors from acting as auditors (art.86) was widely adopted, and companies occasionally stipulated that the auditor should be a professional. More often a professional accountant was actually named as the first person to hold this office. It was no doubt believed that his signature would add greater credibility to the content of the published accounts.

Review

The information today contained in British company accounts is closely controlled and, although there remains scope for innovation, freedom of action is much less than was the case in the nineteenth century when the accounts of registered companies were substantially free from external regulation. It is therefore interesting to ask why companies published audited accounting statements during this early period. A plausible explanation is based on the notion of accounting information as part of the price which management must pay to encourage the public to invest and, for this reason, the level of accountability accepted by management was detailed in the articles of association. The burden placed on management by specially drafted articles was usually significantly less than was envisaged by Table A of CA 1862. This suggests that, to use the terms of agency theory, the level of accountability demanded by shareholders was less than Parliament had expected and, to minimise 'compliance costs', the specially prepared articles were modified accordingly.

The audit requirement enacted by CA 1900 and the accounting provisions contained in the 1906 revised articles incorporated many, but not all, the modifications which were commonly included in specially prepared articles filed during the previous forty years. The official line was summed up neatly by the Davey Committee which admitted to a reluctance to impose burdens likely to deter 'the best class of men from becoming directors' (para.4). The fact that shareholders continued to concur with the practice of publishing accounting information, in broad terms only, was stressed in evidence presented to the Greene Committee in 1926 (*Minutes*, p.lxviii). Attitudes rapidly changed following revelations in the Royal Mail case, culminating in the far more onerous accounting requirements recommended in the Cohen Committee's Report and made legal requirements in 1948.

Postscript. The last quarter of the nineteenth century saw the London Stock Exchange begin to impose a degree of control over the level of accountability required from listed companies. A requirement for companies to send two copies of their accounts to the Stock Exchange was introduced, probably in 1881 when the Stock Exchange's collection of published accounts begins. These accounts were not open for public inspection, but certain information was extracted for inclusion in *The Stock Exchange Official Intelligence.* At the turn of the century the Stock Exchange instructed listed companies to circulate a printed balance sheet and directors' report to members seven days before the general meeting. This is an example of the Stock Exchange introducing publication requirements for listed companies well in advance of their being imposed as general legal obligations.

16

Company Law and Pressure Groups

Introduction

The usefulness of company accounts as the basis for performance assessment and decision making depends on the effectiveness of action taken in dealing with problems arising in each of the following broad areas:

1. Asset valuation and profit measurement, since this determines the extent to which accounting reports succeed in portraying the underlying economic facts.
2. Levels of disclosure, with the ability of user groups to assimilate large quantities of financial data the effective upper limit.
3. Presentation of financial information, including such matters as the desirability of requiring accounts to conform to a prescribed format.
4. External audit requirements designed to add credibility to the information prepared by management for outsiders.
5. Publication and circularisation of financial data to user groups.

The form and content of British company accounts are, today, closely controlled in an attempt to ensure they satisfy perceived user needs in each of the above areas. Regulations are issued by Parliament, the London Stock Exchange, and the accountancy profession. Each regulatory body naturally tends to view the problem of issuing accounting obligations from a different stance. Companies Acts are likely to reflect the economic and political philosophy of the government in power, Stock Exchange regulations are likely to be concerned principally with the requirements of investors in listed companies, while the priorities of practising accountants are likely to loom large in deliberations which result in the issue of accounting standards.

Making new law

Up to 1973 (when Britain joined the European Community) the creation of new company law usually began with the government of the day recognising a problem, such as the lack of regulation which led to 'the notoriety of the circumstances which had attended the concoction, progress and termination of some bubble companies' (Gladstone Committee, first report, p.iii). The traditional source of new ideas for company law reform was the Company Law Amendment Committee (CLAC) appointed by the appropriate government department to investigate the problem. The functions of each committee were to collect evidence regarding possible improvements to company law and to make a report. The committee usually began its task by circulating a list of questions to interested parties and inviting them to submit a written response. The evidence submitted to CLACs naturally reflected the priorities of the individuals or institutions making the submission. The committee then had the difficult job of evaluating a wide range of conflicting ideas, although the practice of direct interview of the various contributors often helped resolve conflict and achieve a consensus.

On receipt of the committee's report, the government of the day decided whether to act upon any or all of the recommendations and, if it decided to act, a Bill was drafted for presentation to Parliament. Altogether 9 CLACs were appointed and reported between 1841 and 1962. It is the purpose of this chapter to provide the essence of the many debates which took place, the conclusions reached and the consequential action taken by Parliament to regulate company accounts.

Today the major source of new legislation is the series of directives on company law. These are drafted by the European Communities Commission, approved by the Council of Ministers and then sent to the governments of member states for enactment as law in those countries. In Britain the government then issues a consultative document setting out the manner in which it proposes to incorporate the content of the directive into UK company law. For example, the EEC's fourth directive, which required standardisation of the annual accounts of limited companies, prompted the government to issue the consultative document entitled *Company Accounting and Disclosure* (Cmnd 7654). The views of interested parties were invited and taken into account when framing the draft Bill which became CA 1981. Standardisation is discussed in Chapter 17.

Gladstone Committee

The first CLAC was appointed in 1841 and reported in 1844; its chairman was W.E. Gladstone. The committee was set up to consider the problem of large partnerships and ended up by inventing the registered company. It concluded that associations of more than 25 should only be allowed to function if registered as companies and that the minimum number of shareholders should be seven.[1]

No accountants submitted evidence to the committee and none sat on it. Actuaries and lawyers presenting evidence strongly advocated the introduction of compulsory accounting requirements, however, and the committee reported that 'periodical accounts, if honestly made and fairly audited, cannot fail to excite attention to the real state of a concern' (p.v). The committee accordingly recommended 'the accounts of every such company to be open to the inspection of the shareholders; and that the annual balance-sheet together with the reports of the auditors thereon, be registered' (p.xiii). These recommendations were immediately implemented by JSCA 1844. Indeed, the original Bill also contained a provision for half-yearly income statements to be presented to shareholders, but this was not included in the Act. The surviving requirements were fairly radical, nevertheless, and not improved upon until CA 1929. Parliament soon had a change of heart and the provisions were repealed in 1856. More onerous, but optional provisions, were instead listed in the model articles of association contained in Table B (see Chapter 15).

Between 1856–94 two further CLACs met and reported – the Watkin Committee (1867) and the Lowe Committee (1877). David Chadwick, accountant, presented evidence to the first of these committees and was a member of the second. Evidence was presented to the 1877 committee by some of the founding fathers of the accountancy profession; Robert Palmer Harding, Samuel Lowell Price and William Turquand. Some attention was devoted to the imposition of a standard form of balance sheet (see Chapter 17), but legislation of interest to accountants was confined to prospectuses (Chapter 17) and the introduction of rules for the reduction of capital (Chapter 14).

Davey Committee

This committee was appointed in 1894 and reported in 1895. By this time the joint stock company was widely used to raise finance from the general public, and accountants had organised themselves on a professional basis. The appointment to the committee of Edwin Waterhouse, a past president of the ICAEW, indicates further government recognition of the contribution accountants could make to the conduct of business life. None of the professional bodies made a submission to the committee, although one was made by Frederick Whinney, also a past president of the ICAEW, in his personal capacity. His fairly radical proposals favoured the publication of a balance sheet containing a classified list of items, an indication to be given of how asset values had been computed, and an annual audit. Harold Brown, a solicitor, cautioned against publicity which would 'injure and check *bona fide* enterprises, and will not stop those which are reckless or fraudulent' (p.77). He believed that directors should be left free to conduct activities 'as far as possible on the lines of a private firm' and claimed that the vast majority of shareholders concurred with this view.

Impressed by the arguments that it should proceed with caution, the committee reported that 'Restrictive provisions which may have the effect of either curtailing the facilities for the formation of companies which bring so much business to England . . . or deterring the best class of men from becoming directors are not to be lightly entertained' (para.4). The committee did, however, adopt a number of Whinney's proposals and prepared a draft Bill for presentation to Parliament. The government instead referred the Bill to the Halsbury Committee (a House of Lords Select Committee) which took a mountain of further evidence and submitted reports to Parliamant in 1896, 1897 and 1898. One notable witness was H.B.Buckley (later Lord Wrenbury), an eminent authority on company law, who argued that a legal requirement to publish a balance sheet would deal 'a death blow to limited liability' and give the system 'such a shock limited liability would go out of fashion' (q.1661).

CA 1900 provided for shareholder appointed auditors to report on whether the balance sheet laid before the AGM showed 'a true and correct view of the state of the company's affairs' (s.23). This recognised the auditor's principal responsibility as being to the shareholders rather than the directors, but the Act said nothing about the qualifications of the auditor (other than that he should not be a director) or the content of the balance sheet. It is not surprising that a contemporary contributor to *The Economic Journal* should have felt driven to complain that 'considering the time spent upon it it is a pity that the Act achieves so little' (1900, p.192).

Loreburn Committee

This committee was appointed in 1905 and reported in 1906. Sir Robert Reid, its first chairman, resigned on being elevated to the peerage (as Lord Loreburn) where he succeeded Halsbury as Lord Chancellor in 1905. He was replaced by C.M.Warmington. Edwin Waterhouse was again appointed to the committee and the SIAA was the first professional body to make a submission to a CLAC. Its memorandum was an extremely modest document and recommended no further legislation. Confidentiality was also favoured by the Council of the Incorporated Law Society which argued that the circulation of information prior to the general meeting, and other accounting matters, should be left for negotiation between management and shareholders. The submission of the London Chamber of Commerce, whose president was James Martin, a future president of the SIAA, was more progressive. It favoured the circularisation of a balance sheet to members, the specification of a minimum content, and the presentation of a profit and loss account to the AGM.

The main recommendation made by the committee was for companies to file with the registrar

> an audited statement, in the form of a balance sheet, containing a summary of its capital, its liabilities and its assets, giving such particulars as may generally disclose the nature of such liabilities and assets, and how the values at which the fixed assets stand are arrived at (para.33, enacted as CA 1907, s.21).

The omission of any specific reference to the profit and loss account balance was intended to allow the directors to omit this item if they believed its inclusion might be detrimental to the company's interest. The Act required companies to publish the balance, if any, of commission paid on the issue of shares or debentures, discount allowed on the issue of debentures, and interest paid out of capital. This approach, which laid down a minimum level of accountability and left it open for the directors to decide how much more should be disclosed to account properly for the resources entrusted to them, we will call the 'minimum disclosure philosophy'.

The introduction of a filing requirement reflects the Loreburn Committee's conviction that creditors had a legitimate right to enquire into the financial position of a company requesting trade credit or a loan. In this respect the committee favoured a broader degree of accountability than had the Davey Committee, which had reached the conclusion that only shareholders should be given a legal right to inspect the balance sheet. In other respects the Loreburn Committee was more cautious than its predecessor, indicating approval of financial secrecy as expressed by the Law Society and implied by the SIAA. The continuing philosophy was one of non-intervention in matters which could be adequately dealt with by private contract between shareholders and management. There was a determined desire not to disturb the status quo. Contemporary opinion, as indicated in *Newton* v *BSA* (1906), attached high priority to confidentiality, if not secrecy, in financial matters. It was necessary to wait until 1929 before obligations along the lines of the recommendations made by the London Chamber of Commerce were put into effect.

Loopholes in CA 1908

Limited liability companies range from the large public corporation, which uses the joint stock structure to raise a substantial amount of money from the investing public, to what are essentially family concerns, incorporated to obtain the protection of limited liability and, possibly, tax advantages for existing shareholders. The question of whether differential accounting obligations should be imposed on these two types of limited company has been a recurring theme in the deliberations of company law reformists.

The terms private company and public company were in common use in the nineteenth century, but it was not until CA 1907 (consolidated in CA 1908) introduced a filing requirement only for public companies that it was necessary to give either of the terms precise statutory recognition. To qualify for private company status, and exemption, the basic requirements were for the company to restrict the right to transfer shares (e.g. by giving the other shareholders the right to veto a proposed transfer), to limit the number of shareholders to 50, and to prohibit any invitation to the public to subscribe for shares or debentures in the company. The popularity of this legislative creation is demonstrated by the fact that 50,000 of the 66,000 registered companies in existence ten years later enjoyed private company status.

The reason for the concession, granted, incidentally, against the advice of the Loreburn Committee, was to protect the financial affairs of private companies from the close scrutiny considered desirable in the case of public companies. It was not long, however, before managers of large companies realised that it was possible to avoid public scrutiny of its financial affairs by transferring some or all of its operating activities to subsidiaries which fell within the definition of private companies and were therefore exempt from the filing requirement.[2]

The failure to state, specifically, that an 'up-to-date' balance sheet should be filed with the registrar provided further scope for businessmen to evade the spirit of the law. It proved legally permissible to file the same statement each year; a procedure, adopted by some companies, which a frustrated registrar found impossible to stamp out. CA 1928 introduced an amended wording to outlaw this practice.

Finally, some company directors took advantage of the opportunity, provided by CA 1908, to omit profit figures from the balance sheet filed with the registrar. The document, as a result, did not balance, and the practice was commented on unfavourably by the registrar of companies in evidence presented to the Greene Committee (*Minutes*, no. 128). The practice was rendered illegal by CA 1928, which obliged the directors to file the shareholders' balance sheet with the registrar.

Wrenbury Committee

This committee was appointed and reported in 1918. James Martin and Sir William Plender were members of the committee. The committee was mainly concerned with the implications of the First World War for the employment of foreign capital in British industries. No positive recommendations were made regarding accounting matters and its report did not result in legislation.

Statutory accounting requirements therefore remained exceedingly modest up to 1928. According to Sidney Pears, the directors 'were within their legal rights [under the 1908 Act] in showing capital, creditors and the balance of profit and loss account, assuming there was a profit, on the one side and sundry fixed assets, debts etc. on the other side' (*Accountant*, 2 February 1929, p.150). In practice many firms did better than this and there was wide diversity in the level of disclosure. This is what one would expect to happen in a substantially unregulated environment, reflecting the extent to which different groups of investors demanded information and the willingness of directors to provide it (see Chapter 11).

Greene Committee

This committee was appointed in 1925 and reported in 1926; its chairman was Wilfrid Greene. Three accountants were appointed to the committee; William Cash, a past president of the ICAEW, Sir James Martin of the SIAA, and Sir William McLintock, a leading Scottish chartered accountant. Memoranda were submitted by the ICAEW, the SIAA, and the Scottish accounting bodies; also by Frank Whinney in his personal capacity. The accountancy profession was, at last, heavily involved in the process of creating new regulations.

There had occurred a great increase in the number of absentee shareholders since the passage of CA 1908, and this implied a corresponding increase in the need for published accounting information. The committee's main accounting interest focused on the reporting procedures of holding companies, which were becoming increasingly common (see Chapter 18), the general level of disclosure in company accounts, and the question of secret reserves.

There is a close resemblance between the accounting proposals of the ICAEW and the Law Society, indicating almost certain cooperation between the two bodies when framing their submissions. Each took a sanguine view of the standard of contemporary financial reporting procedures. On the general question of disclosure in published accounts, the ICAEW echoed the sentiments expressed by Harold Brown to the Davey Committee 30 years earlier:

> the business done by limited companies is, on the whole, transacted by directors and managers, who are honest, and if

> in some cases they disclose in the published accounts less than some people desire the absence of detail is in most cases wise and is generally supported by the shareholders. To give in a balance sheet such detailed information as would afford full protection to creditors might mean the giving of a mass of detail of material value to competitors' (*Minutes*, p.lxviii).

Both the ICAEW and the Law Society reached the conclusion 'that it is impossible by legislation to protect fools from their own folly'.

Some groups were less complacent. Within the accountancy profession, the SIAA pointed out that 'there has been an increasing tendency for the information given in balance sheets of companies to be attenuated' (*Minutes*, p.lxxxiii), and a detailed list of items for disclosure was proposed to deal with the problem. *The Economist* went further and recommended the publication of a profit and loss account.

The question of secret reserves, i.e. undisclosed transfers between the profit and loss account and balance sheet to smooth the trend of reported profit, received a great deal of attention. Comments were generally favourable; both the ICAEW and the Law Society took the view that 'too much disclosure should not be insisted on and the greatest possible freedom should be allowed to those responsible' (*Minutes*, p.xlix and p.lxviii). Looking back, it seems likely that there existed, in the minds of the directors, a substantial divergence between the true reason and the expressed reason for opposing increased publicity. A continuing theme propounded by advocates of secrecy was the need to protect shareholders from the harmful effect on investment values of the increased competition which would result from fuller disclosure. In some instances, more plausible explanations for continued obscurity were the desire to mislead shareholders regarding the true state of their investment, and the determination of directors to safeguard themselves against criticism when profits were low and claims for dividends when results were good.

The committee's conclusion was little different from that of the Davey Committee; 'It appears to us, as a matter of general principle, most undesirable, in order to defeat an occasional wrongdoer, to impose restrictions which would seriously hamper the activities of honest men' (para.9). In general, they were satisfied with prevailing reporting procedures but, drawing heavily on the memorandum submitted by the ICAEW, they did make certain recommendations which were incorporated in CA 1928. These included the following requirements: to prepare a directors' report containing certain specified information; to lay a profit and loss account (which did not have to be audited) before the AGM; to circulate copies of the balance sheet, director's report and audit report at least seven days prior to the AGM, and file these documents with the registrar. A list of minimum items for disclosure in the balance sheet was also submitted to Parliament.

Dicksee was one of the few outspoken critics of contemporary practices. Indeed, the purpose of writing *Published Balance Sheets and Window Dressing* (1927) was to advise company auditors that balance sheets designed to withhold information should not attract their unqualified approval. He did not believe the committee's 'disappointing' recommendations would improve matters much (p.2).

The Act was initially welcomed by the accounting establishment. Later, the official history of the ICAEW observed that 'excellent though the 1929 Act was so far as it went, accountants did not have to wait long before having it painfully brought home to them that it did not go far enough' (Howitt, p.75). The event alluded to was the Royal Mail case which proved that it was still legal for a company to publish technically accurate but grossly misleading information, mainly because of the Act's failure to outlaw the use of secret reserves (see Chapter 12). Indeed, the Act contained implicit approval for secret reserves by requiring the directors only to report the amount 'they propose to carry to the reserve fund, general reserve or reserve account *shown specifically on the [present or subsequent] balance sheet*' (s.123, my emphasis). Other criticisms of the Act are that it did not require holding companies to publish group accounts and only a small number of items were identified for publication. The main ones were: goodwill, patents and trade marks, shares in subsidiaries, and the amounts due to and from subsidiaries. It is somewhat ironic that most criticism has been directed at the accounting content of the report of the CLAC on which the accountancy profession had its largest representation.

Cohen Committee

This committee was appointed in 1943 and reported in 1945. The BOT believed that the time was right for an extension of management's accountability and, in choosing the committee's membership, took care to include people who were likely to be sympathetic to new ideas (see chapter 12). Mr Justice Cohen was appointed chairman and Russell Kettle, who later became president of the ICAEW, was appointed to the committee. Memoranda were submitted by the five professional bodies which gave evidence to the Greene Committee; also the Association of Certified and Corporate Accountants (ACCA) and F.R.M. De Paula, chairman of the ICAEW's taxation and financial relations committee.

A feature of the committee's activities was that it consulted a wider range of interested parties. Attention had previously concentrated on preparers and suppliers of accounting information; groups which naturally have a vested interest in maintaining the status quo. Now, for the first time, the views of users were fully canvassed. These favoured innovation in order to improve the information available for resource allocation decisions. The resulting change in the balance of evidence presented to the committee is reflected in its recommendation for far more demanding legal requirements.

Contemporary reporting procedures were strongly criticised by the ACCA who pointed out that 'Under the law as it now stands as long as the balance sheet is mechanically accurate it can be as obscure and uninformative as the directors may find expedient' (*Minutes*, p.531). But while the Royal Mail case had proved this was true, it was also the case that, by the mid-1940s, the financial reporting procedures of the vast majority of companies were well ahead of prevailing legal requirements. The ACCA's extensive proposals for reform included a detailed profit and loss account commencing with the gross profit figure.

The most radical proposals came from the financial press. *The Economist* submitted a standard form of accounts, including a fully itemised trading and profit and loss account. The main thrust of its evidence was that company law attached too much emphasis to what it called 'security and ownership' and, as a result, gave insufficient recognition to the importance of published profit statements. 'The only true security is earning power, and in our view the profit and loss account is more important, not less, than the balance sheet' (*Minutes*, p.474). *The Economist* also believed that standardised accounting reports, when aggregated, would be of more use to the government as a basis for economic policy making. Support for more demanding regulations came from the editor of *The Financial News* and from the General Federation of Trades Union which emphasised the reporting needs of unions and employees.

The climate of opinion had changed drastically since the Greene Committee reported; whereas confidentiality was then the watchword, 'fullest practicable disclosure' (para.5) was the objective identified in the Cohen Committee's report. The committee's main recommendations, which formed the basis for CA 1947, were as follows: group accounts, usually in the form of a consolidated balance sheet and consolidated profit and loss account, to be published; the company's own profit and loss account, together with group accounts, where appropriate, to be circulated to members prior to the general meeting and filed with the registrar; the audit report to be expanded to cover the profit and loss account and group accounts (but not the director's report[4]); the auditor to be a professional accountant with membership of one of the bodies recognised from time to time by the BOT; and transfers to and from reserves to be fully disclosed.

The committee also identified a comprehensive range of headings for disclosure in the balance sheet and more modest particulars for disclosure in the profit and loss account. To prevent holding companies from concealing the financial results of their business activities, by operating through wholly owned subsidiaries, freedom from the filing requirement was withdrawn for private companies and re-introduced only for 'exempt' private companies, i.e. private companies without a body corporate among their shareholders.

The sharp increase in the level of responsibility assumed by the professional acccountancy bodies, during the 1940s, for the quality of financial reporting procedures was recognised by the Cohen Committee:

> The recent tendency has been to give more information and this tendency has been fortified by the valuable recommendations published from time to time by the responsible accountancy bodies as to the form in which accounts should be drawn up and the information which they should contain (para.97).

Indeed, in framing its recommendations, the committee drew heavily on the ICAEW's submission which was, in turn, based on the Recommendations issued through its Taxation and Financial Relations Committee, beginning in 1942. The committee's recognition of the prime position of the ICAEW in bringing about improvements in financial reporting procedures, and its willingness to provide a back-up system in the form of statutory support for Recommendations which had proved successful, undoubtedly improved the status of each of these.

Jenkins Committee

This committee was appointed in 1959 and reported in 1962; its chairman was Lord Jenkins and one of its members was W.H. Lawson, a former president of the ICAEW. Evidence was presented by the ICAEW, the ACCA, the Scottish Chartered Accountants and the Association of International Accountants. H.C.Edey and Professor W.T.Baxter, both on the staff of the London School of Economics, were the first full-time accounting academics to make presentations to a CLAC. An interesting feature of Baxter's evidence is his concern with full disclosure of financial information, not only for the benefit of shareholders but also as a means of making society as a whole better off – 'The society that fails to provide itself with the best available information is wasting resources, and keeping its income needlessly low' (*Minutes*, p.188).

Correspondents who resisted any extension of existing legal requirements included the Law Society and the ICAEW which argued that 'they have worked remarkably well and may be said to be both necessary and useful and to have achieved substantially the objective of adequate disclosure of information' (*Minutes*, p.1418). The committee again acknowledged the contribution made by the series of Recommendations to the improvement of financial reporting procedures, and concluded that 'it is primarily to the initiative of the professional associations that we must look if the general principles of the Act are to be effectively applied in practice' (para.334). The committee made modest proposals for further legislation, some of which were incorporated in CA 1967.

The Act extended the minimum disclosure requirements applying to the profit and loss account, and a number of additional items of information were identified for inclusion in the directors' report. The consequence of the latter change was that directors' reports tended to be confined to a listing of statutory requirements; the discussion of progress and prospects being transferred to the chairman's review published by large companies. Finally, the dispensation from the filing requirement allowed to 'exempt' private companies was withdrawn. Its purpose had been to provide an element of protection for small family firms whereas, in practice, some exempt private companies were extremely large and influential concerns in whose affairs creditors and employees had a legitimate interest. Withdrawal of the exemption could also be justified on the grounds that limited liability should carry with it the obligation of full publicity irrespective of size. The result of the change was that all companies (large and small) were subject to the same legal requirements regarding the content of the accounts circulated to members and filed with the registrar (differential filing requirements were re-introduced in 1981, see chapter 17). A further consequence was that three times as many companies had to file accounts.

Review

The mechanism for introducing and subsequently reforming company law, discussed in this chapter, lasted for 130 years. The need for a balanced debate was recognised by successive governments which, wisely, did not pack the committees with its own representatives. Membership instead consisted of leading personalities from the business and professional world. A variety of interested parties were consulted, and a wide range of conflicting views was presented to each committee that met. Some groups were keen to impose additional reporting requirements, others favoured maintenance of the status quo, and a few felt company law had already gone too far.

In very broad terms, pressure groups representing the interests of preparers and suppliers of accounting information, such as accountants and managers, rarely favoured substantial additions to existing statutory requirements. In contrast, users of accounting information, such as employees, investment analysts and the financial press, were more demanding. However, there are plenty of examples of an institution changing its position over time, reflecting new priorities, new experiences, and changes in the personalities involved. An example of resistance to change, and subsequent conversion to the need for change, is the ICAEW's initial opposition to group accounting (presentation to the Greene Committee) and its subsequent conviction of the need for statutory regulation (presentation to the Cohen Committee).

As might be expected, the ICAEW exerted a great deal of influence, and more radical proposals from this source would probably have speeded up the development of financial reporting procedures. However, the recommendations it made were carefully thought out and capable of immediate action.

The Companies Acts have helped achieve adequate and uniform reporting standards. This, in turn, has helped foster a sound capital market and achieve a rational pattern of resource allocation. A criticism levelled at the series of Companies Acts is that they have followed improvements in accounting practice rather than anticipating them and causing them to take place. This is substantially true but workable accounting regulations are unlikely to be legal creations, and are more naturally based on voluntary practices developed in an unregulated environment. For example, limited companies today publish audited accounts to comply with the Companies Acts, but they did so prior to 1900 when this was not a requirement. And although it is often said, with some justification, that the Greene Committee's report, and the subsequent Act, were particularly tentative, it must be remembered that the content of the report reflected the balance of arguments received. It is of course possible for legislation to be innovative, though the likelihood of success is greater when the experience of another country is drawn upon to help frame a new measure. This is demonstrated in the next chapter.

17

Standardised Accounts and Prospectuses

Standardised accounts

The Fourth Directive provided for the standardisation of accounting reports published by companies operating in the European Community. At the time the Directive was issued (1978) standardised procedures were already firmly established in France and Germany, but other common market countries were obliged to make significant changes to their existing laws. In Britain, the Directive was given statutory effect by CA 1981.

Prior to 1981 publication requirements imposed on British registered companies were based on the practice of prescribing a minimum level of disclosure without specifying content and form in detail. A persuasive argument in favour of the minimum disclosure philosophy (see Chapter 16) is that it obliged directors to disclose sufficient information to account properly for the resources placed at their disposal, and allowed them ample scope to disclose more should they consider it appropriate. Furthermore, the directors were at liberty to employ whichever method of presentation they considered most likely to communicate effectively the facts reported. The approach implicitly assumes that, given a competitive market for finance, management will endeavour to publish information which provides a useful basis for choosing between alternative investment opportunities.

The discussion which follows shows that the kind of changes Britain was obliged to make, in 1981, were considered on a number of previous occasions. The conclusion usually reached was that standardisation would be detrimental to the long-term development of corporate reporting procedures.

Standardisation in Britain. Standardised financial reporting requirements were, in fact, introduced during the nineteenth century, but for only certain categories of company. In 1868 railway companies were required to produce their accounts conforming to the so-called double account system. Corresponding procedures were subsequently imposed on gas companies (1871) and electric lighting companies (1882) (see Chapter 13). Standard forms of accounts were also prescibed for life assurance companies (1870), industrial and provident societies (1893), building societies (1894), and friendly and collection societies (1896). The objective was to provide a measure of protection for investors by improving comparability and ensuring a reasonable level of disclosure. The above industries were singled out for special treatment because the legislature believed that, in view of the nature and scale of their activities, their financial affairs were of widespread interest. A small minority of the companies affected (mainly life assurance companies) were registered under the Companies Act. The remainder were either incorporated by a special Act of Parliament or formed by registering with the registrar of friendly societies.

The earliest proposal to introduce standardised accounting requirements for *all* registered companies was contained in a draft bill placed before Parliament by the President of the BOT, Robert Lowe, in 1856. He believed that publication of, what was then described as the 'uniform' balance sheet, would improve comparability by outlawing the practice, common under the 1844 Act, of publishing a differently framed statement each year (Edwards, p.230). The standard form of balance sheet was removed from the main body of the Act, during the course of the Parliamentary process, and instead included in the model articles of association which companies might choose to adopt. Few companies published balance sheets in the exact format recommended, or in as much detail, but many adopted the broad pattern (Chapter 15). For example, it became common practice to report the balance of profit as the last item on the liabilities side of the balance sheet, and to present assets in the order of increasing liquidity. In addition, the prescribed format helped institutionalise the British 'wrong way round' balance sheet presentation, with assets on the right and liabilities on the left.

The standardisation debate. A powerful advocate of standardisation during the second half of the nineteenth century was David Chadwick, founder president of the Manchester Institute of

Accountants (1871) and a member of the first council of the ICAEW. In evidence presented to the Watkin Committee (1867) Chadwick unsuccessfully argued that the model balance sheet, contained in Table A, should be elevated in status to a statutory requirement.

Chadwick was elected to Parliament in 1868, and the appointment of a the Lowe Committee (1877) provided him with the opportunity to continue his campaign for standardisation. His Companies Act Amendment (No.2) Bill, which contained both a statutory form of balance sheet and profit and loss account, was specifically referred to the committee for consideration. As a member of the committee Chadwick was in a strong position to press his views, and support for his ideas came from a number of witnesses giving evidence.

The protaganists of standardisation were defeated by the counter arguments presented, in particular, by Sir George Jessel, Master of the Rolls. There are three respects in which accounting statements may be standardised; the financial balances to be disclosed, the format to be used, and the valuation procedures to be adopted. Chadwick's accounts, and other nineteenth-century advocates of standardisation, concentrated on the first two areas but ignored the third. This did not satisfy Jessel who contended that merely to prescribe a standard form and content did not get to the root of the problem and, moreover, gave an appearance of reliability which was illusory and, possibly, misleading. In stating that 'it is not sufficient to put it in form; it is the substance' which is important (*Minutes*, no.2242), Jessel may be regarded as the architect of 'substance over form' as one of the fundamental concepts traditionally underlying British financial reporting practices.

The Davey Committee (1895) also decided against recommending a statutory form of balance sheet on the grounds that 'the character of the business and the different circumstances of the various companies would render such a general form inapplicable' (para. 51). The committee instead favoured the compulsory disclosure of certain minimum financial particulars, leaving it to management to decide how much more to publish. Evidence presented by the SIAA to the Loreburn Committee (1906) contained proposals for amending the specimen balance sheet contained in Table A (*Minutes*, p.85). The committee's report makes no reference to this proposal, and CA 1908, the consolidating statute, omitted the pro forma balance sheet. A small amount of statutory recognition was instead given to the minimum disclosure philosophy as the basis for financial reporting requirements (see Chapter 16).

The Greene Committee (1926) invited views on the 'form and content' of company accounts. Strong resistance to the imposition of a standardised format came from the chartered accounting bodies, and from the SIAA which argued that it was impracticable 'to extend standardised forms of accounts [to registered companies], having regard to the wide variety of businesses involved and the information which the standardised forms would give to trade competitors' (*Minutes*, p.lxxxiii). This summed up the general attitude towards standardisation and was accepted by the committee. However, because the information currently published by some companies was 'of a scanty nature' (para.69), the committee recommended some fairly modest additions to the specified minimum content for published accounts. These were accepted by Parliament and included in CA 1928 (Chapter 16).

In evidence submitted to the Cohen Committee (1945), standardisation was favoured by witnesses who can loosely be described as representing the views of users of accounting statements. The editor of *Financial News*, Hargreaves Parkinson, favoured the imposition of specimen sets of accounts for different trades, and cited the Railway Companies Act of 1911 as an example of standardised accounting requirements which had worked well. *The Economist* pressed for a change of attitude on the grounds that reliable information regarding the progress of registered companies was an indispensable basis for government economic policy. Standard forms of balance sheet and profit and loss account were presented as part of its evidence (*Minutes*, pp.476–77).

Opponents of standardisation included the ICAEW which put forward the usual 'diverse businesses' argument and also contended that

> Over the last two decades, and particularly in the last year or two, considerable and not unimportant developments have occurred in the forms of balance sheets and profit and loss accounts and the absence of standardisation by statute has undoubtedly facilitated these. There seems no reason to think that the end of development has been reached and the encouragement of flexibility as to form, whilst insisting that at least certain information should be supplied, seems to the Institute a policy which in the long run would be most beneficial to the shareholders in companies and to business generally (*Minutes*, p.388).

The accountancy profession was also opposed to standardisation because it was thought to deprive the auditor of the need to exercise professional judgement and might relegate his job to a relatively routine mechanical process.[1]

The arguments against standardisation were accepted without reservation by the Cohen Committee which instead recommended a substantial development of the minimum disclosure philosophy (see Chapter 16). CA 1947 signalled the government's awareness of the need for directors to be made more accountable to shareholders and the general public, but the continuing school of thought was that a strong measure of flexibility should be permitted to those responsible for compiling the annual accounts.

The early 1960s saw general satisfaction with the quality of published financial information and continued opposition to standardisation. In evidence presented to the Jenkins Committee, Professor Baxter, a persistent critic of the close regulation of accounting procedures, warned that 'the law should lay down minimum requirements for accounts, but in no way cramp experiment, innovation, and the development of new concepts' (*Minutes*, p.188). He paid tribute to the success achieved by British company law in this respect, and warned against any departure from the traditional cautious approach. In his judgement 'No reform at all would be far better than regulations that start as a floor but end as a ceiling'. In other words, the objection to detailed legal regulations was that they would place accountancy in a statutory straight-jacket. To remain relevant accountancy must respond to changing business needs; a process which might be impeded by detailed legal regulations established in an earlier period and in a different business environment.

The Companies Act 1981. Against this background CA 1981, which introduced standardised formats (now set out in CA 1985, schedule 4, part I) for the use of registered companies, marks a sharp break with tradition. A minor degree of flexibility is, however, allowed under the new system. Companies may choose from two balance sheet formats and four profit and loss account formats. Both balance sheets contain the same headings and the only difference is the method of presentation – format 1 uses a vertical layout and format 2 a horizontal layout. The profit and loss accounts offer a choice between two alternative approaches, each of which may be presented in a vertical or horizontal format. The essential difference between these two approaches is in the method used to classify items of expenditure. Formats 1 (vertical) and 3 (horizontal) analyse expenses by function, and disclose figures for cost of sales, distribution costs and administrative expenses. Format 2 (vertical) and 4 (horizontal) analyse expenses by type of input, and show figures for raw materials, staff costs, depreciation etc.

Apart from the alternative formats, there are a number of other provisions designed to meet the criticism that standardisation prevents innovation and hinders the preparation of accounts in the form most suitable for a particular company. For example, certain items may be combined with others where the amount involved is immaterial, and any item may be shown in greater detail than is given in the standard format. Most important of all, however, is the 'true and fair override'. Directors are *required* to provide additional information, not contained in the standard disclosure requirements, where failure to do so would result in the publication of accounts which do not give a true and fair view. In addition, departure from the standard format is *required* where compliance would prevent a true and fair view from being given. Where this happens, the directors must give details of the departure, reasons for it, and its financial effect by way of note.

CA 1981 introduced less onerous (called 'modified') disclosure requirements for what are described as 'small' and 'medium-sized' companies. These categories of company are identified by reference to the following criteria: turnover, the balance sheet total for gross assets, and the average number of employees. Small companies need file with the registrar neither a profit and loss account nor a directors' report, while the amount of information to be disclosed in the balance sheet and the notes to the accounts is significantly reduced. Medium-sized companies are allowed to file an abridged profit and loss account and need disclose, by way of note, neither turnover nor an analysis of turnover and profit. The concessions apply only to accounts filed with the registrar of companies; full information must be given in the accounts presented to members. The Act has therefore reintroduced the practice of relieving what are often essentially family concerns from the close public scrutiny considered desirable in the case of larger companies.

Origin of CA 1981. We have seen that the Act affected British financial reporting requirements in a manner which could not have been forecast by studying the provisions of earlier Companies Acts and the deliberations of CLACs. The break with tradition occurred because the accounting requirements imposed by CA

1981 (similarly CA 1980) are, in part, continental in origin, and have been adopted as part of the process of harmonising laws within the European Community. In Britain, where the traditional emphasis has been on 'truth and fairness' and 'substance over form', financial reporting developed as an independent discipline with incremental changes made to disclosure requirements as the need was demonstrated. In West Germany (where many of the regulations contained in CA 1981 originated) the position was quite different; detailed formats, disclosure requirements and measurement rules were in operation because financial reporting practices were traditionally controlled by legal (company and tax) regulations.[2]

The European Parliament gave the job of preparing the preliminary draft of the Fourth Directive to a working party chaired by a West German, Professor Elmendorff. It is not therefore surprising that the first version of the Directive, published in 1971, bore a close resemblance to the prevailing West German legal regulations. The true and fair override, which was absent from German law, did not appear in the initial draft. Its introduction was the result of pressure from the British government, where the requirement that accounts should show a 'full and fair' or 'true and correct' or 'true and fair' view has been enshrined in company law since 1844. An important feature of each of these terms is that they remain undefined and leave the final decision to the individual judgement of the accountant.

The valuation rules introduced in 1981 (now contained in CA 1985, schedule 4, part II) also owe their introduction to German law. Many of the rules are familiar and consistent with established British accounting practice, but it is an area of regulation which company law previously chose to avoid. The introduction of such regulations in the endeavour to improve comparability of accounting statements nevertheless makes a great deal of sense. At the same time it must be borne in mind that the new rules inevitably leave major areas still open to the exercise of individual judgement.

Because of their continental origin, some of the regulations were at variance with prevailing accounting practice and have caused difficulties. For example, the requirement to value stock at the lower of cost or net realisable value is seen to conflict with the standard practice of recognising attributable profit on long-term contracts, while the requirement to write off purchased goodwill over its useful life contravened the practice, sometimes followed, of retaining the asset indefinitely at cost. It proved necessary to re-examine the content of certain SSAPs in an attempt to deal with these anomalies.

Although CA 1981 is mainly continental in origin, it must be acknowledged that, since the Jenkins Committee met and reported (1962), there had been a sharp revision of views regarding the appropriate degree of regulation of accounting reports. The series of SSAPs, which aimed for and achieved closer control of reporting procedures than had the series of Recommendations, no doubt helped create a climate favourable to the acceptance of more rigid legal regulations. Certainly the British accountancy profession fought less hard against the Fourth Directive than against earlier attempts to standardise accounting reports. After initially expressing serious misgivings, the profession adopted a more conciliatory policy. This, no doubt, reflected a clear recognition of the political realities. By the time Britain joined the European Community, discussions concerning the form of the Fourth Directive were well advanced and, with the West German officials extremely active, the standardisation concept was firmly entrenched.

Prospectuses[3]

Prospectuses, in the broad sense of the term, were common during early speculative phases, such as occurred at the time of the South Sea Bubble. These documents took the form of newspaper advertisements, hand bills, and circulars of all varieties. Street-hawking was not uncommon. Many of these 'prospectuses' were extremely unreliable.

Errors occur even today, especially when the prospectus is issued by a new company with no experience to draw upon. It is also quite natural for the promoters of a new company to be optimistic about its prospects. Both these possibilities must be accepted. Fraudulent misrepresentation is in a quite different category, but is also a possibility, particularly in the distant past when there were few, if any, regulations in force. Promoters often attempted to convince potential subscribers that the company was more soundly based than was actually the case. One way of doing this was to misrepresent the formation date. For example, a barrister advised the Gladstone Committee that a company, actually created in 1836, claimed that it was established in 1796 (*Minutes*, no.5). Another method of deception, popular in the past, was to insert the names of well known personalities as directors without their consent.

Regulations date from JSCA 1844 which required a copy of every prospectus addressed to the general public to be filed with the registrar. No content was specified and even the filing requirement was repealed by JSCA 1847, because it was considered 'very burdensome to the promoters' (s.4). This action was taken without reference to the registrar of companies who expressed disapproval in evidence presented to the Wilson Committee, 1853 (*Minutes*, no.162). No statutory provisions were in force between 1847 and 1867 when the Companies Act of that year made a modest start at defining the content of the prospectus; the dates and names of parties to any contract entered into by the company prior to the prospectus being issued were to be stated.

Contemporary practices left much to be desired. The case of *Oakes* v *Turquand* (1867) contains an interesting criticism of the prospectus issued by Overend, Gurney & Co., of which William Turquand (the ICAEW's first president, 1880–82) was the official liquidator. Chelmsford, L.C. observed:

> It is said that everything which is stated in the prospectus is literally true, and so it is. But the objection to it is, not that it does not state the truth so far as it goes, but that it conceals most material facts with which the public ought to have been made aquainted, the very concealment of which gives the truth which is told the character of falsehood'.

In essence, the prospectus was technically 'true', in detail, but certainly not 'fair' in the impression it conveyed.

Turquand was invited to give evidence to the Lowe Committee (1877) where he recommended the inclusion of a profit forecast (*Minutes*, no.534). A solicitor giving evidence recommended that, in the case of companies already in existence, the prospectus should include a copy of either the balance sheet submitted to the last general meeting or one made up to a date not more than one month before the issue of the prospectus (*Minutes*, no.824). These proposals were not adopted. The Directors Liability Act 1890 made directors and promoters liable for misstatements even though they were not fraudulently made; in 1948 this liability was extended to experts, such as accountants, whose statements were included in the prospectus.

The last quarter of the nineteenth century saw the conversion of many family firms into public companies and the first important spate of merger activity. The prospectuses issued to advertise new issues usually contained an auditor's report despite the absence of statutory regulations. No doubt the promoters judged that its inclusion increased the prospects of a successful issue. Unilever, then Lever Brothers Limited, was first introduced to the investing public in 1894. The document issued in support of an invitation to subscribe for 5 per cent cumulative preference shares to be listed on the London Stock Exchange, although brief, contained the main essentials. The report by Cooper Brothers & Co. (reproduced in Hodgkins, p.40) ran as follows:

> We have examined the books and accounts of Lever Brothers, and Lever Brothers Ltd, soap manufacturers, of Port Sunlight, near Birkenhead for the seven years ending 31 December 1893.
>
> We have acted as auditors of the company since its formation in 1890.
>
> The business has increased in extent in each succeeding year, and the annual average net profit has been–

For the seven years	£66,331	per annum
For the last five years	£79,561	per annum
For the last three years	£111,013	per annum
For the year 1893	£147,250	

> Interest on Partners' and borrowed capital has not been charged against the profit.
>
> The whole of the outlay on advertising has been deducted and provision, in our opinion ample, has been written off for depreciation.
>
> The books show that in 1893, goods were invoiced to more than sixteen thousand customers in the United Kingdom, in addition to customers in the Colonies and foreign countries. The total sales exceeded in amount one million pounds sterling.

In evidence given to the Davey Committee (1895), the Portsmouth Chamber of Commerce recommended that, where a company was established to take over an existing business, the prospectus should contain the most recent statement of the old company's assets and liabilities and a statement of its profits over the last three years, each certified by a professional accountant (p.120).

The requirements introduced in 1900 were closely in line with the committee's more modest recommendations. These included proposals for the prospectus to be filed with the registrar, and for the names and addresses of the auditors (if any) of the company to be stated. An interesting curiosity is that, in earlier times, unqualified individuals described as 'auditors' were sometimes listed in the prospectus to provide an element of window dressing. In view of the fact that CA 1900 specified no professional qualifications it has been said, perhaps a little unfairly, that statutory approval was now provided for this practice (Hein, p.318).

In 1907, a requirement for companies to file a statement in *lieu* of a prospectus, where a prospectus was not filed, was introduced to cope with the common practice of avoiding the provisions of CA 1900 by issuing shares to the promoters of the company, or the vendors of property transferred to the company, who, in turn, resold the shares either privately or on the stock market.

Between 1908–28, some companies avoided issuing a prospectus by selling all the shares to an issuing house which then sold them to the general public. The document used for this purpose was called an 'offer for sale'. From 1929 any document by which a company's securities were offered to the general public, including any advertisement of an issuing house, was to be deemed a prospectus issued by the company itself and subject to similar legal requirements.

A ploy used in the 1920s to conceal falling profits was to publish the *average* figure reported over, say, the previous five years. In evidence presented to the Greene Committee (1926), the SIAA recommended that this practice should be outlawed (*Minutes*, p.lxxxii). The Law Society specifically recommended that the actual profits reported and dividends paid for each of the last five years, or since the date of incorporation whichever was the shorter, should be reported on by the auditors; also that there should be an accountant's report containing similar information about the profits of any business to be purchased from the proceeds of the issue (*Minutes*, p.xlv). These proposals were accepted and enacted, except that the period to be covered was specified as three years rather than five. The Law Society's further recommendation that the auditor's report and the accountant's report should be made by a chartered or incorporated accountant was not accepted at this stage.

A wide range of proposals were made to the Cohen Committee (1945), many of which were included in CA 1948. This resulted in a significant extension of the auditor's and accountant's reports. In particular: the period covered by the profit record was extended to five years; the most recently published statement of assets and liabilities are now required for both the company making the issue and any company to be taken over with the proceeds; and the rates of dividend paid on each class of share over each of the last five years are to be given. Where the company issuing the prospectus is a holding company, similar information is required in respect of the consolidated results. It was also decided that the reports should be made by members of a professional body approved by the BOT.

Recommendations on accountant's reports in relation to prospectuses were issued by the ICAEW's Taxation and Research Committee in 1949 (No.13) and 1953 (No.16). These recognised that figures, previously published, might require amendment for inclusion in the prospectus in view of the fact that the document is used as the basis for assessing future prospects. Matters which give rise to the need for adjustments include: the availability of new information (e.g. where a material bad debt had been suffered but not provided for when the accounts were initially issued); the existence of non-recurrent sources of revenue and expenditure; changes in the accounting principles employed; and the failure to comply with accepted accounting principles. Additional disclosures were also required, e.g. of depreciation charged during the period covered by the prospectus. The London Stock Exchange subsequently introduced requirements for the auditor's and accountant's reports to cover a ten-year period, and for the disclosure of the amounts of the directors' emoluments paid and waived.

The contents of the prospectus are today regulated by section 56 and schedule 3 of CA 1985, as expanded by schedule 2 of the Stock Exchange's *Admission of Securities to Listing* (the Yellow Book).

18

Accounting for Subsidiaries and Associated Companies

Economic developments

The unincorporated enterprise and the proprietorship company remained dominant in most industries until the last quarter of the nineteenth century. These, today, remain important features of the business scene, but the large scale limited liability company accounts for the major proportion of economic activity undertaken in the private sector of the economy. One advantage enjoyed by this type of company is its access to a wider range of possible sources of finance, and this has facilitated growth, either by extending its existing business activities (internal growth), or by merging the activities of two or more separate legal entities (external growth). Early spurts of merger activity occurred in Britain between 1895–1902 and 1916–22.

The first phase of merger activity (1895–1902) was mainly confined to textiles, brewing, iron and steel, cement, wallpaper and tobacco. Combinations normally took the form of asset acquisitions, though the industrial-type holding company (the operating company which also holds shares in other companies) did begin to emerge around the turn of the century. The investment holding company (a non-operating company whose assets consist exclusively of shareholdings in other companies) was not unknown at this time but became more common during the second merger period; the Nobel Dynamite Trust, a forerunner of Nobel Industries, was an isolated example of an investment holding company formed prior to the First World War. Combinations in the second phase of merger activity (1916–22) mainly affected iron and steel, armament and associated engineering, electrical, chemical, lead manufacture, photographic materials, textiles and the food trade.

A combination based on the purchase of assets produces an immediate accounting problem; it is necessary to set a value on individual assets taken over for inclusion in the acquiring company's books. Once this has been done, however, the assets are accounted for in the usual way. Where the combination is based on the purchase of shares, the total price paid is recorded in the acquiring company's balance sheet as the cost of the investment, and no further accounting entries initially need to be made. But the following question subsequently arises: 'What additional information should be made available to the shareholders of the holding company (broadly defined as a company which holds more than 50 per cent of the equity shares of another company) to enable them to assess the value of their indirect interest in the subsidiary?' This chapter examines the British response to this problem.

Legal entity based accounts

Financial reporting requirements, at the beginning of the twentieth century, focused on companies as separate legal entities. CA 1900 implied a requirement for directors to present an audited balance sheet (the 'legal' balance sheet) to shareholders attending the AGM,[1] while CA 1907 required non-private companies to file an audited statement 'in the form of a balance sheet' with the registrar of companies (s.21). The 1907 Act established definite incentives for the formation of holding companies because directors, wishing to conceal financial information from investors or the general public, could form a subsidiary company to undertake some of the holding company's business activities. Indeed, exemption from the filing requirement was soon described as the main advantage of incorporating as a private company.[2]

The problem went even deeper. Because subsidiaries were separate legal entities, their results were accounted for by the holding company on the cash basis. The investment was recorded at cost and profits were reflected in the holding company's accounts only when a dividend transfer was made. Even then it was unusual for the amount of the dividend to be disclosed separately. Often there was no similarity whatsoever either between the book value and real value of the investment or between the dividends received and the subsidiary's actual results.

Legal entity based financial reports therefore provided ample scope for profit smoothing. When the reported results of the holding company were buoyant, profits were 'stored up' in the books of the subsidiary and, at the same time, provision might be made for losses incurred by another member of the group. In the reverse situation, large dividend transfers could be made by the subsidiary to boost the reported results of the holding company. Clearly, the usefulness of accounting information as a basis for assessing financial performance was, in these circumstances, undermined. The need for a new method of financial reporting was obvious to some, but the response of the business community and accountancy profession was slow.

The problem recognised

In December 1922 Sir Gilbert Garnsey presented a paper entitled 'Holding Companies and their Published Accounts' to the London members of the ICAEW. The lecture was published in *The Accountant* and, later, in book form. Garnsey emphasised the accounting problems presented by this relatively new form of business organisation, and expressed considerable doubt whether publication of only the holding company's legal balance sheet was satisfactory. He believed that it should be supplemented by sufficient additional data to enable users to observe the financial position of the group as a whole.

Garnsey proposed three alternative methods: to publish also the separate balance sheets and profit and loss accounts of each subsidiary; to publish a separate summary combining the assets and liabilities of all the subsidiaries; and to publish, either separately or in addition to the holding company's balance sheet, a consolidated balance sheet and profit and loss account of the entire undertaking, i.e the profits, losses, assets and liabilities of the holding company and its subsidiaries would be combined as if they formed a single entity.

Garnsey's lecture is an important landmark in the development of group accounting in Britain. Because he was a partner with a leading firm of chartered accountants (Price, Waterhouse & Co.), presenting his views to the London members of the ICAEW in a forceful and lucid fashion, he could not be ignored. The lecture provoked a great deal of controversy in the financial press but, in a climate of professional conservatism and general complacency with the quality of reporting standards, his efforts did not, immediately, have a dramatic effect.

Group accounts; some early examples

The earliest British example of a consolidated statement, known to this writer, was published by the directors of the Pearson & Knowles Coal and Iron Co. Ltd in 1910. The directors first considered the possibility of publishing a consolidated balance sheet in 1907, and a draft statement was prepared. For some reason the plan was abandoned, but it was later revived when the company needed capital to finance the establishment of a new company. The prospectus issued in 1910 drew attention to an important limitation of the legal balance sheet, namely that it failed to give a proper indication of the value of the company's investment in its wholly owned subsidiary. Clearly, the intention was to disclose a strong financial position in order to make the share issue appear more attractive. The directors must have been pleased with the result; from 1910 a consolidated balance sheet was published as part of the company's annual accounts.

A better known pioneer of group accounting is Nobel Industries. A statement displaying a summary of the group's assets and liabilities was included in the 1922 chairman's report. Sir Josiah Stamp, a distinguished economist and civil servant, and a stern critic of the secretive accounting practices employed during the 1920s, was secretary of Nobel Industries. It is likely that he encouraged the directors to improve the company's reporting practices.

The number of companies publishing group accounting information increased at a modest rate throughout the 1920s, and they experimented with a variety of reporting procedures additional to those proposed by Garnsey. These included publication of a consolidated balance sheet *instead* of the legal balance sheet and use of the equity method of accounting. The equity method involves the following relatively simple adjustments: the investing company's share of the profit or loss of the subsidiary company, for the year, is entered in the profit and loss account; in the balance sheet, the holding company's share of post-acquisition retained profits is added to both the cost of the investment and the reserves of the group. The relative popularity of the various methods changed considerably during the 1920s. The equity method received a great deal of support to begin with but, by the end of the 1920s, the publication of a supplementary consolidated balance sheet was the most favoured option.

Greene Committee

The accounting practices of holding companies were examined by the Greene Committee (1926). There was some support for the statutory imposition of disclosure requirements. For example, the Scottish professional bodies thought it desirable for holding companies to publish either separate statements for each subsidiary or a summary of their results. Surprisingly, Garnsey was not invited to give evidence, though views were sought from a number of other leading accountants, including Francis D'Arcy Cooper who was a powerful adversary of Garnsey on the issue of whether group accounts should be published.

It is likely that the committee attached a great deal of weight to D'Arcy Cooper's evidence in view of the fact that he was chairman of Britain's largest conglomerate, Lever Brothers Ltd. His company used the equity method to account for the results of subsidiaries but, in other respects, it was by no means at the forefront in developing financial reporting procedures. In the balance sheet for 1923, an entry for the company's aggregate investment in 'associated' companies comprised over £54m among assets which totalled just under £68m. *The Economist* sarcastically observed that 'a little more information here would be welcome' (1924, p.733). Two years later the same journal commented that 'the reports of Messrs Lever Brothers have been distinguished by obscurity and the scantiness of the information which they have afforded to shareholders' (1926, p.724). Not surprisingly, D'Arcy Cooper opposed legislation commenting that 'The matter is one, I submit, between the shareholders and the directors' (*Minutes*, p.lx).

In the face of further opposition from the Law Society and the ICAEW, the committee concluded that 'In view of the divergence of opinion on this and cognate matters we only find ourselves able to make recommendations of a quite limited character' (para.71). The committee's main recommendations, incorporated in CA 1928, were for the balance sheet disclosure of investments in subsidiaries, amounts due to subsidiaries and amounts due from subsidiaries. In addition, there was a requirement to state how the profits and losses of subsidiaries had been dealt with in the accounts of the holding company. Businessmen soon realised that there was no need to quantify the amount involved; the legal obligation was usually satisfied by merely drawing attention to the fact that reported profits had been computed after taking credit for dividends received from subsidiaries and making provision for their losses. A quantitative indication was rarely provided of the relationship between profits earned by subsidiaries and dividends received from them, or between losses suffered and provided for.

Slow progress

The rate of adoption of group accounting procedures was slow, particularly compared with the US where, by 1910, consolidated accounts were a common feature of financial reporting. It has been suggested that one barrier to progress was the absence of sufficient expertise, among accountants, in preparing these statements. Certainly it was a neglected area in professional examinations; candidates sitting the ICAEW's examinations, for example, were first required to prepare a consolidated balance sheet in 1925, and such questions did not feature regularly in that examination until much later. Some support for the idea of a possible link between slow development and a lack of professional competence was provided by the observation, made to the Greene Committee, that 'infrequent use of consolidated reports was due to the fact that they were difficult to prepare' (*Minutes*, p.167).

The general reluctance of British management voluntarily to publish group accounting information was undoubtedly another important factor, despite D'Arcy Cooper's assertion that 'if directors considered that the publication of an amalgamated balance sheet was in the interests of their shareholders, they would no doubt publish it' (*The Times*, 3 June 1925). The following comment made by Garnsey, six years later, appears more consistent with the available evidence: 'perhaps the real opposition to any but the most essential changes in the form of the published accounts often comes from boards of directors who are not all imbued with the desire to give their shareholders as much information as possible' (1931, p.103). The scope which the traditional legal entity based accounts provided for concealing information on assets and liabilities, and smoothing the pattern of reported profits has already been mentioned. Indeed, the Greene Committee agreed that one of the main reasons for structuring business activity through subsidiary companies was to avoid 'disclosure of matters relating to what in substance is the business of the parent company' (para.87).

Company accounts are, of course, primarily the directors' responsibility, but accountants undoubtedly exert a considerable influence over their form and content. No attempt is made to rank managers and accountants in an order of responsibility for the slow rate of adoption, but it does seem that the British accountant took on a less vigorous role than might have been expected. Whereas practising accountants in the US were actively delivering lectures and writing books on this topic during the first decade of the twentieth century, British accountants remained silent, at least in public. One reason for this might have been an indigenous prejudice against change, another that the British accountant considered any strong initiative to be unprofessional, and a third that he simply did not consider it an important problem.

The existence of perceived, if not real, legal barriers also delayed change. Prior to 1928 there was no requirement that the shareholders' statutory balance sheet should be confined to the strict legal entity, but this obligation was usually implied by the company's articles; Table A's model provision, usually adopted, stated that the balance sheet should set out the 'property and liabilities of *the company*'. Similarly, CA 1907 required *the company's* balance sheet to be filed with the registrar (s.21). CA 1928 used a similar wording ('assets and libilities of *the company*') to imply a statutory obligation for a legal entity based balance sheet to be presented to shareholders.

None of these provisions, of course, prevented directors from either presenting supplementary consolidated accounts to shareholders or filing them with the registrar. However, directors might well have been reluctant to risk confusing users by publishing two balance sheets; certainly the more recent proposal to publish inflation adjusted accounts as well as historical cost accounts was resisted on these very grounds. Emphasis on the legal entity basis is, therefore, likely to have delayed the publication of supplementary consolidated accounts; a practice which did not gain momentum until the 1930s.

A limitation of consolidated accounts stressed by early writers is that they are of little use to creditors in judging solvency, since their claims are restricted to the assets of the legal entity which has received the money or the goods. The consolidated balance sheet does not distinguish between the assets of individual companies, and this makes it impossible for creditors to identify the security for their debt.

Lack of demand is, however, the most important single factor explaining the delay. The information requirements of the British investing public do appear to have been less exacting than, for instance, those of its counterpart in the US. This reflects the British tradition of allowing directors a free hand to manage the company's affairs, rather than saddling them with disclosure requirements which might hamper entrepreneurial initiative. For protection, shareholders instead relied principally on the statutory audit, with the right to obtain information by asking pertinent questions at the AGM available as an additional minor safeguard.

Regulations introduced

The publication of supplementary consolidated statements slowly gained ground during the 1930s, in common with other financial reporting developments. The effect of the Royal Mail case on the use of secret reserves has received the bulk of the accounting historians' attention (see Chapter 12). However, that case involved an intricate web of companies enabling Kylsant to publish information which materially misrepresented the group's financial results. For example, in the absence of a requirement to publish consolidated statements, he was able to inflate reported profits by making inter-company transfers of dividends and conceal the massive overall gearing of the group. These revelations underlined some of the limitations of legal entity based accounts and motivated some companies to publish consolidated statements. A further impetus for this process was provided by the 'trail blazing' accounts published by the Dunlop Rubber Co. in 1933 on the initiative of De Paula (see Chapter 11).

From 1939 the London Stock Exchange required directors of holding companies, seeking a quotation, to undertake to issue shareholders with a consolidated balance sheet and profit and loss account. Recommendation 7, issued by the ICAEW in 1944, provided formal encouragement for *all* holding companies to publish group accounts, normally in the form of consolidated statements. Statutory support for these procedures received general, though not unanimous, approval in submissions made to the Cohen Committee. The committee's proposals, which adopted the essential features of Recommendation 7, were included in CA 1948.

Post-war economic developments

Except for the busy period 1918 to 1922 there were relatively few takeover bids during the inter-war years. This has been attributed to the fact that a significant proportion of most companies' shares remained in the hands of private families and company directors. Where takeover bids did occur, they were normally made through the directors, and in those few cases where shareholders did attempt to intervene, they do not seem to have been successful. The justification for the directors conducting negotiations was to preserve secrecy. A reason put forward for the lack of shareholder success and for the shortage of contested bids was the poor quality of the financial information made generally available.

For a variety of reasons business combinations have occurred on a vast scale during the post-war period. Rising affluence, which helped develop markets both at home and abroad, underlined the advantages of the large unit which could exploit operational techniques based on the division of labour and economies of scale. Government legislation in the 1950s helped remove restrictive practices and, unintentionally, encouraged combinations in order to avoid the increased level of competition which would otherwise result (Hannah, pp.167–69). An important factor facilitating business combinations, during this period, was the gradual weakening of the degree of control exerted by families of the original entrepreneur.

A specific incentive for takeovers, which began to gain pace during the 1950s, was share price undervaluation caused partly by post-war government restrictions on the level of dividends, and partly because managers, shareholders and the financial markets were slow to become aware of the effect of inflation on property values. Charles Clore, a 'self-made man', became famous as a result of a series of massive investments in companies which possessed under-utilised assets. Starting from an ice rink in Cricklewood, he became the effective owner of a vast array of shoe shops, stores, car distributors and engineering companies. His activities were matched by Jim Slater, and many others, in the 1960s.

During the post-war period it became the usual practice for expansion to be undertaken by bidding for and acquiring shares in other companies. It has also been found convenient to organise different divisions of large companies as separate subsidiaries. The fact that nearly all the larger public companies are today holding companies has naturally resulted in a great deal of attention being devoted to the appropriate method of accounting for their operations.

Acquisition method and merger method

The purchase of shares in a subsidiary may be paid for either in cash, or by issuing shares or loan stock in the holding company (a share exchange), or by any combination of these three possible forms of consideration. Where the transaction is entirely for cash, the terms 'acquisition' or 'takeover' are considered appropriate as the former shareholders of the subsidiary company have no further involvement with the activities of the group. Where an exchange of shares occurs, the term 'merger' often describes the event better, particularly where the companies are of roughly equal size. In the latter case, shareholders are said to 'pool' their interests and become joint shareholders in the holding company so that no resources leave the group.

The accounting methods used to report these events assume, in the case of an acquisition, that an 'arms length' transaction has occurred; in the case of a merger the accounting is done as if the companies have always been members of the same group. These contrasting circumstances can result in the adoption of very different methods for recognising profits and valuing assets:

> *Profits* Under the acquisition method pre-acquisition profits of the subsidiary are treated as capital. Under the merger method pre-acquisition profits remain available for distribution on the grounds that the subsidiary's former shareholders continue as joint investors in the enlarged group. Indeed the consolidated profit and loss account includes the new subsidiary's profits for the whole year even though the acquisition is unlikely to have been made on the first day of the accounting period.

> *Assets* Under the acquisition method the purchase consideration is recorded at market price (giving rise to a share premium account), and the subsidiary's individual assets are re-stated at their 'fair values' for the purpose of preparing the consolidated accounts. This usually results in the creation of a figure for goodwill representing the difference between the two totals. Under the merger method, securities issued as purchase consideration are recorded at their nominal value, assets remain at their existing book values (subject to necessary adjustments to apply common accounting policies), and no goodwill arises on consolidation.

Advantages accruing to management and/or the shareholders, as the result of applying the merger method, are that the pre-acquisition profits of an acquired subsidiary remain available for distribution, and higher profits are reported in future years because depreciation is charged on existing book values instead of on the, usually higher, fair values. Furthermore, the need to depreciate consolidated goodwill or write it off against reserves does not arise.

The merger method has long been popular in the US. It was also used to account for a number of well-publicised British mergers in the late 1960s and early 1970s, e.g. GEC-AEI (1968), BMC-Leyland (1968) and Trust House-Forte (1970). Indeed, an exposure draft on the subject was issued in 1971, but doubts about the legality of the method under CA 1948 led to its withdrawal. The preparation of group accounts on the acquisition basis was given formal recognition by SSAP 14 (Group Accounts, 1978), and the decision in the tax case *Shearer* v *Bercain* (1980) confirmed the suspicion that merger accounting did in fact contravene CA 1948. The grounds for the decision were that the the 1948 Act obliged companies to record shares issued, as consideration, at their market price (the procedure used under the acquisition method) rather than at their nominal value (the procedure used under the merger method).

CA 1981 legalised merger accounting in certain circumstances, and gave retrospective approval to companies which had previously adopted this procedure. SSAP 23 (Accounting for Acquisitions and Mergers, 1985) fleshed out the bare legal provisions. This Standard permits, but does not oblige, holding companies to adopt merger accounting where certain conditions are met, including the following: an offer is made for all the equity and voting shares; at least 90 per cent of the fair value of the consideration for equity shares acquired is in the form of equity shares issued by the holding company; and at least 90 per cent of the target company's shareholders accept the offer.

In view of the advantages of merger accounting, listed above, it is not surprising that some companies choose to use this option where the various conditions are satisfied. A further, even more popular, option has been to use 'merger relief', introduced by CA 1981, s.37 (now CA 1985, s.131) to combine certain aspects of acquisition accounting and merger accounting. Section 131 allows companies to record purchase consideration (shares and/or loan stock) at par value where the circumstances giving rise to a merger exist, i.e. a share premium account does not have to be created. The accounting procedure employed may be described broadly as follows: the purchase consideration (shares and/or loan stock) is recorded at par value; the tangible and identifiable intangible assets (goodwill is ignored) taken over are reported in the consolidated accounts at fair value; and the difference is credited to a merger reserve. There is a strong suspicion that the merger reserve is sometimes used to make generous provision for the reorganisation costs associated with the merger and to write down current assets to a conservative value. This procedure, an example of what is known as 'the big bath', is designed to help the directors report favourable results in the years immediately following the merger.

Associated companies

During the 1960s it became increasingly common for companies to conduct part of their activities through other companies in which less than a 50 per cent equity interest was acquired and, therefore, escaped the group accounting provisions of the CA 1948. Effective control was exercised, however, either through some form of partnership agreement or because the remaining shareholdings were widely dispersed. Fuller disclosure was demanded in order to remove obvious opportunities for investing companies to manipulate their reported results in the same way as had holding companies during the inter-war period. The matter was referred to the Accounting Standards Committee (ASC) which concluded that, where management assumes a measure of direct responsibility for the performance of an 'associated company' by actively participating in its commercial and financial policy making decisions, the investing company should present a full account to its members.

The committee decided that the objective of full disclosure could be achieved by extending conventional group accounting procedures to incorporate information concerning the activities of associated companies. This obliged the committee, first to define an associated company and, secondly, to decide what additional information should be published. The answers to these questions are contained in SSAP 1 entitled Accounting for the Results of Associated Companies (1971). An associated company is broadly defined as one where the investing company is in a position to exercise significant influence over its affairs. This is presumed to be possible where the investing company owns more than 20 per cent of the equity voting rights and plays an active part in decision making, usually through representation on the board of directors. The method chosen to account for associates was the equity basis, i.e. the procedure used by some companies to account for subsidiary companies during the 1920s but which went out of fashion.

Review

The present system of group accounting has evolved gradually during the twentieth century. It is a good example of the development of accounting procedures and regulations to cope with new circumstances, and it illustrates the ability of pressure groups to resist successfully their statutory imposition. It is interesting, with the benefit of hindsight, to contrast the relative strengths of the arguments of those who opposed legislation, in the 1920s, such as the ICAEW and D'Arcy Cooper, with reformists such as Garnsey. Garnsey's views better stood the test of time and it seems reasonable to conclude that the various objections to the introduction of group accounting requirements, when closely examined, often amounted to little more than what Watts and Zimmerman would consider excuses designed to conceal 'naked self-interest'.

The history of group accounting also illustrates the impact of regulations on financial reporting practices. Emphasis given to legal entity based financial statements helped deter the development of more relevant financial procedures up to, at least, the 1930s, while CA 1929 quite possibly discouraged the further use of equity accounting for subsidiaries.[3] CA 1948 provided a strong impetus for acquisition accounting, whereas the 1981 Act reintroduced merger accounting as a possible alternative.

One may assume that the procedures described in this chapter were devised, by and large, to help ensure the publication of more reliable data as the basis for investment decisions. On the whole this objective has been achieved, though arbitrary definitions have produced scope for window dressing. To give a single example: although a more subjective test is identified by SSAP 1, the 20 per cent equity interest is usually the main criterion used to decide whether shares in another company are to be accounted for as an associate, on the accruals basis, or as an investment, on the cash basis. Knowledge that an associate has run into difficulties, and is due to report poor results, can cause management to sell a few shares and reduce its interest to, say, 19.5 per cent. The associated company is then treated as an investment unless a determined, and courageous,[4] auditor insists on compliance with the spirit of the law. If results subsequently improve, the investing company can re-enter the market. Similar adjustments may be made around the 50 per cent level of shareholding, depending on whether the holding company wants to incorporate the assets and liabilities of its subsidiary in the consolidated accounts.

19

Recommendations and Standards

Limitations of published accounts

Accounting statements have a comforting appearance of complete accuracy because precise figures are given for each of the items reported in the profit and loss account and balance sheet, and because the use of double entry causes the principal accounting statements to articulate with one another and balance. The economic reality is very different and, despite improvements designed to meet earlier criticisms, published accounts remain under attack. In the early part of the twentieth century their informational value suffered because of obscurity, excessive summarisation, the use of secret reserves, the failure to publish a profit and loss account, and the absence of group accounts. Today's perceived deficiencies include the lack of forecast information, the omission of assets and liabilities from the balance sheet, the failure to take account of changing prices, and the increasing use of what has become known as 'creative accounting', i.e. the deliberate selection of accounting practices designed to transmit a message which management wants user groups to believe, rather than to portray what has actually happened.

Over the years financial reporting practices have been the subject of growing criticism in the accounting literature. A feature of accounting texts, published up to the 1930s, was that they accepted existing practice and concentrated mainly on explaining how the job should be done. It is also probably fair to say that these writers were doers rather than thinkers, although there were exceptions. Dicksee and De Paula (profiled in Kitchen and Parker, p.51 and p.81) strongly criticised contemporary practices and made great efforts to bring about improvement. But even these individuals accepted the basic features of the existing system and were mainly concerned with refining it and ensuring that best practices received general support. Wholesale critics of conventional accounting practices such as Sweeney and MacNeal, in the US, and R.S. Edwards in Britain, began to voice their opinions in the 1930s.

During the post-war period there has been a reappraisal of what has been described as

> the traditional view that there should be a single set of financial statements prepared on a single principle (such as the traditional historical cost method), culminating in a single profit figure (the 'bottom line' of the income statement) which encapsulates the total performance of the business entity during a period (Tweedie and Whittington, p.2).

Advocates of dramatic changes include Edwards and Bell (current value), Chambers (net realisable value), Baxter (deprival value), and T.A.Lee (cash flow accounting). Other financial reporting developments which have received enthusiastic support, from certain quarters, include the publication of profit and cash forecasts, segmental reports, value added statements, future investment plans, dividend policies, and special purpose accounting reports.

Theoretical framework

Some argue that financial reports are deficient due to the absence of a sound conceptual basis underpinning their preparation. During the twentieth century there have been numerous attempts to construct a general theory of accounting against which present practices might be judged and which might form the basis for the development of new practices and procedures. The first organised attempts in Britain to develop a framework of accounting principles were made by the Accounting Research Association (ARA) and the SIAA.

The ARA was formed in 1936 on the initiative of a number of teachers at the LSE (including R.S.Edwards) and a few practitioners. Its first meeting was addressed by Sir (later Lord) Josiah Stamp. Over the next five years the ARA made some significant contributions to the literature, although it is doubtful whether these much influenced professional people, who, in the main, ignored theory and considered the profit figure to be an automatic product of the double entry process. Activities were interrupted by the war and much of the impetus was lost.

William Baxter (who contributed to the series of pamphlets published by ARA) picked up its work when appointed professor of accounting at the LSE in 1947. David Solomons also joined the staff at around this time and began his influential contributions to the history and theory of accounting. Both were active in the Association of University Teachers of Accounting (now British Accounting Association) formed in 1946, and they edited much needed volumes entitled *Studies in Accounting* (Baxter, 1950), and *Studies in Costing* (Solomons, 1952). Harold Edey joined the LSE in 1949 and, 'under the guidance of Baxter and Edey [Solomons moved to Bristol University in 1955] the interests of successive members of staff have centred on the theoretical foundations of financial and management accounting' (Dev, p.7).

The SIAA established a research committee (1935) to stimulate interest in current and future professional developments. It sponsored a number of useful publications, but perhaps its most significant contribution was the establishment of the journal, *Accounting Research*, in 1948. The aim was to 'make a real contribution to the theoretical and practical development of accountancy'. The journal was extremely successful and brought together articles and book reviews written by professional and academic accountants from all over the world. The SIAA also created the Stamp-Martin chair of accounting (1952) in honour of Lord Stamp and the SIAA's former president Sir James Martin. The chair was tenable at Incorporated Accountants Hall and Sewell Bray was appointed the first, and only, professor.

It is thought that the activities of the SIAA's research committee did much to help establish accounting as a respectable university subject in Britain, and to emphasise the importance of continuing accounting education which should not stop with the final professional examination. The committee was disbanded in 1957 when the SIAA merged with the chartered bodies. The ICAEW had provided no encouragement for the ARA and it was equally uninterested in the activities of the research committee. *Accounting Research*, rumoured to have been considered of no practical relevance by some of the ICAEW's leaders, survived integration just one year (Zeff, 1972, p.27). The Stamp-Martin chair was also discontinued, and the Institute's scant regard for academic accountancy was further reflected in *The Report of the Committee on*

Education and Training (1961) which preferred correspondence courses to university tuition.

The late 1960s and early 1970s saw a turning point in the profession's, and especially the ICAEW's, attitude towards the *academe*. Edey was appointed to the ASC in 1969 and to the ICAEW's Council in 1970. A revival of interest in the conceptual framework was indicated by the president's assertion (1971) that 'much more time and effort must be devoted to fundamental research into the theory and practice aspects of accountancy' (quoted in Zeff, 1972, p.49). The journal *Accounting Research* was resurrected and renamed *Accounting and Business Research*. It is thought that this action owed much to the efforts of Bertram Nelson who was a strong supporter of academic education; he had been president of the SIAA, 1954–56, and an ICAEW Council member when *ABR* was launched. In 1971 a further decision was made to establish a chair of accounting at the University of Lancaster where finance was also provided for a research centre in accounting. Edward Stamp was appointed to the chair and made director of the centre; Sir Ronald Leach, who had entered into a fierce public dispute with Stamp a couple of years earlier (see later in this chapter), became the chairman of the centre's board of trustees.

One of the most ambitious schemes for improving financial reporting practices has been the attempt by the Financial Accounting Standards Board (FASB – the US standard setting body) to develop a 'conceptual framework' for accounting defined as 'a coherent system of interrelated objectives and fundamentals that can lead to consistent standards and that prescribes the nature, function and limits of financial accounting and financial statements' (1976, p.2). The idea is the creation of a general theory which can provide 'all the answers'.

In the late 1970s, the ICAEW's research committee commissioned Richard Macve to conduct a survey of the large amount of work undertaken under the auspices of the FASB. His report (1981) shows that, despite a great deal of research having been undertaken and money spent since the mid-1970s, there is little evidence of real progress having been made. The report also helps to demonstrate the unlikelihood of ever establishing a conceptual framework which will serve as a panacea for the solution of accounting problems. The more realistic conclusions are that accounting is rather less scientific than some seem to have believed, and that to report complex economic matters, effectively, is extremely difficult and inevitably involves exercising a great deal of subjective judgement. This has now also been recognised in the US where, since publication of the disappointing Statement of Financial Accounting Concepts 5 (1984), little further progress is expected.

User decision oriented approach

A less ambitious, and more practical, approach towards constructing a 'theory' of financial reporting is contained in *The Corporate Report*, a discussion paper issued by the ASC in 1975. The approach involves identifying users of accounts, assessing what information they require to reach decisions, and deciding how this information might best be provided. Views have developed over the years about which groups possess a legitimate interest in the financial affairs of limited companies. It was agreed at a fairly early stage that shareholders and creditors fell into this category, but the recognition of much broader obligations is a relatively recent development. *The Corporate Report* broke new ground by giving explicit recognition to the existence of *five* additional user groups; employees, the government, financial analysts and advisers, the business contact group (including customers and competitors), and the general public.

The report's emphasis on greater disclosure, including statements of future prospects and corporate objectives, initially stimulated a great deal of controversy and opposition from the business community. It was overshadowed by the issue of the government sponsored Sandilands report, in the same year, and any momentum was lost as the inflation accounting issue took centre stage. It has been suggested that the diversion of attention from the broad issues raised in *The Corporate Report* was greeted with great relief by some of the profession's leaders (Peasnell, p.246)

Interest in the user decision oriented approach is mainly confined, at present, to the academic community. Little progress has been made in assessing how the broad informational requirements identified by the report might be met, and how the diverse and sometimes conflicting priorities of particular user groups might be satisfied by publishing a single general purpose corporate report. The user decision oriented approach to theory construction therefore appears promising but much more work needs to be done. The result has been a continued allegiance to what might be described as the *inductive* approach to theory construction. The practice of company law amendment committees was to observe existing practices, identify those considered to represent best practice, and make their adoption a statutory requirement. To a large extent this is the approach which has been adopted and extended by the accounting bodies when issuing Recommendations and SSAPs.

Recommendations on accounting principles

Up until 1942 the ICAEW devoted its attention almost entirely to administrative matters. Its main contribution to the development of technical competence, among its members, was the organisation of professional examinations. No technical material was published; guidance was limited to the publication of counsel's opinion on controversial issues, and the unofficial comments made, or papers published, by leaders of the profession. The failure to take a stronger initiative in the regulation of financial reporting procedures was particularly unhelpful in view of the profession's consistent opposition to the imposition of statutory regulations and, in the evidence presented to successive CLACs, it was usually left to non-accountants to put forward radical proposals for reform (see Chapter 16).

The establishment of the Taxation and Financial Relations Committee in 1942 (re-named the Taxation and Research Committee in 1949 and the Technical Advisory Committee in 1964) represented a major break with the tradition of non-interference. Part of the reason for the change of heart was press criticism, in *The Economist*, of the professional bodies' failure to provide help and advice to accountants in 'the front line' (1942, p.392). The committee consisted of both practising and non-practising accountants and its purpose was to offer guidance to members about procedures which it considered to represent best practice.

Between 1942–69, 29 Recommendations were issued; their purpose was to identify acceptable accounting practices and, thereby, encourage their adoption. The committee was extremely active from the outset; six Recommendations were issued by the end of 1943. The last of these dealt with Reserves and Provisions; the topic which had caused the accountancy profession so much embarrassment in the Royal Mail case (see Chapter 12). In the aftermath of this case there was general agreement that the use of secret reserves to bolster current earnings should be disclosed, but disagreement persisted about the need to reveal the creation and existence of reserves at the balance sheet date. The new Recommendation required full disclosure of movements on reserves and of the balance at the accounting date. Recommendation 7, which favoured the publication of consolidated accounts by holding companies, further demonstrated the ICAEW's willingness to issue guidelines which were ahead of prevailing practice (see Chapter 18).

It was, however, the ICAEW's proposals for the valuation of trading stock that the committee's chairman (De Paula) hailed as 'the most revolutionary of any of the recommendations issued to date by the Council' (quoted in Zeff, 1972, p.16). The crucial point seems to have been that, although it permitted various methods of cost identification, it emphasised the need to apply the chosen procedure consistently over time. The aim was to discourage companies from switching between accounting methods in order to distort the trend of the reported profits.

The series of Recommendations proved acceptable to the business community and are thought to have significantly improved reporting practices (Zeff, 1972, p.23).[1] Widespread compliance was partly due to the extremely thorough consultation process organised by the ICAEW, and partly because companies were allowed to choose from a range of approved practices, i.e. flexibility was the price paid for acceptance. In an article written in 1965 Chambers estimated that, even assuming compliance with existing Recommendations, it was possible to come up with 'a million sets of mutually exclusive rules, each giving a true and fair view of the company's state of affairs and its profits!' (p.15). Chambers concluded that 'where there are so many possible rules there are in effect no rules'.

It was a few more years before this diversity in accounting practice became the subject of public criticism. In the mid-1960s the British accountant's ability to prepare, for publication, entirely reliable factual statements of a company's financial position was generally accepted. The popular view was that the accounting process was time consuming, painstaking, meticulous, and even boring, but that it was all worthwhile because the end result was a reliable statement of a company's financial position. The accountant no longer enjoys immunity from public criticism and the quality of his work is constantly being challenged as are the standards prevailing in many of the other established professions.

The more critical attitude towards accountancy in the UK stems from a series of events in the late 1960s, among which the GEC–AEI takeover is perhaps the best known. In October 1967, GEC (General Electric Company) made a takeover bid for the shares of AEI (Associated Electrical Industries). Often the directors of a company which is the subject of a takeover bid wish to resist the move, and one of the defensive tactics employed by the directors of AEI was to circulate its shareholders with a document explaining the advantages of retaining their present investment, and informing them that the company's forecast profit for 1967 was £10m.

The takeover bid was nevertheless successful and when AEI's 1967 accounts were eventually published, in April 1968, they revealed a loss of £4.5m. An obvious explanation for the massive discrepancy might have been that substantial errors were made when preparing the forecast, but an investigation showed that this was not the case. The forecast for 1967 was prepared late in the year (October), so only a small element of estimation was required, and this function was efficiently performed. The discrepancy was mainly caused by the new management team making more conservative accounting estimates and assumptions when valuing AEI's assets.

The general public, buoyed up by the media, was shocked to discover that accountancy was not the precise science they had believed it to be, and that the level of reported profit was substantially a matter of opinion concerning the values of business assets. Further revelations at the time of the Rolls Razor collapse and the Leasco–Pergamon affair (1969) reinforced these doubts. Public concern was fuelled by Professor Edward Stamp's public denunciation of the absence of firm accounting practices (*The Times*, 11 September 1969). An important reason for the public outcry was a failure to appreciate the nature of the problem. Different individuals will view the same economic facts in a different light, especially where there is a change of managerial strategy involved. But the profession was not, and possibly is still not, particularly good at explaining this fact.

Sir Ronald Leach, senior partner of Peat Marwick Mitchell & Co., and 'the unfortunate president of the English Institute at that time' (his own words) was 'besieged by members demanding action from the council to stem the mounting criticism of the profession in the press' (Leach, p.5). In an article, also published in *The Times* (22 September 1969), Leach objected to the tenor and, to some extent, the content of Stamp's criticisms, drew attention to the achievements of the accountancy profession, and emphasised the problems of profit measurement, particularly in relation to forecasts.

Statements of standard accounting practice

The ICAEW's leaders nevertheless perceived a need to act quickly. In December 1969 the ICAEW publicised 'its determination to advance accounting standards by narrowing the difference and variety in accounting practice' which destroyed comparability between the accounts of one business and another. The ASC was set up to do the job and other leading professional bodies soon joined, save the Chartered Institute of Public Finance and Accountancy which began to participate in 1976. The composition of the ASC was revised, and broadened, in 1983 to incorporate the views of users of accounts (such as bankers and analysts) who need not be accountants.

The standard setting process can briefly be described as follows. The ASC identifies a topic requiring attention and, usually, one or more research studies are undertaken. A discussion paper and/or a Statement of Intent may be published to elicit public reaction.[2] An Exposure Draft (ED) is then prepared, publicised, and circulated for comment to the relevant committees of the various professional bodies. It is also the subject of discussion in meetings between the ASC and organisations particularly affected by the topic under consideration. The project receives more attention at this stage because businessmen realise that the SSAP is unlikely to differ significantly from the ED unless changes, deemed desirable, are proposed and accepted. Increased interest is also a consequence of the fact that the debate enters the public domain, and quite often comments and criticisms of the ASC's proposals appear in the national and technical press. A SSAP is prepared in the light of views received, and circulated to the major accounting bodies for approval and publication.

The committee was provided with an ambitious initial programme of work; 20 problem areas were identified for treatment within five years. It has taken rather longer in some cases. For example, Accounting for Goodwill (SSAP 22) was not issued until 1984 and Accounting for Acquisitions and Mergers (SSAP 23) until 1985. Nevertheless, a great deal of progress has been made; by the end of 1975 (the first five years) eleven standards had been issued; there are now (June 1988) 24 SSAPs which deal with both the valuation of assets and liabilities and the way in which the information relating to those items should be disclosed in the accounts.

SSAPs do not have specific legal backing, and while it is true that a number of their main provisions are incorporated in CA 1985, it remains necessary, even in these cases, to refer to the SSAPs for operational details. Significant departures from standards should be disclosed and explained in the financial statements and, where practicable, their financial effect quantified and reported. Professional accountants working in industry and in practice are expected to encourage compliance. The auditor should refer to departures in his report unless he believes that non-compliance is justified and adequately disclosed in the accounts. Failure to observe standards renders a member liable to disciplinary action from the appropriate professional accountancy body, but there has been criticism of the failure of the professional bodies to take strong action in such cases.

Pragmatic standards

The rule makers may be convinced that a new standard is needed to deal with a particular problem and that they have devised the best theoretical solution, but there are a number of important constraints on the implementation of chosen procedures. Problems include the difficulty of achieving widespread acceptance of a standard and the effect of changing circumstances. These can be illustrated by examining the development of certain standards.

A choice of methods. SSAP 22 Accounting for Goodwill was issued in December 1984 and took effect for accounting periods beginning on or after 1 January 1985. Initial discussion began way back in 1974 and the gestation process was beset with problems. Companies had previously experimented with a variety of methods to account for purchased goodwill. These included: (a) permanent retention at cost in the balance sheet; (b) showing it in the balance sheet as a permanent deduction from shareholders' equity, without actually writing the item off - the 'dangling debit'; (c) immediate write off against reserves; (d) amortisation through the profit and loss account. SSAP 22 favours the adoption of method (c), but it does, as a second choice, permit companies to adopt method (d). It rules out methods (a) and (b). Where method (d) is employed, the Standard says that amortisation should be on a systematic basis over the asset's 'useful economic life'.

The difficulty of obtaining consensus support for a particular treatment was a feature of the ASC's deliberations from the outset. The initial working party on goodwill (set up in 1974) was split down the middle, and so it was divided and instructed to make separate reports. When the reports were reviewed the ASC was similarly divided - half favoured immediate write off and half the capitalise and amortise scheme. The matter was shelved. CA 1981 brought the problem back into focus by giving statutory approval to the two methods. The Act indicated no preference for either approach and ED 30 (the initial draft of the revised SSAP 22) adopted a similar flexible approach.

Why does SSAP 22 favour immediate write off? The probable explanation is that this method was in use by the vast majority of listed companies at the time the Standard was introduced; its popularity attributable to the fact that the need to make a write off against reported profit is avoided. It is therefore tempting to conclude that the Standard is more in the nature of a confirmation of existing practice than a rational assessment of available alternatives. Indeed, it is perhaps a little surprising that the Standard did not come out wholly in favour of direct write off. Once again, however, there were practical considerations. CA 1981 clearly permitted amortisation which severely weakened the position of auditors faced with strong minded directors determined to follow this approach. Also, the reserves of some companies might be at a low level and direct write off an impossible option, unless the directors are willing to report a negative reserve.

Changing circumstances. Experience has shown that the acceptability of standards depends on the accountancy profession's willingness to recognise that there are few accounting problems for which there exist definitive answers. Therefore, when business circumstances alter, standards must be revised. The evolution of the Standard for deferred tax is a good example of the pragmatic approach taken, increasingly, by the ASC.

Deferred taxation was not on the original agenda of the ASC but was 'listed for action' in 1971 (Zeff, 1972, p.84). The initial discussion focused on two main issues: whether to require companies to make a provision for deferred taxation;[3] and, if so, whether to adjust amounts previously set aside for any change in the rate of corporation tax. The first question was answered in the affirmative and SSAP 11, Accounting for Deferred Taxation, was issued in 1975. The second question was avoided by allowing two alternatives; companies could either retain the provision at its original figure, 'the deferral method', or restate it to take account of increases or decreases in future tax liabilities due to corporation tax changes, 'the liability method'.

SSAP 11 provoked widespread opposition, as soon as it was published, from a number of influential groups including the CBI. In 1970 first year allowances (FYA) were introduced, initially at 60%, to encourage capital investment in plant and machinery. The rate was soon (1972) increased to 100%, i.e. the entire capital cost could be written off immediately for tax purposes. With raw material prices rising rapidly, stock appreciation relief was also brought in (1972) to remove 'holding gains' from taxable profit. The combined effect of these measures, for many companies, was to reduce the current corporation tax charge but produce a substantial potential future tax liability. Critics of SSAP 11 argued that, as timing differences were unlikely to reverse in the foreseeable future, the requirement to make *full* provision severely distorted the published accounts. The accountancy profession's initial response was to delay implementation of SSAP 11; later (1978) the Standard was withdrawn. Its successor, SSAP 15 (1978), introduced a radical innovation; companies were permitted to provide only for those timing differences expected to 'crystalise', i.e. reverse in the foreseeable future (*partial* provision).

It is the accountancy profession's policy to review, periodically, the operation of SSAPs, but the re-examinaton of SSAP 15 was no doubt prompted by the Finance Act 1984 which withdrew stock appreciation relief and began to phase out the 100 per cent FYA on plant and machinery. The revised version of SSAP 15 (May 1985) requires companies to make partial provision, i.e. the option to make full provision was withdrawn. The Standard also removes the choice between the liability method and the deferral method by settling on the former. This seems to make sense in view of the greater likelihood of deferred liabilities 'crystalising' following the fiscal changes of 1984. Again approval was given to the procedures which had proved popular with UK companies.

Inflation accounting

The origin of some of the basic ideas underlying inflation accounting has been traced to the debate on rate regulation in the US during the last quarter of the nineteenth century, but it is the inter-war years that saw the development of an inflation accounting literature (Tweedie and Whittington, pp. 17–34). In view of the high inflation rates in France and Germany (indeed hyper-inflation caused the collapse of the German mark in 1923), it is not surprising to discover that important contributions were made by writers from those countries. Much of the literature dealt with the adjustment of accounts for changes in the general price level. But German writers also supported the restatemant of assets at their replacement cost, and this approach was advocated by authors in the Netherlands and the US.

Canning's *The Economics of Accountancy* (1929) was designed to encourage accountants to adopt the economists' forward looking approach to profit measurement, which discounts future cash flows to present value. In recognition of the intractable practical problems this approach entails, however, Canning accepted replacement cost or net realisable value as surrogates for present value in certain circumstances. The use of replacement cost was also favoured by Bonbright (1937) who developed the notion of 'deprival value' or 'value to the business' on which CCA is based. The best known inter-war publication is Sweeney's *Stabilised Accountancy* (1936), acknowledged not only as the authoritative early work on CPP but also because it pioneered the development of real terms accounting (RT).[4]

In Britain, little interest was shown in the topic of inflation accounting until the post-war period when rapidly rising prices caught the attention of the professional accountancy bodies. The ICAEW issued two Recommendations; No.12 gave unreserved support for the continued use of HCA but, after criticism, No.15 signalled a minor tactical retreat by advocating the continued use of HCA 'unless and until a practical and generally acceptable alternative is available'. Certain other professional accountancy bodies were more sympathetic to the need for change; reports by the research committees of the Association of Certified and Corporate Accountants and the Institute of Cost and Works Accountants recommended the use of replacement costs. The Scottish Institute recommended experimentation with supplementary accounts reflecting price changes. The more conservative attitude of the ICAEW prevailed, partly because it was widely regarded as the leading professional body, and partly because of a return to relatively low rates of inflation.

The inflation accounting issue was shelved by the profession for the best part of two decades, and the opportunity to work out better accounting methods during a period of relative price stability was lost. Some academics continued to stress the need for change. In the US, a particularly important contribution was made by Edwards and Bell (1961) who further developed replacement cost accounting into an operational model which contained a number of features – e.g. a division of historical cost profit into two components: 'current operating profit' and 'residual holding gains' – which played an important part in the development of CCA. In Britain, Professor Baxter's energetic campaign for fundamental reform met with little response.

British companies instead experimented with a variety of *ad hoc* adjustments designed to take some account of changing prices. Periodic revaluations of fixed assets, with the surplus credited to a revaluation reserve, were made quite early on, and ICI and Unilever are examples of well known companies that used this procedure. A second adjustment popular in some quarters was to base depreciation on the replacement cost of fixed assets. Where companies had also revalued their fixed assets, the total charge was debited to the profit and loss account and credited to accumulated depreciation. Where companies continued to state fixed assets at historical cost, the replacement element was debited to the profit and loss appropriation account and credited to a replacement reserve.

As a further manifestation of the more enlightened attitude displayed by the ICAEW in the late 1960s, a discussion document entitled *Accounting for Inflation* (1968)[5] was published. This advocated the publication of supplementary statements based on CPP. The document provoked little immediate interest but, with the sharp upturn in the inflation rate in the early 1970s, businessmen at last became convinced of the need for a fundamental re-examination of HCA. The accountancy profession decided to tackle the subject but, 'in view of the importance of carrying all parties', favoured a government backed official inquiry (Morpeth, p.44). According to Morpeth, the government's initial view was that the problem should be dealt with by the profession and other interested parties, and it was against this background that the ASC prepared and issued ED 8 entitled Accounting for Changes in the Purchasing Power of Money (1973). This advocated the use of CPP.

Soon afterwards (July 1973) the government changed its mind and joined the debate by appointing its own committee on inflation accounting chaired by Francis Sandilands. It is rumoured that this step was taken because the government was uneasy about the introduction, for businesses, of a system which might imply the need to index government debt. The committee's appointment placed the profession in a quandary; whether to persist with CPP and risk government disapproval or await the committee's findings before taking action. The heroic decision was to press ahead and Provisional

Statement of Standard Accounting Practice 7 (1974) was issued pending publication of the government's report. It provided for the publication of supplementary statements based on CPP.

Application of the standard ran into immediate difficulties because of the requirement to recognise, as profit, the unrealised gains from holding debt during a period of rising prices. This particular criticism was fuelled 'by the property crisis of 1974 when it was claimed that under PSSAP 7 the most apparently profitable companies were often those closest to bankruptcy' (Morpeth, p.45); i.e. high gearing, which produced large paper profits, also fostered financial instability. The report of the Sandilands Committee, published in the following year, undoubtedly damaged the prestige of the ASC. It was severely critical of CPP (see, for example, para.439) and instead favoured the adjustment of company accounts for specific price changes. To add insult to injury the committee recommended that the ASC should be charged with the responsibility for developing the system called CCA. The profession had little option but to comply with government wishes and, in 1976, produced ED18 which was rejected by the ICAEW's own members as unnecessarily complex and unworkable. SSAP 16, issued in 1980, proved that the third attempt is not always lucky; this measure lasted a little longer but proved unpopular with companies and its mandatory status was withdrawn in 1986.

These failures should not be viewed as evidence of the irrelevance of accounting for changing prices. On the contrary, the fact that the various schemes have provoked strong opposition points in the opposite direction. More specifically, it is because CCA has such a dramatic effect on reported profit that it produces a good deal of unease within the business community. Comments made in the directors' report of Pilkington Brothers plc, for 1986, are particularly illuminating. The company had been an enthusiastic supporter of CCA but reverted to historical cost because 'the directors believe that the present policy places the group at a disadvantage when its reported results are compared with the majority of United Kingdom companies which account for tangible assets on a historical cost basis'. Also revealing is the directors' further assertion that 'within the company, the directors will continue to assess performance in inflation accounting terms'.

The ASC's present position (June 1988) is that information about the effect of changing prices should be provided where relevant to a proper appreciation of a company's results and financial position. CCA is still considered the most appropriate scheme for the great majority of economic entities and, where prices are changing at a significant rate, companies are urged to make adequate disclosures. The basic principles of SSAP 16, together with supplementary material, were published as an official *Handbook* (1986) for use as an authoritative reference work. A minority of companies continue to publish CCA data as do certain nationalised industries. Indeed the Byatt report, presented to the Government in 1986, concluded that CCA provided a better framework for reporting the results and assessing the performance of nationalised industries.

The choice is not of course simply between inflation adjusted accounts and HCA; today the majority of listed companies publish accounts containing *some* assets which have been revalued. According to Macdonald these 'modified historical cost accounts' are now 'almost the sole barometer as to the real worth of a company's asset backing' (pp.3–4). This half-way house may be viewed as an attempt to overcome some of the major drawbacks of HCA by giving recognition to increases in the value of selected assets. A problem is the entire lack of standardisation in this area, giving rise to considerable variety in accounting practice regarding both the regularity of valuations and the range of assets subject to revaluation – freehold and long leasehold land and buildings being most preferred and, within these categories, shops and offices rather than industrial property (Macdonald, pp.3–10).

Statements of recommended practice

Most SSAPs apply to all companies; exceptions are Accounting for Source and Application of Funds (SSAP 10) which does not apply to companies with turnover or gross income of less than £25,000 a year and Earnings per Share (SSAP 3) which applies only to listed companies. In July 1983 the ASC announced that, in future, SSAPs will be issued only on 'those matters which are of major and fundamental importance and affect the generality of companies'. They will therefore be few in number. This has been welcomed by businessmen as an indication of the fact that Britain may not go down the path of the Americans where the FASB had issued well over 90 standards by the beginning of 1988).

The Statement of Recommended Practice (SORP) has been developed to deal with issues which do not meet the criteria which are considered to justify the issue of an SSAP, i.e. they are to cover matters of importance, but not of major and fundamental importance, and matters which only apply to certain types of companies.

SORPs may be developed by the ASC through a similar consultation process as applies for SSAPs, or by people within a particular industry for ultimate approval by the ASC. Industry based SORPs, approved by the ASC, are called 'franked SORPs'.

SORPs have a similar status to Recommendations; they are considered to represent best practice and compliance will be encouraged, but they are not mandatory in the sense that departures must be disclosed. To date (June 1988) two SORPs have been issued – on Pension Scheme Accounts and Accounting for Charities. Disclosures about Oil and Gas Exploration and Production Activities, prepared by the Oil Industry Accounting Committee, became the first franked SORP in March 1986. In view of the criticism of SSAPs it may be that SORPs are seen as a less contoversial way of encouraging improvements in financial reporting practices.

Review

The formulation and issue of standards, without first developing an accepted conceptual framework, has been criticised by some as bad in principle and likened to a 'fire fighting' exercise. Sir Ronald Leach, chairman of the ASC from its inception until 1976, justifies the issue of standards on the grounds that 'if we had held up the issue of standards for this purpose [the development of a conceptual framework] we should have wasted precious years' (p.11). Edey has added the following reasons for introducing standards in the controversial area of profit measurement: first, to reduce the scope for management 'to regard accounting statements as tactical or strategic weapons . . . instead of intelligence reports for the world at large'; secondly, to raise the level of public debate by 'bringing to the surface fundamental issues that have hitherto been glossed over in practice' (1977, p.303). All this is undoubtedly correct and has happened. At the same time, experience has also shown that the issue of regulations which do not fit into a coherent theoretical structure can give rise to inconsistencies and loopholes which are exploited by management in conjunction with its legal advisers. On the other hand, there is no reason to suppose (and both the literature and US experience confirms this) that it would, by now, have been possible to develop a consistent conceptual basis for financial reporting which would have been well defined, generally acceptable, and capable of satisfactory application to all situations and events.

PART V

DEVELOPMENT OF A PROFESSION

20

Professional Accountants at Work

Early developments

A small number of individuals managed to make a living out of accounting during the eighteenth century. One such man was William Cuthbertson, who began to practice in Glasgow and has been described as the originator of the accountancy profession in that city (Stewart, p.74). On the whole accountants remained thin on the ground. The directories give the following figures: London, 1 in 1776 and 5 in 1790; Liverpool, 1 in 1783 and 5 in 1790; Bristol, 2 in both 1783 and 1808. Scotland did rather better, perhaps reflecting more harmonious links with the legal profession in that country; the Edinburgh directories list 7 accountants in 1773 and 17 in 1805, and a Glasgow directory 6 in 1783.

The demand for accounting data increased during the Industrial Revolution and methods of financial control devised by businessmen met with varying degrees of success (see Chapter 8). On the whole they coped fairly well without significant help from practising accountants, but it is likely that they would have coped even better if their records had been more accurate. Increases in the numbers of accountants practising in London reflects a fairly rapidly growing demand for their services: 24 in 1809–11, 47 in 1817, 73 in 1822–24, 107 in 1840, and 264 in 1850. The formation of partnerships is a further indicator of the need for specialist expertise. William Cuthbertson's son Donald joined him as a partner in 1810. Other early Scottish firms of accountants include Keith & Horne (1820), McEwan & Auld (1836), and Brown & Pearson (1835). Early English examples are Quilter, Ball & Co. (1832), Youngs & Co. (1840), Deloitte (1845), Harding and Pullein (1848), Turquand & Edwards (1850), Cooper Brothers & Co. (1854).

William Quilter was described in his obituary (d.1888) as 'the pioneer of the present generation of public accountants'' (reproduced in Parker, 1980). The firm Quilter, Ball & Co. established its reputation investigating the affairs of railway companies, in the aftermath the 'railway mania' (see Chapter 13), but their involvement was not initially welcomed by the leading railway publication, *Herapath's Journal*. A barrage of editorial abuse included claims that the firm's recommendation for a continuous audit was designed only to ensure that 'a continuous employment should be found for Messrs. Quilter & Co., with an army of clerks', that their charges were excessive, 'three guineas a day (six hours?) for each of the principals' and it dismissed them as 'mere professional accountants' (1849, p.1,001) 'with no other railway knowledge in their head than that a railway is an iron road, upon which locomotives draw trains' (1850, p.720). The firm was also facetiously described by *Punch* as 'Rug, Bullet & Co.'

It is unlikely that these were widespread views. The firm was called in to assist the committee of inquiry into the South Eastern Railway; 'the nature of the inquiry rendering the assistance of a professional accountant indispensible' (*Railway Times*, 1849, p.502), the committee investigating the Midland, and a number of others, possibly including the London, Brighton and South Coast where the committee's report refers to the fact that they engaged the assistance of an 'experienced accountant' (*Herapath's Journal*, 1848, p.434). A further indication of Quilter's standing is that he was invited to give evidence to the 1849 Monteagle Committee on the audit of railways.

Worthington believes that 'the disastrous period of 1847–48 did more than anything else to place professional accountancy on a solid and substantial basis' in this country (p.47). The profession made steady progress and a further boost was provided by the need to undertake investigations prior to the flotation and following the failure of numerous public companies in the 1860s. But although these were boom years for accountants, it still took some time for an extremely capable young accountant to become established. Edwin Waterhouse, a founding partner of Price, Waterhouse & Co., began to practice on 24 February 1864, putting up his brass plate outside No.11 Old Jury Chambers. His diaries tell us that 'no work came in for some weeks, and I began to think I might have made a mistake . . . my father had given me £2,000 to start on which, with my small savings, made a sum of £2,078 18s 5d, and I made calculations and estimates as to how long, with compound interest,

I could subsist on this sum at my current rate of expenditure'. In May 1865 he accepted Samuel Lowell Price's invitation to join together in partnership because it 'seemed to open out chances of quickly obtaining wider experience, while ensuring a more steady practice' (quoted in Edwards, 1986, p.675).

A major difference between the accountancy profession at the end of the last century and today is the present dominance of a relatively small number of extremely large international firms. In 1900, Deloitte, Dever & Griffiths was one of the largest firms with just four partners and 80 staff (even this was considered a daring increase from 32 in 1882). This contrasts with the position in 1987 when, its successor, Deloitte Haskins & Sells, ranked fourth among the 'big eight', had 224 partners, 3821 employees and a fee income of £121.1m.

Firms of accountants tend to cope very well with economic change and, despite national and international mergers, a number of today's partnerships are instantly recognisable as successors of their nineteenth-century counterparts. Deloitte, Dever & Griffiths are now Deloitte, Haskins & Sells, Cooper Brothers & Co. have become Coopers and Lybrand, W.B. Peat & Co. is now known as Peat Marwick McLintock, and Price, Waterhouse & Co. has changed least of all to Price Waterhouse. The modern day equivalents are of course the product of numerous takeovers and mergers. For example, the following firms already formed by the time the ICAEW was established (1880) are now part of Ernst & Whinney: Harold E. Clarke & Co., Mayo, Thornbury & Co. (both Birmingham), H.W. & J. Blackburn (Bradford), Charles Ware & Co. (Bristol), J.T. Smith & Co., D.E. Wallace & Co. (both Edinburgh), Brown, Fleming & Murray, Reid & Mair (both Glasgow), Joe Sharp & Co. (Huddersfield), A.C. Palmer & Co. (Leicester), Harding, Whinney & Co., Mason & Son, Turquand, Youngs & Co. (all London), Parkinson, Mather & Co., Thomas Smethurst & Co., J. Townley Trotter & Co., Charles R. Trevor & Co. (all Manchester), Thomas Bowden Sons & Nephew, Holmes Dudley & Co. (both Newcastle) (Jones, pp.256–59).

Range of services provided

We will see that there is a great deal of truth in the assessment that the British accountancy profession 'was born through bankruptcies, fed on failures and fraud, grew on liquidations and graduated through audits'.

Insolvency

The nineteenth century was marked by periods of rapid expansion followed by deep financial crises which produced numerous insolvencies. One quarter of the companies incorporated with limited liability were dissolved within three years, and nearly 70 per cent within 20 years. 1866 was a particularly disastrous year for business; the failure of Overend, Gurney & Co. with liabilities of £18m produced the worst panic seen in the City since 1825 when 25 banks suspended payment. As is still the case industrial collapse provided accountants with rich pickings. Evidence presented to the Watkin Committee (1867) shows that accountants were appointed liquidators of 259 companies with a total capital of over £92m. As an indication of the lucrative nature of this work, Turquand and Harding, appointed receivers of Overend, Gurney & Co., earned £71,000 in fees and £14,000 in expenses over a period of 13 years (Jones, p.43). Out of gross fees of £29,845 earned by Harding, Whinney, & Gibbons in 1867, £25,447 came from insolvency work (ibid., p.47). No doubt this was a little exceptional; of the 259 appointments to the position of liquidator in 1866, this firm obtained 61 of them.

The importance of insolvency and bankruptcy work to early professional firms is further indicated by the content of petitions for Royal Charters made by some of the professional bodies. For example, the Edinburgh and Glasgow Societies' petitions (1853) emphasised work done on behalf of the Court, trusteeship and actuarial work; they make no reference to auditing, tax or cost accounting. Twenty-seven years later the ICAEW's submission stressed liquidations and bankruptcy work and, according to Parker, the reference to auditing 'appears to be almost an afterthought' (1986, p.20). Again there is no mention of taxation or cost accounting. Contemporary commentators make the same point in a different fashion: according to a disgruntled partner in a failed banking firm 'Accountants make their fortunes from the misfortunes of others' (Worthington, p.4), while Ernest Cooper observed that 'to be seen talking to or having your office entered by an accountant was to be avoided, particularly in the stressful times of 1866' (p.43).

Various statutes helped, both directly and indirectly, to provide accountants with this type of work. The Bankruptcy Act 1831 (applying to England and Wales; Scots law is founded on the Bankruptcy Act 1856) provided for the appointment of officers, designated 'official assignees', to liquidate estates on behalf of creditors. Some accountants were appointed to this office; others increasingly employed professional accountants to help them carry out their task. CA 1862 established the position of official liquidator, usually filled by an accountant, and the Act was re-named 'the Accountant's friend' by a grateful profession. The Bankruptcy Act 1869 abolished the position of official assignee and instead created the position of trustee to distribute the debtor's estate. Professional accountants could be appointed *directly* to this position, rather than only through an intermediary official, and this resulted in an even greater volume of bankruptcy work.

A hint of competition between the new and the established professions is given by Mr Justice Quain's complaint (1875) that 'The whole affairs in bankruptcy have been handed over to an ignorant set of men called accountants' (quoted in Worthington, p.73). However, in 1883 some of this work was lost when the new Bankruptcy Act abolished the position of trustee in bankruptcy, and reintroduced the middle-man, now called the official receiver. Pixley described the 1883 Act as a 'direct attack upon the profession' (p.203). Official intervention provoked strong opposition from accountants and lawyers.

Bankruptcy and liquidation work today remain lucrative sources of income for many professional firms, particularly during periods of deep economic recession.

Auditing

The first job of the professional accountant when appointed auditor, in the nineteenth century, was often to sort out the company's records. De Paula has remarked that, in the 1890s, 'It was by no means uncommon to find primitive records upon a single entry basis or alternately most complicated double entry systems' (p.22). A major part of the accountant's work was therefore to introduce an efficient system of double entry. Some examples of the exceptionally slow adoption of double entry bookkeeping, by very large companies, is the Sun Fire Office, founded in 1710, which did not introduce this system until 1890 and the Capital and Counties Bank which used single entry until it merged with Lloyds in 1918 (Jones, p.23).

Statutory requirements. A statutory requirement for directors to arrange for the preparation and audit of registered companies' accounts was in force between 1844–56, and was reintroduced in 1900 (see Chapter 15). Compulsory audit requirements were also introduced for particular categories of company; railways (1867), water companies (1871), building societies (1874), banks (1879), insurance companies (1909) and industrial and provident societies (1913).

In some general statutes the option to appoint a professional accountant, as auditor, was explicitly stated at an early stage. An Act of 1875 referred to the possibility of the audit of friendly societies (introduced in 1829 in recognition of the large quantities of funds at their disposal) being carried out by a 'public auditor' (s.35). Municipal corporations were placed in a similar position by an Act of 1890. In a few instances the appointment of a professional accountant to the position of auditor was made compulsory; the Building Societies Act 1894 stated that 'one at least of the auditors shall be a person who publicly carries on the business of an accountant' (s.3), while the Industrial and Provident Societies Act 1913 stipulated that the appointment should be made from a list of public auditors drawn up by the Treasury (s.3). The Electric Lighting (Clauses) Act (1899) provided for the accounts to be 'examined and audited by such competent and impartial person as the Board of Trade appoint' (s.6).

During the twentieth century various statutory provisions have been introduced to strengthen the position of the auditor of registered companies, e.g. CA 1907 protected the auditor from unexpected dismissal at the AGM by providing for at least two weeks notice to be given of the intention to nominate a different auditor (s.19). It was not until 1947, however, that public registered companies were required to appoint professional accountants as auditors (s.23). The profession was granted a monopoly of all company audits (private as well as public) in 1967. The accounting bodies whose members are today authorised to act as auditors of registered companies are listed in CA 1985, s.389.

We can see that the government was slow to provide *general* support for the development of the professional audit; on the other hand it left the decision to the market and did not take on private sector work itself, though the possibility has been considered from time to time. Indeed, the Monteagle Committee (1849) recommended the government appointment of a public auditor to act in conjunction with the company's own auditors. The proposal was contained in an unsuccessful bill presented to Parliament later that year.

Amateur shareholder/auditors. In the absence of monopoly rights the professional accountant had, first, to oust the amateur auditor who was firmly entrenched for a variety of reasons. These included the initial shortage of professionally qualified accountants, the idea that the audit was a fairly straightforward matter, and the fact that the directors welcomed the appointment of individuals who were unable to ask difficult technical questions.

The need for a share qualification was indicated both by the Companies Clauses Consolidation Act (s.102) for statutory companies, and Table A (art.86) for registered companies. Arguments in favour of this requirement were that, at this time, a shareholder was more likely to possess a technical knowledge of the company's affairs, also that he had a financial interest in ensuring that the job was done properly. This latter point was also cited as an argument against appointing a shareholder, i.e. because he had a personal interest in the amount of dividend declared, he might be tempted to accept an inflated figure for reported profit. A further drawback of the share qualification was the probable absence of a suitably qualified accountant from the body of shareholders. Dicksee was outspoken in his criticism of the amateur auditor because he had 'seen too much of their shortcomings, and of the inexpressible misery and distress that has been caused by their scandalous incompetency, to feel any desire to deal gently with their failings' (p.141). A sometimes bitter contest resulted in eventual victory for the professional.

The appointment of the professional accountant as independent auditor dates from the 1840s and, in common with many other British accounting developments, was closely connected with the growth of the railways. In many cases the professional was called in by a railway company's shareholder/auditors to improve both the standard of the audit and the form of the published accounts. William Welch Deloitte, for example, was called in by the Great Western Railway's auditors in 1849. The directors' report tells us that this action was taken without reference to the Board – an early example of the auditor exercising his independence – but the directors appear to have been satisfied with the appointment, presumably because they realised that a clean report provided stronger evidence of the authenticity of the accounts (Edwards, 1985a, p.38). In a similar vein the auditors' report on the London and North Western Railway's 1849 accounts refers to the engagement of 'Mr J.E. Coleman, a professional accountant of eminence, whose employment by the Bank of England and other public establishments will, doubtless, secure to his report (appended hereto) the confidence of the proprietors' (*Railway Times*, 1850, p.188).

In 1850 the Midland Railway's directors reported that 'with a view to placing the accounts of the company on a basis more satisfactory to the shareholders, the directors have obtained the services of a public accountant'. William Jordan, as well as the shareholder/auditors, signed much improved accounts including, for the first time, a balance sheet. At the South Eastern Railway company Quilter, Ball & Co. were appointed by the auditors to help with the July 1850 accounts. The auditors' report tells us that, 'In compliance with our request to the Board of Directors, a balance sheet is appended to the accounts' (Edwards, 1985a, p.38). William Quilter quite probably helped bring about this change.

This process continued and statutes requiring the accounts of railways and registered companies to be audited merely recognised existing practice. An exception occurred in the case of banks who were slow to follow suit because of concern about client confidentiality. They made general provision for the appointment of auditors only after it became a statutory requirement in 1879 (see Chapter 12). Edwin Waterhouse was one accountant who was successful in obtaining a share of this work for his firm which was invited, in the 1880s, to become joint auditor to both the National Provincial Bank of England and the London and Westminster Bank.

Despite the slow start auditing soon became the main source of income for professional firms. In 1905, the *Encyclopaedia of Accounting*, placed it at the head of the list; in sharp contrast to 50 years earlier when it hardly merited a mention (Jones, p.51). The achievement of the early British practitioners in establishing the professional audit as the principal protection for shareholders is underlined by the knowledge that, in other countries, alternative safeguards took precedence. In the US the principal protection was the publication of full financial information designed to enable users to make their own evaluation of management performance and corporate progress, whereas in certain European countries standardised accounts were employed (see Chapter 17).

Nature and scope of the audit. Nichol's Case (1878) decided that the auditor was principally responsible for the detection of error and fraud. Judged by today's standards these seem rather limited objectives but, at a time when joint stock companies were at an early stage of their development, error and fraud were important causes of company failure. Other contributory factors, about which the auditor could do little, were fluctuations in economic conditions between boom and slump, the absence of a sound basis for proposed activities, and management inefficiencies.

Towards the end of the nineteenth century the court reached the conclusion that it was unreasonable to expect the auditor to detect *all* errors and frauds. Where collusion occurred, for example, it was recognised that the detection of fraud would be almost impossible. Certainly the cost would be prohibitive. *Re Kingston Cotton Mill* (1896) decided that the auditor's principal duty was to excercise a reasonable amount of skill and care, and that the detection of error and fraud was mainly management's responsibility. As Lopes, L.J. put it:

> Auditors must not be made liable for not tracking out ingenious and carefully laid schemes of fraud, when there is nothing to arouse their suspicion and when those frauds are perpetrated by tried servants of the company and are undetected for years by the directors.

Provided matters *appeared* to be in order the accountant was not expected to be unduly suspicious, but if his suspicion was aroused he was expected to examine the matter in detail.

An important question, still not adequately answered today, was how far the auditor needed to 'dig' in order to discover whether his suspicions should be aroused. During the second half of the nineteenth century the auditor's investigation was often confined to a simple comparison of the balance sheet with the underlying records which were checked only for numerical accuracy (the 'mechanical audit', see Chapter 15). According to Sir George Jessel (Master of the Rolls), even the comparison with the underlying records was often not as thorough as it should have been.

> I have had the auditors examined before me, and I have said, 'You audited these accounts?' 'Yes.' 'Did you call for any vouchers?' 'No, we did not; we were told it was all right, and we supposed it was, and we signed it'. Nothing is checked as a rule; I do not say it is the case in every company, but with most companies; everything is taken for granted until it turns out to be all wrong (Lowe Committee, 1877, q.2192).

The mechanical audit was the focus of the court's attention in *London Oil Storage Co.* v *Seear, Hasluck & Co.* (1904) where the balance sheet figure for cash agreed with the cash book but not with the physical cash balance which the auditors had not verified. The court decided that the auditor had a general duty to check the balance sheet information not just with the records but also with the underlying economic facts.

The initial development of audit practices is likely to have been hindered by the absence of authoritative texts that could be referred to by practitioners. This impediment was removed by the publication of Dicksee's classic volume *Auditing: A Practical Manual for Auditors* in 1892. Dicksee's major contributions were to draw a clear distinction between accounting and auditing, and to identify the latter as an independent activity involving careful investigation of the relationship between the final accounts and the underlying economic events, rather than merely 'calling over the accounts' (*Accountant*, 9 August 1947, p.85).

The decision in *re London and General Bank* (1895) signalled the possible need for a change in the direction of the audit by indicating that the auditor had a responsibility for the quality of the information contained in the accounts. Lindley said that it was the duty of an auditor 'to ascertain and state the true financial position of the company at the time of the audit'. The need for the auditor to report fully to shareholders on the results of his audit, rather than merely to attach the word 'audited' to the balance sheet, was also stressed. Legislation, beginning with CA 1900, expressly referred to the auditor's duty to report on the accounts, but made no reference to any obligation to detect errors and fraud perpetrated during the year.

Despite these 'straws in the wind', for the next twenty years the audit continued to focus principally on the detection of error and fraud rather than the content of the published accounts. Preoccupation with legal responsibilities was no doubt reinforced by the fact that much of the influential early accounting literature, such as the books written by Pixley (1881) and Dicksee (1892), had a heavy legalistic bias, e.g. Parker has calculated that 131 out of 290 pages in Dicksee's book comprised extracts from relevant statutes and the reports of cases dealing with the questions of divisible profit and the liability of auditors (1986, p.38). As these were the basic textbooks used to prepare for professional examinations, their impact must have been enormous.

During the inter-war period a change of audit emphasis occurred. This change reflected the growing demand, from shareholders, for financial information as the basis for investment decisions, rather than simply as a means of confirming that everything was in order. It therefore became the auditor's responsibility to report on the reliability of the financial position disclosed in the balance sheet and, as time went on, the fairness of the reported profit figure. The audit was no longer looked upon as a kind of fraud-squad investigation; the efficient method for coping with irregularities was to prevent the loss occurring rather than to discover it had taken place.

Relegation of error and fraud detection to a secondary audit objective was facilitated by management developing improved systems of internal control in at least the larger companies. The auditor's concern with error and fraud was mainly confined to circumstances where it affected the quality of the information reported in financial statements. These developments resulted in the following changes in audit procedures; there was a move towards test checking transactions rather than vouching each item individually; and greater interest was shown in the valuation of assets and liabilities.

The focus of the audit has therefore transferred from the accounting records to the accounting reports; from checking the technical accuracy to verifying the quality of the information disclosed. The growing emphasis on the audit as a means of enlightening shareholders regarding the state of their investment caused secret reserves, which made a lot of sense from the creditors point of view, to fall out of favour. Increased attention was instead focused on the importance of earning capacity as the basis for corporate performance assessment. Judicial and public criticism at the time of the Royal Mail case (1931) helped remove the obsession with purely legal responsibilities and, instead, resulted in an increased emphasis on the moral and ethical obligations of the accountant (see Chapter 12).

It is interesting to note that, at this time, the literature seems to have followed rather than led changes in contemporary best practice. By the 1930s Pegler and Spicer's *Practical Auditing* was established as an authoritative work, and a comparison of 'The objects of an audit' sections in the sixth (1933) and seventh (1936) editions of this book is relevant. Whereas the former identifies the detection of error and fraud as the 'two principal reasons for which an audit may be instituted' (p.5), the latter states that 'the main object of an audit is the *verification* of accounts and statements prepared by a client [and] the detection of error and fraud must be regarded as incidental to such main object' (p.5).

Investigations

It was probably the reputation established by Quilter, Ball & Co. for sorting out errors and inconsistencies in railway company accounts that encouraged amateur shareholder/auditors to turn to professional accountants to help with their preparation and audit. Investigations undertaken to detect a suspected fraud or to quantify the amount of a known defalcation also became increasingly common. An early example was William Welch Deloitte's engagement by the auditors of the Great Northern Railway to look into the famous Redpath frauds in 1856. Leopold Redpath was the company's registrar of share and stock transfers and, in that capacity, had control over recording the entire transaction. His frauds enabled him to maintain an address in Regent's Park, where he lived 'in a style of great elegance', and a country residence in Weybridge. It was discovered that his frauds involved sums totalling £150,000. Deloitte must have done a good job. The directors of the Great Western and the Lancashire & Yorkshire subsequently instructed him to examine their stock registers in order to reassure anxious shareholders (Kettle, pp.22–24).

Investigation work became increasingly important during the last quarter of the nineteenth century, dealing with such matters as the examination of a company's financial condition and the detection of fraud. The conversion of a privately owned business into a public company, as a means of raising new finance, was also a common occurrence during this period, and a report on the company's earnings, prior to conversion, was an indispensible element of the prospectus issued to potential investors. The reporting accountant was then often appointed auditor, e.g. at the Shelton Iron, Steel and Coal Co. Ltd where Deloitte, Dever, Griffiths & Co. were appointed in 1890. The development of the accountant's report for inclusion in the prospectus is examined in Chapter 17. The preparation of reports on profit forecasts issued in the endeavour to resist an unwelcome takeover bid, and investigations of the target's affairs where there is a friendly bid, are further common feature's of the modern accountant's work load.

The advantages to be gained from engaging professional expertise was also recognised by the government at an early stage. Peter H. Abbott's examination of the method of keeping the public accounts, on behalf of Commissioners appointed in 1831 by Lord Grey, is a notable early example (Quilter's obituary in Parker, 1980), although his recommendation that public sector accounts should be placed on the double entry basis was not acted upon. Quilter himself undertook 'investigations into the Government Stores at Weedon, [and made] confidential reports to the Board of Trade on the financial position of private firms desirous of converting themselves into limited liability companies'. William Turquand was also actively involved in this type of work. By 1847 he had been made an official assignee under the Bankruptcy Act 1831, and, like Quilter, he was sometimes appointed by the BOT to investigate and report on companies wishing to obtain a certificate of registration with limited liability under the 1855 Act (Jones, p.34).

Later in the century (1887) Frederick Whinney and Edwin Waterhouse were asked to investigate the accounts of the Woolwich Arsenal for a Parliamentary committee under the chairmanship of Lord Randolph Churchill. Waterhouse's personal diary notes certain reservations concerning the value of their report, but it seems to have been well received as there followed invitations to advise on the accounts of other departments of the War Office and also of the Admiralty. Moving on to the twentieth century, William Plender acted for the Metropolitan Water Board which acquired the London water companies in 1903 and, five years later, he acted for the purchasers to help establish the Port of London Authority. In 1911, the year he was knighted, he investigated conditions of work and remuneration under the National Insurance Act.

The First World War is an important landmark in government use of accountants to provide financial expertise. Gilbert Garnsey, for example, was appointed to the Ministry of Munitions, which had been established to help maximise the contribution to the war effort of industries supplying goods to the forces. Garnsey and J.H.Guy prepared a report severely critical of the accounting procedures operated by the Ministry which, in common with the systems operating in other government departments, were designed principally to show whether money allocated by Parliament was used for its intended purpose. Their investigations revealed that undue concentration on cash accounting, rather than accruals accounting, had resulted in large losses of money due, for example, to the Ministry's failure to maintain an adequate record of amounts due from contractors. They recommended reorganisation of the accounting system on a commercial basis, and major innovations included the replacement of single entry by double entry accounting, and the periodic preparation of a production (income and expenditure) account and balance sheet, which were previously little used in government accounting. In the Comptroller and

Auditor General's view these changes had a very favourable influence on the Ministry's accounts for the latter part of 1917–18 and for the subsequent period (Edwards, 1985b, p.487). The new procedures were extended to other government 'trading' departments in the immediate post-war years.

The appointment of professional accountants to undertake Department of Trade and Industry investigations under CA 1985, ss.431–32, and government appointments for many other purposes are today commonplace.

Cost accounting and management consultancy

Interest in costing developed in the last quarter of the nineteenth century as profit margins declined, industry became more competitive and capital intensive, and overheads more important. Solomons has described this period as a 'costing renaissance' (p.17) though it was one led by engineers rather than accountants (Parker, 1986, p.41).

In view of the profession's success in obtaining large slices of work in new areas, there is surprisingly little evidence of accountants providing management accounting services before 1900, either directly or on a consultancy basis. This anomaly may be explained on grounds of snobbery; employment in the service of traders not being considered professional work. Another possibility is that the professional accountant simply lacked the entrepreneurial and innovative skills needed for this kind of work. Certainly American accountants were much more active in this area and Anyon has commented that English accountants were 'looked upon as rather slow and stupid and while admittedly honest, were not considered over capable' (p.20). A further factor might have been the desire to avoid accusations of a possible conflict of interest at a time when the profession was striving to establish the auditor's independence as a crucial characteristic. A final explanation for the slow development of consultancy services is simply that businessmen became keenly interested in costing techniques only after the turn of the century when Britain came under greater pressure from its trading rivals.

The twentieth century has seen professional accountants increasingly engaged by companies to provide business advice. The second half of the 1920s saw the start of a drive towards the rationalisation of industry; an idea introduced from Germany. In 1933 Whinney,

Smith & Whinney were invited to help devise a scheme for the amalgamation of companies engaged in the cotton industry. Edgar Jones points out that this was a

> situation unheard of in the nineteenth century, where a firm of accountants was being requested not simply to check a company's books, but to arrange a complete scheme of merger and reorganisation which placed them at the very root of managerial decision-taking (p.161).

It also became common for accountants to be called in to reconstruct individual companies, e.g. Sir Thomas Smethurt and C.J.G.Palmour's scheme for salvaging the affairs of the Belsize Motor Company at Clayton, Manchester (ibid., p.160). Garnsey was also active in this area, taking a leading part in schemes for reconstructing and reorganising numerous leading companies including, Armstrong, Whitworth & Co. Ltd, William Beardmore & Co. Ltd, Cable & Wireless Ltd, Lipton Ltd, Marconi's Wireless Telegraph Ltd and Spillers Ltd.

Sometimes more formal links were established between the accountant and the company to which a service was supplied. For example, Van den Bergh's appointed (1909) Basil Mayhew to the Board of Meadow Dairy to look after their interests. Later (1926) Mayhew acted as consultant to Bowaters. A further natural development has been for professional accountants to give up professional practice and move into industry. The 1920s saw chartered accountants become industrial leaders; a trickle at this stage later became a flood. For example, in 1923 Francis D'Arcy Cooper took up the appointment of vice-chairman with Lever Brothers, becoming chairman in 1925. In the years that followed he achieved a 'complete metamorphosis of Lever Brothers from a private empire owned and controlled by one man into a public company administered by professional management' (Wilson, p.132).

Professional firms today register separate companies to provide specialist management consultancy services. Reasons include the desire to give separate corporate status to this important area of activity, the value placed on the protection provided by limited liability, and the facility corporate status provides for giving non-accountants, who are ineligible for partner status, a prestigious title such as director.

Taxation

Since the beginning of the last century there has been an enormous growth in both the number and complexity of taxes levied in this country, also in the weight of taxation.

The taxation of asset transfers on death goes back many centuries. Modern legislation dates from the introduction of probate duty in 1694. This lasted until Harcourt's famous budget of 1894, which brought in estate duty, later replaced by capital transfer tax (1975) and, in turn, by inheritance tax (1986). These have been described as discretionary taxes paid by people who dislike their family even more than they dislike the Inland Revenue. This is the exceptional situation and accountants have been at the forefront devising schemes to keep the taxman's share to the minimum.

New taxes have often been introduced, or extended, to help cope with some form of national emergency; for example, income tax was introduced by Pitt (1799) to help finance the Napoleonic Wars. The accountant's services have been required to help companies comply with statutory obligations, e.g. the administration of PAYE, and to devise ways of reducing the tax burden by ensuring that income arises in a tax exempt or, at least, a tax favourable form. The demand for tax avoidance schemes is naturally most pressing when income tax rates are high, such as in the fiscal year 1952/3 when the top marginal rate was 97.5 per cent on all income, and between 1974–78 when it was 98 per cent on investment income.

Other major taxes which have provided 'grist for the accountant's mill' include capital gains tax and corporation tax (both introduced 1965), and value added tax (1973). The last of these gave rise to the need for more reliable business records and for periodic returns to be made to H.M.Customs and Excise.

Sources of fee income, 1987

An indication of the relative financial importance of different activities, in modern times, can be obtained from the annual survey conducted by *The Accountant* into the fee income of UK accounting firms. The 1987 survey showed that the 'big eight' obtain 7 per cent of their fee income from insolvency work, 55 per cent from audit and accountancy, 17 per cent from management consultancy and 21 per cent from tax (investigation work was not separately identified). Firms naturally showed relative strengths in different areas; Coopers & Lybrand earned 12 per cent of its total fees from insolvency, Ernst & Whinney relied on the traditional areas of audit and accountancy for 66 per cent of its income, Arthur Andersen received 33 per cent from management consultancy, and Arthur Young 28 per cent from tax. In general the smaller firms continued to rely more heavily on audit and accountancy for fee income, though some saw management consultancy as offering the greatest potential for growth and specialised in that area (*Accountant*, 30 June 1987, pp.7–9).

21

Professional Associations

Objectives of professionalisation

There are different views about the nature and purpose of professions and their professional associations. The 'altruistic' approach regards professions as providing services which make a distinctive contribution to the smooth operation of society, that they possess specialist knowledge and self-discipline, and that the high level of prestige and financial reward enjoyed are a fair price for these services. The 'cynical' assessment is that the professions comprise groups of individuals pursuing self-interest, striving to convince others of their entitlement to professional recognition and reward, and doing a job which is just enough to satisfy clients and maintain their professional status. It is an approach which sees the accountant as 'street wise' profit maximiser rather than a selfless servant of society.

Developing the more cynical scenario, professional associations are created to improve social status and financial rewards by achieving control over the supply of a particular service within the market for skilled labour, rather than as the natural and inevitable result of performing a distinctive and valued function. Success is of course likely to be achieved only if consumers are convinced of the value of the professional service. The association therefore aims to highlight and reinforce 'the socially valued traits of trustworthiness, independance and dependability' (Willmott p.559). The achievement of professional objectives is more or less guaranteed if the association is given the seal of approval, ideally in the form of monopoly rights, from a powerful group such as the government.

It is therefore argued that the service is valued not only on the basis of its intrinsic worth but also on how well it fits in with the structure of society and the existing economic order which the profession itself is able to influence. Professional associations are seen as '*primarily*, but not exclusively, political bodies whose purpose is to define, organise, secure and advance the interests of their (most vocal and influential) members' (Willmott, p.556). Chapters 16–19 contain examples of professional accounting associations going about their work.

Creation, amalgamation and fragmentation

In the year 1800 only the church, the law and medicine were recognised as professions. The nineteenth century saw the development of the service sector, however, with a number of jobs previously performed by the owner/manager taken over by specialists. This division of labour was a natural consequence of industry becoming more complex as the economy developed. By 1900 the following new professions were well established: accountancy, engineering, architecture, pharmacy, veterinary surgery, dentistry and actuarial science. The professions were undoubtedly a development which occurred in response to economic and social needs, and the job of the professional associations was to build on these needs.

The initial reason for the proliferation of accounting associations was because they originated on a local basis. Amalgamations produced a national organisation but dispersion subsequently took place for the following reasons: to overcome barriers to entry in the form of cash premiums and examinations imposed by the established organisations, and to cater for accountants supplying specialist accounting techniques. Some of these events are now summarised.

The ICAEW was formed in 1880 as a result of the merger of provincial societies – established in Liverpool (1870), London (1870), Manchester (1871), and Sheffield (1877) – with the Society of Accountants in England (1872). The Society of Accountants and Auditors (SAA), formed 1885, went through name changes in 1908 (SIAA) and 1954 (Society of Incorporated Accountants) before it merged with the chartered bodies in 1957. The Scottish organisations set up in Edinburgh (1853), Glasgow (1853) and Aberdeen (1867) merged to form The Institute of Chartered Accountants of Scotland in 1951 (ICAS). The Institute of Chartered Accountants in Ireland (ICAI) was formed in 1888.

The appearance of two Scottish associations nearly twenty years earlier than any of their English counterparts has been attributed to the availability of more practical (and superior?) education, more favourable (to accountants) bankruptcy laws and close links with the legal profession. The Scottish courts, which were far more willing to recognise the standing of the independent accountant than were courts in England, regularly referred accounting questions to practitioners for investigation and report. Many of the early Scottish accountants, particularly in Edinburgh and Aberdeen, received part of their training in legal offices or had family connections with the legal profession (Stewart, p.6 and p.15).

A 'second wave' of professional associations emerged to accommodate accountants who, for one reason or another, found it difficult to gain entry to the existing bodies. A particular impetus for their formation, from 1903, being the Revenue Act of that year which authorised an accountant (defined as a person who had been admitted as a member of an incorporated society of accountants) to represent clients before the general commissioners. New bodies included the Corporation of Accountants in Scotland (1891), the Institute of Certified Public Accountants (1903), the London Association of Accountants (1904), and the Central Association of Accountants (1905). The initial willingness of these bodies to embrace all aspiring accountants did not last long. Once the monopoly position of the existing bodies was breached the 'new boys' lined up with the old establishment to form a new order.

The London Association of Accountants, for example, began by opening its doors to all practising accountants but, by 1919, passing the final exam was a compulsory condition for admission to entry. In 1939 it combined with the Corporation of Accountants in Scotland to form the Association of Certified and Corporate Accountants, ACCA (renamed the Association of Certified Accountants in 1971, and the Chartered Association of Certified Accountants in 1984). In 1941 the ACCA absorbed the Institute of Certified Public Accountants which had already joined forces (1932) with the Central Association of Accountants.

Throughout this process there has rarely been any shortage of work for accountants; indeed, it was the ready availability of paid employment that gave rise to the formation of rival organisations. These new bodies succeeded in enhancing the position of their members, thereby demonstrating the advantages of a formal association and the apparent failure of the market to make a rational assessment of services offered.

Additional organisations were established to meet the specialist needs of accountants working in the public sector and in industry.

The Corporate Treasurers' and Accountants' Institute was formed in 1885 to represent the interests of municipal accountants. It changed its name to the Institute of Municipal Treasurers and Accountants (IMTA) in 1901 and, since 1973, has been known as Chartered Institute of Public Finance and Accountancy (CIPFA). The Institute of Cost and Works Accountants (ICWA) was formed in 1919 to cater for accountants in industry. It was renamed the Institute of Cost and Management Accountants (ICMA) in 1972, and the Chartered Institute of Management Accountants (CIMA) in 1986.

Many of these bodies established professional journals to act as a focal point for debate, a vehicle for official pronouncements and as a place for marketing specialist skills. *The Accountant*, first published 1874, had close connections with the ICAEW for many years. The official publication of the SIAA was the *Incorporated Accountants Journal* (1889), later renamed *Accountancy* and now the mouthpiece of the ICAEW. The ICWA established *The Cost Accountant* (now called *Management Accounting*) in 1921. The public sector journal, *Financial Circular* (1896) was re-named *Local Government Finance* (1926) and is now called *Public Finance and Accountancy*. The Scottish journal is *The Accountant's Magazine* (1897), while the Certified Accountants launched *The Certified Accountants' Journal* (now called *Certified Accountant*) in 1905. Numerous other professional journals were inaugerated and perished due to lack of interest, mergers and takeovers.

Statistics

If we judge success by size, the British professional accountancy bodies have accomplished a great deal. In 1904 there were just over 4K chartered accountants in Britain and about 2K incorporated accountants. In 1957, when the ICAEW and the SIAA merged, there were 38K chartered and incorporated accountants. Qualified membership of each of the major accounting bodies at the end of 1986 was as follows (student membership in brackets): ICAEW 84K(16K), ACCA 28K(70K), CIMA 26K(40K), ICAS 12K(2K), CIPFA 9K(2.5K), and the ICAI 6K(2K). There is also a junior body, called the Association of Accounting Technicians, which had 12K(25K) members. It is generally believed that the demand for accountants in an 'information based economy' is likely to continue to grow.

The ICAEW has the largest proportion of its members in private practice, 50 per cent compared with 40 per cent of the Scottish Institute and 30 per cent of ACCA. Except for the members of CIPFA, nearly all qualified accountants work in the private sector; in 1975, for example, only 3 per cent of the members of non-CIPFA bodies worked in central or local government. CIPFA members overlap with members of other bodies only in nationalised industries and public sector organisations such as the national health service.

The age profile of the profession is young. In 1987, for example, almost 50 per cent of the ICAEW's members were under 35 and two-thirds aged under 45. It remains mainly a non-graduate profession although the position is changing fairly rapidly. Today the accountancy profession is a massive consumer of graduate talent, taking one in ten students leaving British Universities with a first degree.[1] There is also a move towards more women accountants. In 1960 there were just 342 female members of the ICAEW (less than 1 per cent of the total membership) and by 1982 the proportion had crept to just 3 per cent. But the position will soon change as 28 per cent of new students registering in 1983 were women. In September 1986 CIMA admitted its 1000th female member.

There are major international differences in the number of professional accountants. For example, accountancy has achieved greater prominence as an independent profession in Western Europe than in Eastern Europe. But even within Western Europe there are major variations; in 1982 the UK boasted 116K qualified accountants compared with 10K in France and 4K in West Germany.[2] These differences no doubt reflect variations both in the structure of society and in the ability of accountants to sell their services.

Professional associations at work

The broad objectives of professionalisation were considered at the beginning of this chapter. The more specific functions of a professional organisation are as follows: to distinguish competent practitioners from the incompetent and downright dishonest; to ensure members behave in an ethical manner; to raise the quality of the service provided; to provide advice for members on how to discharge their duties; and to ensure that members are adequately rewarded for the work they do. The areas of activity discussed below are together designed to achieve these aims.

Ethics and specialisation. An important initial reason for forming a professional body is to provide its members with a respectable identity, and on 9 January 1868 *The Times* urged the formation of an Accountants' Institute

> to exclude the herd of disreputable persons, who act merely as the tools of delinquent directors and officials, or the lowest class of attorneys, and whose knowledge of their calling has generally been derived from personal experience of failure in every other pursuit they have tried (quoted in Worthington, p.81).

According to Frederick Whinney, the problem was exacerbated because, during the 1870s, numerous individuals believed they simply had 'to put up a plate and designate themselves as [accountants], in order to become rich men' (Howitt, p.4). Worthington put it more strongly and colourfully: 'this opportunity of easily acquiring some of the circulating medium was seized upon with alacrity by many shabby genteel nondescripts to display their latent and mobile abilities on anything connected with estimates, returns, or accounts' (p.41).

To help counter the above problems the ICAEW broke new ground by including in its Charter (1880) what might be broadly described as a code of conduct or professional ethics. Obligations imposed on members included requirements that they should not accept commissions from solicitors and that they should not carry on any occupation other than that of being a public accountant. Although part of the reason for this restriction was that some accountants associated with activities considered undesirable, also important was the determination of the early leaders to identify accountancy as a distinct discipline requiring full-time attention. The Charter also imposed a ban on advertising (lifted 1984). This has, of course, never prevented surreptitious touting for work.

Entry Barriers. We have seen that new societies were formed, from time to time, to challenge the monopoly of existing organisations. The initial reaction of the establishment was aggression and ridicule but, after varying periods of warfare, the new body either collapsed or gained in strength and became a part of the establishment. Amalgamation often then followed.

The ICAEW described the initial membership of the SAA as 'a formidable array of clerks of all kinds – rent collectors, corn merchants, shopkeepers, valuers, collectors of taxes, bailiffs, secretaries of various concerns, civil engineers, schoolboard clerks, overseers, timber agents, tobacconists, pawnbrokers and manure merchants' (*Accountant*, 1886, p.160). Later on *The Accountant* described the newly formed London Association of Accountants as consisting of 'Questionable characters who make the dregs of the profession' (1908, p.514).

The development of cost accounting during the first couple of decades of the twentieth century was similarly looked down upon by the established bodies. The general view was that these 'cost accountants' were little more than industrial book-keepers, technicians or clerks. Undoubtedly costing systems were of an uneven quality, and a government investigation (1916) noted their virtual absence even from some very large companies (Loft, p.141). The need for improved procedures increased 'hand in hand with the general transformation of industry as business strove to meet wartime requirements' (ibid., p.146). More efficient costing systems were also needed to help with post-war reconstruction and in 1919 the ICWA was formed to act as a focal point for accountants working in industry, many of whom were members of professional accountancy bodies which had made no attempt to provide them with the skills needed for this work. Hence the ICWA's objective was to fill this gap by encouraging 'the development of scientific costing, to hold examinations and award qualifications' (Stacey, p.99).

Leading industrialists such as Lord Leverhulme and Sir Herbert Austin showed tremendous enthusiasm for the new venture (Loft, p.153), in contrast with outright opposition from the existing bodies. The Charter application was resisted by the ICAEW and the SIAA, which had quickly learned the rules of the game, on the grounds that 'such persons are not employed in professional work but in the service of traders' (*Accountant*, 5 May 1923, p.683). Despite this antipathy, the ICWA succeeded in delineating its area of operation and identified cost accounting as a separate and independent profession.

Education and training. The standard of entry to the profession is regulated by the professional bodies; the government has, in the past, played no part.[3] Preparation for entry typically consists of two elements; the completion of a period of apprenticeship and a series of examinations. The purposes of apprenticeship are to guarantee adequate experience and professional competence. In the ICAEW's case, the apprenticeship (first called articles and now the training contract) was five years for O level entrants, until this category was phased out in the early 1970s, four years for A level entrants and three years for graduates. Continuing professional education and training after qualification date from 1978.

The purposes of the examination system are to check whether an individual has achieved the level of intellectual ability and professional knowledge needed to discharge the duties of a practising accountant. The ICAEW held its first examinations for admission in 1882 and, until 1892, they contained an oral element, though this was used merely to enlarge upon written answers. Oral exams were also used for a short time after the Second World War to test soldiers who had passed written exams in German prisoner of war camps.

The titles to the six papers of the first final examination of the ICAEW were as follows: bookkeeping; partnership and executorship accounts; auditing; the rights and duties of liquidators, trustees and receivers; bankruptcy and company law; mercantile law and the law of arbitration. The questions initially had a verbal rather than a numerical emphasis. Economics was not introduced until 1934, taxation and cost and management accounting were given little attention until 1947, statistics was introduced in 1965, and financial management ten years later.[4] Optional papers in economics and statistics were set between 1922 and 1934 (Freear).

Over the years the exam pass rate has varied considerably, though the general trend has been downwards despite the increasing proportion of graduates entering the profession. This suggests that entry standards are being continuously raised. Low pass rates have led to suggestions that the professional bodies control entry to keep rates of pay high. Such allegations have been strenuously, but not always persuasively, rejected. Some bodies, such as the ICAS are closely involved in the education and training of potential members. Others, such as the ICAEW, have confined their activities to that of an examining body, leaving preparation for the professional exams to correspondence colleges and private sector 'cram' colleges.

Further restrictions on entry, imposed in earlier times, were based on wealth and sex. Payment of a premium for articles, which was sometimes as much as 500 guineas – a substantial figure – confined the profession to the sons of the reasonably well off. A natural response was the establishment of an alternative route to professional status. The SAA, for example, formed in 1885, instead arranged for a ten-year apprenticeship and a modest payment during articles. The London Association (1904) welcomed women members from the outset and was the first to do so. The first women member of the ICAEW was Mary Harris Smith admitted, in 1920, following the Sex Disqualification (Removal) Act of 1919. She had been making unsuccessful applications for membership since 1891, rejected on the technically doubtful grounds that the Royal Charter was expressed in the male gender.

Links with universities. A fair number of early Scottish accountants obtained a part of their education at university, although few of them graduated. It was not unusual for young men to attend some classes at Scottish universities without the intention of proceeding to a degree, and aspiring accountants went along to acquire a knowledge of the law of bankruptcy. On the whole, however, the development of the accountancy profession in Britain has, until recently, owed very little to the universities. During the last quarter of the nineteenth century, universities were established in many of the busy provincial cities, but accounting was rarely offered. Even in 1912, only the following offered degrees containing an accounting element: Birmingham, where Dicksee was Professor of Accounting 1902–6, Manchester, Leeds, Liverpool, and the LSE where accounting was available only as an optional subject.[5] There were no formal university connections until the recognition of the 'relevant' degree in 1945 and, in 1957, there were still only three full-time chairs in England (Birmingham, Bristol and the LSE) and two part-time chairs in Scotland. The rate of development has speeded up significantly since about 1970; the number of full-time chairs in England, Scotland and Wales, had risen to 30 by 1976 and to over 50 by 1987. Geoffrey Whittington became the first Oxbridge Professor of Accountancy in 1988.

It has been suggested that one reason why accounting has struggled to achieve academic status in Britain is because universities saw themselves as institutions capable of producing the 'well-rounded gentleman' rather than an individual trained to enter the market. The large increase in the number of university graduates, the heavy demand from industry for financially trained personnel, the consequent rise in salaries, and the increased complexity of the accounting function have together conspired to change attitudes and practices. Another reason for the growth, in numbers, of the graduate entrant is that these students do a lot better in their professional examinations, thereby increasing the efficiency of a firm's investment in that area. The high grades now demanded from students wishing to study accounting at university is, however, a reflection of the continued lack of public resources devoted to this expanding area. The gap is partly filled by the professional firms which provide a modest amount of funds for staff and equipment, and help, on a part-time basis, with lecture courses and tutorials.

Regulation of reporting practices. The government policy of minimum interference placed on the professional accountancy bodies the responsibility for raising standards of financial reporting by providing guidelines for members to follow. They were slow to accept the challenge but, since the early 1940s, they have been increasingly active in this area (see Chapter 19).

Registration and integration. Accountancy bodies, in common with other professional associations, have endeavoured not only to control the supply of personnel but also the demand by obtaining official recognition of the *need* for the services offered, such as an annual audit (see Chapter 20), and by obtaining a monopoly position in the *provision* of these services. State registers do in fact exist listing individuals entitled to practice certain occupations and professions. The need for a register is sometimes to protect the public, e.g. in medicine. There are also cases where groups have successfully petitioned for a register despite the absence of any demonstrable public need, e.g. architects. Accountants have been less successful despite strenuous efforts in this direction.

Soon after its formation the ICAEW began to take an interest in political affairs. Two types of audit had been evolved for local government by 1880; the district audit (undertaken by government paid officials) dates from 1844, and the elective audit (undertaken by individuals, probably amateurs, appointed by the ratepayers) was given legislative sanction by the Municipal Corporations Act 1835. In 1888 the ICAEW attempted to get a provision written into the local government bill confining appointment, to the position of local government auditor, to members of the ICAEW. This naturally provoked opposition from the SAA, and the lack of success was quite possibly the result of this public squabble. The right to appoint a practising accountant as auditor in individual cases, however, was endorsed by Parliament's approval of the

Accrington Municipal Corporation Act (1890) which provided for this to be done.[6]

The last decade of the nineteenth century and the first decade of the twentieth century saw numerous attempts made to obtain a monopoly position for the ICAEW and the SAA (SIAA from 1908) by the establishment of a register of qualified accountants. These attempts failed, partly because the leading bodies were unable to reconcile their conflicting interests, and partly because of vigorous opposition from the new, smaller, bodies who were excluded. A further factor was the profession's failure to convince the government that such a move would be in the public interest.

The majority of appointments to the position of 'public auditor' under, for example, the Friendly Society Act 1875 (see Chapter 20), nevertheless went to members of the ICAEW, SAA or SIAA after 1890. Members of other bodies remained eligible for this work, but the services provided by certain members of the London Association of Incorporated Accountants, between 1916–19, were deemed unsatisfactory and, in 1920, Parliament confined the appointment to members of the two leading accounting bodies (Stacey, p.41). The Municipal Corporations (Audit) Act 1933 confined appointment as local governmment auditor to chartered accountants, members of the SIAA, the London Association, which was back in favour, and the Corporation of Accountants in Scotland (Stacey, pp.44–50).

Demands for a general register were revived in the 1930s and the accounting bodies were invited to present evidence to a BOT committee chaired by Viscount Goschen. Opposition came from the ICAEW which argued that this would result in a 'levelling down' of standards. The conclusion, once again, was that a register was not in the public interest. Such a register was, for example, considered likely to impose unnecessarily high costs on private companies who could themselves investigate the reputation of an auditor they wished to engage. The committee also took the view that a register was impracticable in view of the numerous professional bodies in existence and the difficulty of defining the scope of the professional services supplied by accountants.

During the 1940s and 1950s a number of attempts were made by the senior accounting bodies to establish a 'public accountants' council' to keep a register of 'respectable' accounting bodies and to issue a licence for accountants to practice. It was partly because of the failure of these initiatives, again due to internal wrangling, that, in 1957, the ICAEW and the SIAA merged with the objectives of providing a more unified public image and to prevent harmful competition, particularly for staff, between the two bodies.

Following this merger there were six major accountancy bodies in Britain; the three chartered bodies, the ACCA, the IMTA and the ICWA. In a determined attempt to integrate the profession the ICAEW produced a scheme, in 1970, under which the ACCA, IMTA, and ICWA would be dissolved and their members would join one or other of the chartered bodies and be called chartered accountants. It was a sign of the growing divisions within the ICAEW, between the small and larger practitioners, that this initiative was rejected by the 'backwoodsmen' who believed the change would result in a dilution of their status as chartered accountants.

Integration was intended to remove misunderstanding arising from the multiplicity of professional designations, and to enable the profession to speak with one voice on matters of professional, national and international importance. Clearly the bulk of the membership were unwilling to exchange the known value of their chartered qualification for the possible greater benefits of unity. A compromise solution worked out over the next few years was the establishment (1974) of the Consultative Committee of Accounting Bodies (CCAB), 'to develop joint representation on matters of common concern'. Or as Woolf put it: 'The CCAB was the phoenix which rose from the ashes of the 1970 integration proposals' (p.31).

An impetus for this development, as with the formation of the ASC, were the number of important scandals and perceived professional failures that occurred in the late 1960s and early 1970s. The creation of the CCAB with three sub-committees concerned with accounting standards, auditing practices and professional ethics was also, to some extent, designed to meet the threat of government interference if the profession failed to put is own house in order. The path of the CCAB has not been entirely smooth. Even internally there has been dissention, mainly as a result of the ICAEW's numerical dominance on the committee. Recent (1987) illustrations of disquiet are the ICAS's criticism of the financial cost of its contribution to the CCAB, and recurring differences of opinion on how to cope with the problem of inflation accounting.

In view of the size of the main bodies, and their different specialisations, complete integration is perhaps becoming less rather than more likely.

Social Status

The appointment of accountants to government committees, their engagement to undertake investigations on behalf of the government, and the receipt of honours, are all indicative of a rise in the accountant's social status. Quilter gave evidence to the Monteagle Committee (1849), and other witnesses during the nineteenth century included William Turquand, Samuel Lowell Price, James Edward Coleman, John Ball, Robert Palmer-Harding, David Chadwick and Frederick Whinney. Chadwick was the first accountant appointed to a company law amendment committee (1877), but the entries for accountants in the *Dictionary of Business Biography* show that, during the twentieth century, accountants have undertaken a massive range of government work.

The first accountant to receive a knighthood was Sir Robert Palmer-Harding (1890) but this seems to have been in recognition of his services as chief official receiver, a post he took up after resigning from the profession. Sir William Barclay Peat was knighted in 1912. During the First World War professional accountants were heavily engaged in management of the war effort by introducing efficient procedures for controlling the supply of raw materials and, later, food. This undoubtedly improved their status with the Government and resulted in numerous knighthoods and other honours being granted. Today, honours lists invariably include a plentiful supply of accountants in one capacity or another, although lawyers, for example, still do rather better.

Review and prospect

Professional accountants have shown themselves to be a highly practical, enterprising, flexible and ambitious body of men, and of late women, who quickly organised themselves on a professional basis and soon became an accepted part of the establishment. Over the years they have efficiently identified new opportunities for development and provided a range of services which are highly valued by society, at least in cash terms. Progress has been made in competition with a number of other professional groupings, including lawyers, bankers and actuaries. Success has been achieved partly because the accountancy profession has shown itself to be more innovative and industrious than its competitors, partly because it proved capable of supplying the best service, and partly because it has benefited increasingly from statutory recognition and support.

There is no doubt that individual associations have played an important part in fostering their members' interest though, in the absence of integration, this has sometimes been at the expense of sister organisations. There is, at present, a feeling in some quarters that the large firms of chartered accountants have outgrown the need for an institution to represent their interests and are quite capable of looking after themselves. One problem is the differential priorities of the large firms and their clients (often household names themselves) on the one hand, and the small local practice on the other. The difficultly of framing standards which are equally appropriate for the international conglomorate and the proprietorship company is one manifestation of this difficulty.

The diversification of large practices has also raised doubts whether these firms are any longer professional in the altruistic sense of the word and have instead become a part of big business. As a leading US accountant put it (the comment would apply equally in Britain): 'there has been an erosion of that self-restraint, conservatism, and adherence to basic professional values at a pace and to an extent that is unprecedented in the profession's history' (quoted in Zeff, p.110). The problem seems to be growth at all costs and, in an endeavour to reach the 'big eight', or become the biggest of the big eight, the competitive edge is greater than ever before. Preoccupation with growth has resulted in a rapid movement away from auditing (the one area where the government recognises the need for a professional accountant's specialist skills), and into consultancy. This has produced a 'change [in] the balance of the professional mindset – moving farther from an audit mentality and toward a consulting mentality' (Zeff, p.110). This diversification has brought accounting firms into competition with businesses which have no professional and competitive constraints and, in such circumstances, adherence to traditional professional standards is seen as a handicap.

There is reasonable ground for the concern that partners in professional firms now give first priority to high salaries in the short term rather than the provision of a valuable service for society linked with adequate long-term financial rewards. If accountancy is to maintain its current status, built up over many years, it is important for accountants to realise the need to ensure some correspondence between their own personal interests and those of the community as a whole.

Appendix A

Table of Cases

1849 Burnes v Pennell, 9 English reports, 1181
1867 Oakes v Turquand, L.R.2.H.L.325
1869 Stringer's case, L.R. 4 Ch.App.475
1875 Ashbury Railway Carriage and Iron Co. v Riche, L.R.7 H.L.653
1877 re Ebbw Vale Steel, Iron and Coal Co. Ltd, 4 Ch.D.827
1878 Nichol's Case, 47 L.J. Ch.415
1879 re City of Glasgow Bank, 4 App.Cas.547
1879 Davison v Gillies, 16 L.R.Ch.344
1882 Flitcroft's Case, 21 L.R. Ch.519
1886 re Midland Land and Investment Corporation, Ltd, unreported except for shorthand reporter's notes in Palmer, *Company Precedents*, 1912, pp.904–06.
1887 Trevor v Whitworth, L.R.12 App.Cas.409
1889 Lee v Neuchatel Asphalte Co., 41 Ch.D.1
1889 Glasier v Rolls, 42 Ch.D.436
1892 Lubbock v British Bank of South America, 2 Ch.198
1894 Verner v General and Commercial Investment Trust, Ltd, 2 Ch.239
1895 re London and General Bank (No.2), 2 Ch.673
1896 re Kingston Cotton Mill Co. Ltd (No.2), 2 Ch.279
1898 Cox v Edinburgh and District Tramway Co. Ltd, 1898, discussed in Edwards, Ronald S., 'The Nature and the Measurement of Income', in *Studies in Accounting*, edited by W.T.Baxter, p.296.
1901 Foster v New Trinidad Lake Asphalte Co. Ltd, 1 Ch.208
1904 re Hoare and Co. Ltd, 2 Ch.D 208
1904 London Oil Storage Co. v Seear, Hasluck & Co., 31 Acct.L.R.1
1906 Newton v Birmingham Small Arms Co. Ltd, 2 Ch.378
1918 Ammonia Soda Co. Ltd v Chamberlain, 1 Ch.D 266
1931 Rex v Lord Kylsant and another, reported in *The Royal Mail Case* edited by Collin Brooks.
1932 re Westminster Road Construction and Engineering Co. Ltd, Acct.L.R.8
1960 Westburn Sugar Refineries Ltd v IRC, S.L.T.297
1961 Dimbula Valley (Celyon) Tea Co. Ltd v Laurie, Ch.353
1980 Shearer v Bercain, 124 S.J.292

Appendix B

Table of Statutes

1285	Remedies against Servants and Accountants	13 Edw.1, c.11
1601	Poor Law Act	43 Eliz.1, c.2
1719	Royal Exchange and London Assurance Corporations Act ('Bubble' Act)	6 Geo.1, c.18
1739	County Rates Act	12 Geo.2, c.29
1790	Glamorganshire Canal Company	30 Geo.3, c.82
1801	Surrey Iron Railway Company	41 Geo.3, c.33
1823	Northampton Gas Light Company	4 Geo.4, c.96
1825	Bubble Companies, etc. Act	6 Geo.4, c.91
1826	Country Bankers Act	7 Geo.4, c.46
1829	Friendly Societies Act	10 Geo.4, c.56
1831	Bankruptcy Act	1&2 Will.4, c.56
1834	Trading Companies Act	4&5 Will.4, c.94
1835	Municipal Corporations Act	5&6 Will.4, c.76
1837	Chartered Companies Act	7 Will.4 & 1 Vict., c.73
1842	Newcastle and Darlington Junction Railway Company	5 Vict., sess.2, c.80
1842	Mines and Collieries Act	5&6 Vict., c.99
1844	Factory Act	7&8 Vict., c.15
1844	Lancaster and Carlisle Railway Company	7&8 Vict., c.37
1844	Railway Regulation Act	7&8 Vict., c.85
1844	Joint Stock Companies Act	7&8 Vict., c.110
1845	Companies Clauses Consolidation Act	8&9 Vict., c.16
1845	Railway Clauses Consolidation Act	8&9 Vict., c.20
1846	Railway Act	9&10 Vict., c.105
1847	Gas Works Clauses Act	10&11 Vict., c.15
1847	Water Works Clauses Act	10&11 Vict., c.17
1847	Joint Stock Companies Act	10&11 Vict., c.78
1855	Limited Liability Act	18&19 Vict., c.133
1856	Joint Stock Companies Act	19&20 Vict., c.47
1856	Bankruptcy Act	19&20 Vict., c.79
1858	Joint Stock Banks Act	21&22 Vict., c.91
1860	Gas (Metropolis) Act	23&24 Vict., c.125
1862	Companies Act	25&26 Vict., c.89
1867	Railway Companies Act	30&31 Vict., c.127

1867	Companies Act	30&31 Vict., c.131
1868	Regulation of Railways Act	31&32 Vict., c.119
1869	Bankruptcy Act	32&33 Vict., c.71
1870	Life Assurance Companies Act	33&34 Vict., c.61
1871	Gas Works Clauses Act	34&35 Vict., c.31
1871	Metropolis Water Act	34&35 Vict., c.113
1874	Building Societies Act	37&38 Vict., c.42
1875	Friendly Societies Act	38&39 Vict., c.60
1877	Companies Act	40&41 Vict., c.26
1879	Companies Act	42&43 Vict., c.76
1882	Electric Lighting Act	45&46 Vict., c.56
1883	Bankruptcy Act	46&47 Vict., c.52
1890	Accrington Municipal Corporations Act	53&54 Vict., c.63
1890	Directors' Liability Act	53&54 Vict., c 64
1893	Industrial and Provident Societies Act	56&57 Vict., c.39
1894	Building Societies Act	57&58 Vict., c.47
1896	Friendly Societies Act	59&60 Vict., c.25
1899	Electric Lighting (Clauses) Act	62&63 Vict., c.19
1900	Companies Act	63&64 Vict., c.48
1902	Metropolitan Water Companies Act	2 Edw.7, c.41
1903	Revenue Act	3 Edw.7, c.46
1907	Limited Partnerships Act	7 Edw.7, c.24
1907	Companies Act	7 Edw.7, c.50
1908	Companies (Consolidation) Act	8 Edw.7, c.69
1909	Assurance Companies Act	9 Edw.7, c.49
1911	Railway Companies Act	1&2 Geo.5, c.34
1913	Industrial and Provident Societies Act	3&4 Geo.5, c.31
1919	Sex Disqualification (Removal) Act	9&10 Geo.5, c.71
1928	Companies Act	18&19 Geo.5, c.45
1929	Companies Act	19&20 Geo.5, c.23
1933	Municipal Corporations (Audit) Act	23&24 Geo.5, c.28
1947	Companies Act	10&11 Geo.6, c.47
1948	Companies Act	11&12 Geo.6, c.38
1967	Companies Act	c.81
1976	Companies Act	c.69
1980	Companies Act	c.22
1981	Companies Act	c.62
1985	Companies Act	c.6

Appendix C

Government Committees

1844 Gladstone Committee. Select Committee on Joint-Stock Companies. Report and Minutes of Evidence, BPP 1844, vii, 1.

1849 Monteagle Committee. House of Lords Select Committee on the Audit of Railway Accounts. First, Second and Third Reports, Minutes of Evidence and Appendix, BPP 1849, x, 1.

1852/3 Wilson Committee. Select Committee on Assurance Associations. Report and Minutes of Evidence, BPP 1852/3, xxi, 1.

1867 Watkin Committee. Select Committee on Limited Liability Acts, 1867. Report and Minutes of Evidence, BPP 1867, x, 393.

1877 Lowe Committee. Select Committee on the Companies Acts. Report and Minutes of Evidence, BPP 1877, viii, 419

1895 Davey Committee. Departmental Committee on Joint Stock Companies. Report and Minutes of Evidence, BPP 1895, lxxxviii, 151.

1896/8 Halsbury Committee. House of Lords Select Committee on the Companies Bill. Report and Minutes of Evidence, BPP 1896, ix, 171, BPP 1897, x, 97, BPP 1898, ix, 19.

1906 Loreburn Committee. Company Law Amendment Committee. Report and Minutes of Evidence, BPP 1906, xcvii, 199.

1910 Cole Committee. Departmental Committee on Railway Accounts and Statistical Returns. Minutes of Evidence, BPP 1910, lvi, 357.

1918 Wrenbury Committee. Company Law Amendment Committee. Report, BPP 1918, xii, 727.

1926 Greene Committee. Company Law Amendment Committee. Report, BPP 1926, ix, 477. Minutes of Evidence, 1925, Non-parliamentary.

1945 Cohen Committee. Committee on Company Law Amendment. Report, BPP 1945, iv, 793. Minutes of Evidence, 1943–45, Non-parliamentary.

1962 Jenkins Committee. Company Law Committee. Report, BPP 1962, xii. Minutes of Evidence, 1960–61, Non-parliamentary.

1975 Sandilands Committee. Report of the Inflation Accounting Committee, Cmnd 6225, HMSO, London.

1986 Byatt Committee. Accounting for Economic Costs and Changing Prices, Report to HM Treasury by an advisory group, HMSO, London.

Notes

Chapter 2

1. This is a variant of the categorisation contained in Baladouni (1977), from which much of the material in this section is taken. The first period is a sketch of worldwide developments, the second relates to Europe and the third and fourth specifically to Britain.
2. One important exception was the imposition of the double account system on certain categories of statutory company (see Chapter 13).
3. Their theories are summarised and demolished by de Ste Croix and in the appendix to Macve, 1986.

Chapter 3

1. This revelation is less surprising when attention is drawn to the fact that mathematical calculations of considerable complexity must have been made in certain pre-literate societies in order to create the megolithic constructions used for astronomical observations in places such as Carnac, Brittany (Yamey, p.127).
2. Charge and discharge accounting was still widely used in Britain during the middle ages. The general format of the charge and discharge statement, prepared at that time, is given in Chapter 4.

Chapter 4

1. The content of this section draws heavily on Chatfield, pp.20–24.
2. The office of Master of the Rolls was established, in 1285, to act as the custodian of the pipe-roll. At this time the position carried no judicial responsibilities.
3. The content of this section is based mainly on Jones's article.

Chapter 6

1. This approach was also used where an incomplete or disorganised system of double entry was in operation (see Chapter 8).
2. Lister's analysis has been criticised by Hopwood and Johnson for a number of reasons which include Lister's failure to take account of recent research.
3. Reference is made in Chapter 5 to the fact that it is not entirely clear whether Pacioli's trial balance was prepared *before* or *after* closing balances on revenue and expenditure accounts to the profit and loss account.

Chapter 8

1. An even broader interpretation is provided by Malthus who wrote (1820) that 'stock is a general term, and may be defined to be all the material possessions of a country' (quoted in Tucker, p.85).

2. This is an example of a persistent accounting problem. Today, however, a much more limited range of assets are omitted because of valuation problems. The main ones are 'created' goodwill and research expenditure.

Chapter 9

1. The twelve country banks in existence in 1750 grew to 660 by 1824. They were unincorporated enterprises which often lent money, short term, to high risk business. They operated from a single locality and used a growing army of bill-brokers to provide mobility of capital between different geographical areas (Alderman, p.46).

Chapter 10

1. Even today, however, repairs and renewals accounting is considered appropriate in certain circumstances. For example, the 1987 accounts of Greenall Whitley state that 'no depreciation is provided on non-industrial freehold and leasehold properties as it is the group's policy to maintain them, out of expenditure charged to revenue, to a standard which ensures that their estimated aggregate residual values exceed net book amounts'.
2. This is a reference to the Regulation of Railways Act of 1868, which imposed a system of financial reporting – the double account system – that some consider to have ruled out the possibility of making a charge for depreciation (see Chapter 13).

Chapter 11

1. Much of the material in this chapter is taken from Edwards, 1981, which was an investigation of the financial reporting practices of iron and steel companies.
2. Between 1844–1981 numerous companies acts introduced new accounting regulations. In addition major consolidations occurred in 1862, 1908, 1929, 1948 and 1985 (see Appendix B). The provisions of many of these acts, particularly the later ones, took effect on a range of different dates specified in the act or subsequently set out in Orders in Council or Statutory Instruments. This chapter, and others, usually quote the year of the companies act which introduced a new regulation, rather than the date when it took effect.
3. Today assets and liabilities may be omitted from the balance sheet by making use of 'special purpose vehicles'. This is a technique whereby equal amounts of assets and liabilities are transferred to a 'subsidiary' which does not have to be consolidated because of the way in which owner-ship is arranged. The usual procedure is for the 'holding' company to own 50 per cent of the shares and a friendly financial institution, such as a bank, to hold the other 50 per cent. The rights of the financial institution to participate in profits are, however, severely restricted.

Chapter 12

1. The accounts of the Royal Mail Steam Packet Co. Ltd were not issued under the Companies Act, as it was a chartered company, and the prosecution of the chairman and auditor was under the Larceny Act 1861. The lessons of this case, however, were considered to have a general application.
2. In the US, a quite different mechanism for investor protection was established at about this time. Intense discussion of financial reporting practices following the 'great (stock market) crash' of 1929 led to the establishment of a supervisory body called the Securities and Exchange Commission. Accounts filed with the SEC must comply with generally accepted principles and practices as developed by the accountancy profession. Compliance is effectively guaranteed because failure to do so results in the suspension of a company's quotation. Whether a similar procedure should be adopted in Great Britain has been the subject of intermittent debate.

Chapter 13

1. Clauses Acts relating to railways 1847, water 1847, gas 1847 and 1871, and electricity 1899 worked in a similar way.
2. Experimentation with depreciation accounting was, however, discontinued in the 1850s (see Chapter 10).
3. The forms of accounts prescribed for electric lighting companies 29 years earlier (1882) contained separate entries for a depreciation charge on leasehold works, on buildings, and on plant and machinery, while the accounts prescribed for gas companies (1871) contained an entry for leasehold lands.
4. There was of course considerable variation between companies, and probably even more variation between industries. It must also be noted that the railways have been researched most fully, though the accounting practices of other public utilities appear to have followed the same broad pattern.
5. The possible inadequacy of the charge has already been noted of course. It should also be noted that, within industry generally the widespread inclusion of a depreciation charge, calculated on a systematic basis, was also a slow process (see Chapter 11).

Chapter 14

1. A realised profit (capital or revenue) is usually regarded today as one which has arisen as the result of a sale at 'arms length'.
2. A requirement was introduced for the disclosure of exceptional profits and losses; this matter is now dealt with in more detail by SSAP 6 and CA 1985.
3. The decision in *re Hoare and Co. Ltd* (1904) has been cited (Gower, p.233) as authority for the proposition that the directors might, alternatively, base a distribution on accumulated profit where a loss was suffered during the current accounting period, but this interpretation has been challenged by French (p.323).

4. Problems of course occur where there is a conflict between accepted accounting practice and a specific provisions contained in the Companies Act (see Chapter 17).

Chapter 15

1. Order of the Board of Trade, dated 30 July 1906, substituting a new Table A for that contained in the first schedule to the Companies Act 1862, S.R.& O.1906, No.596, L.15.
2. Auditing guideline 11, entitled Financial Information issued with Audited Financial Statements (1985), now requires the auditor to review the chairman's report (and any other information contained in the accounts for which he has no explicit statutory responsibility) for any 'material inconsistency' or 'misleading' information and, if appropriate, refer to the matter in his report.

Chapter 16

1. The maximum number of partners was reduced to 20 in 1856 although this rule was relaxed for certain professional firms, including accountants, in 1967. The minimum number of members for private companies was put at 2 when this category of company was introduced in 1907. The minimum of 2 was extended to all companies in 1980.
2. It was possible for the holding company to own all but one of the shares which would be held by a director to satisfy the legal requirement for private companies to have at least two shareholders.
3. Bircher believes that the receptiveness of the BOT to the need for change (they had resisted the SIAA's campaign for reform in the 1930s, see Chapter 12), can be put down to 'the change in social attitudes engendered by the war and the need, as the war drew to a close, to address the issues of rebuilding the economy in the post-war period' (p.119).
4. CA 1981 imposed on auditors a statutory duty to check whether the information given in the directors' report is consistent with that contained in the financial statements on which they are reporting (s.15).

Chapter 17

1. Developments post-CA 1981 indicate that these suspicions may have been, to some extent, well-founded. There are signs that the content of company accounts is now controlled by the detailed letter of the law, rather than by the spirit of the law and the traditional concepts of truth and fairness.
2. The Germans initially developed uniform formats, however, for management accounting purposes. The first comprehensive chart of accounts was published in 1911 and was used by industry during the First World War (Nobes, p.45). In 1927 Schmalenbach, a leading accounting professor and writer, devised model charts for different industries and, in order to achieve close control over the allocation of resources throughout the economy, the Nazis made the adoption of

these charts compulsory. They introduced a similar system into France in the early 1940s. The use of uniform formats for published financial statements were made compulsory in Germany, in 1931, and in France in 1947.

3. Much of this section draws on Hein, ch.8.

Chapter 18

1. This obligation was inferred from the requirement for auditors to report 'on every balance sheet laid before the company in general meeting' (s.23).
2. A further advantage claimed for private company status was the facility it provided for minimising the impact of death duties on the family business (*The Incorporated Accountants Journal*, 1910–11, pp.461–67).
3. CA 1929 emphasised the obligation to report *the company's* assets, and this may have been interpreted as ruling out the use of equity accounting since the subsidiary's retained profits clearly did not belong to the holding company (Edwards and Webb, p.40).
4. There is a risk that the directors will turn to a firm of accountants willing to take a more flexible approach, and in today's more businesslike and less professional climate, there is a strong likelihood that the new work will be welcomed.

Chapter 19

1. At the same time, the fact that the Recommendations were non-mandatory proved an important drawback when attempting to persuade an obstinate client to accept best accounting practice (Leach, p.4).
2. The former contains a full examination of the matter under consideration, whereas the latter focuses more directly on the main issues.
3. The payment of tax is deferred where, for example, expenditure is allowable for tax before it appears as a deduction in the published accounts (e.g. see first year allowances below).
4. The inflation accounting debate is fully examined in Tweedie and Whittington. Chapter 1 also contains a series of simple examples which clearly explain the basic principles of, and differences between the following:
   a. Historical cost accounting (HCA).
   b. Current purchasing power accounting (CPP). This involves the adjustment of HCA for changes in the purchasing power of money as measured by the general price index.
   c. Current cost accounting (CCA). This is the version of replacement cost accounting which involves restating assets at their 'deprival value' or 'value to the business'. This uses replacement cost or recoverable amount, whichever is the lower, where recoverable amount is the higher of present value and net realisable value.
   d. Real terms accounting (RT). This bases CPP adjustments on replacement costs rather than historical costs.

5. The paper was written by W.E.Parker but published anonymously. Parker was president of the ICAEW, at the time, and there was unease that the document might be regarded as Institute policy if the author's name was known.

Chapter 20

1. The obituary awards the accolade 'practical founder of the profession of public accountants in this country', to Peter H. Abbott, referred to later in this chapter.

Chapter 21

1. The ICAEW's 1987 intake consisted of approximately 6000 trainee accountants, of which 1500 were relevant and 4000 non-relevant graduates. The Scottish Institute took about the same proportion of graduates (90 per cent), but the other professional bodies less.
2. Part, but by no means the whole, of the difference is due to narrower definitions in France and Germany, where the term professional accountant is confined to people working in private practice performing the traditional functions of the accountant and auditor, i.e. taxation and management consultancy are excluded.
3. Traditionally the British accounting profession has been self-regulatory, but this may be changing. The Financial Services Act 1986, for example, which makes provision for the supervision of businesses providing investment advice, is seen by some as leading, in due course, to greater state control through organisations such as the Securities and Investments Board.
4. The ICAEW's recently published consultative paper *Training the Business Professional* (1987) sets out a new examination structure which contains papers entitled 'Business Strategy and Planning' and 'Commercial and Financial Decisions' to 'provide the newly qualified with an excellent grounding in business affairs' (p.12).
5. In the US, by way of contrast, over one hundred universities offered options in accountancy to over 3500 students in 1914. In the German Empire eleven technical universities were in existence by 1900 and these introduced cost accounting courses before the First World War. The business schools, of which there were eight by 1920, 'made business economics into a respected applied science' (Locke, p.12).
6. The right of local authorities to appoint their own auditors was withdrawn in 1982, and transferred to the audit commission which may appoint either a district auditor (employed by the commission) or a firm of professional accountants to do the job. Since this change was made the amount of local authority work undertaken by firms of chartered accountants has significantly increased.

References and Bibliography

Chapter 1

American Accounting Association, 'Report of the Committee on Accounting History', *Accounting Review*, 1970, Supplement, p.53.

Baladouni, Vahe, 'The Study of Accounting History', *The International Journal of Accounting*, Spring 1977, p.53.

Baxter, W.T., 'Accounting History as a Worthwhile Study', *Accounting Historians Notebook*, Spring 1981, p.5.

Carr, E.H., *What is History?*, Macmillan, London, 1962.

Goldberg, L., 'The Future of the Past in Accounting', *The Accountant's Magazine*, October 1974, p.405.

Lee, Geoffrey, A., 'The Coming of Age of Double Entry: The Giovanni Farolfi Ledger of 1299–1300', *The Accounting Historians Journal*, Fall 1977, p.79.

Lee, T.A., 'The Evolution and Revolution of Financial Accounting: a Review Article', *Accounting and Business Research*, Autumn 1979, p.292.

Lister, Roger J., 'Accounting as History', *The International Journal of Accounting*, Spring 1983, p.49.

Mumford, Michael, 'The End of a Familiar Inflation Accounting Cycle', *Accounting and Business Research*, Spring 1979, p.98.

Newgarden, Albert, 'Accounting and Accountants: An Anthology', in *Accounting, a book of readings*, edited by Gerhard G.Mueller and Charles H.Smith, Holt, Rinehart & Winston, 1970.

Parker, R.H., 'The Study of Accounting History', in *Essays in British Accounting Research*, edited by A.Hopwood and M.Bromwich, London, Pitman, 1981, p.279.

Postan, M.M., *Fact and Relevance: Essays on Historical Methods*, Cambridge University Press, Cambridge, 1971.

Yamey, B.S., 'Some Reflections on the Writing of a General History of Accounting', *Accounting and Business Research*, Spring 1981, p.127.

Yamey, Basil, 'The Relevance of the Study of Accounting History', in *Selected Papers from the Charles Waldo Haskins Accounting History Seminars*, edited by James F.Gaertner, the Academy of Accounting Historians, 1983.

Chapter 2

Baladouni, Vahe, 'The Study of Accounting History', *The International Journal of Accounting*, Spring 1977, p.53.

Baxter, William T., 'Accounting History as a Worthwhile Study', *Accounting Historians Notebook*, Spring 1981, p.5.

Baxter, W.T., 'Accounting Roots and their Lingering Influence', in *Selected Papers from the Charles Waldo Haskins Accounting History Seminars*, edited by James F.Gaertner, The Academy of Accounting Historians, 1983, p.135.
Bird, Peter, *Accountability: Standards in Financial Reporting*, Haymarket Publishing, London, 1973.
Brief, Richard P., 'Nineteenth Century Accounting Error', *Journal of Accounting Research*, Spring 1965, p.12.
Brief, Richard P., *Nineteenth Century Capital Accounting and Business Investment*, Arno Press, New York, 1976.
Chatfield, Michael, *A History of Accounting Thought*, Robert E.Krieger Publishing, New York, 1977.
de Ste. Croix, G.E.M., 'Greek and Roman Accounting', in *Studies in the History of Accounting*, edited by A.C.Littleton and B.S.Yamey, p.14.
Grassby, R., 'The Rate of Profit in Seventeenth-Century England', *English Historical Review*, 1969, p.748.
Hopwood, Anthony G., 'The Archaeology of Accounting Systems', *Accounting, Organizations and Society*, 1987, p.207.
Hoskin, Keith W., and Richard H. Macve, 'Accounting and the Examination: a Genealogy of Disciplinary Power', *Accounting, Organizations and Society*, 1986, p.105.
Littleton, A.C., *Accounting Evolution to 1900*, American Institute Publishing Co., New York, 1933 (reprinted by Russel & Russel, New York, 1966).
Littleton, A.C. and B.S.Yamey, *Studies in the History of Accounting*, Sweet & Maxwell, London, 1956 (reprinted by Arno Press, New York, 1978).
Littleton A.C. and V.K.Zimmerman, *Accounting Theory: Continuity and Change*, Prentice-Hall, Englewood Cliffs, N.J., 1962.
Macve, Richard H., 'Some Glosses on Greek and Roman Accounting', *History of Political Thought*, 1986, p.233.
May, G.O., 'The Influence of Accounting on the Development of an Economy, Railway Retirements and Depreciation', *The Journal of Accountancy*, March 1936, p.171.
Stone, Williard, E., 'Antecedents of the Accounting Profession', *The Accounting Review*, April 1969, p.284.
Yamey, B.S., 'Some Reflections on the Writing of a General History of Accounting', *Accounting and Business Research*, Spring 1981, p.127.

Chapter 3

Chatfield, Michael, *A History of Accounting Thought*, Robert E.Krieger Publishing, New York, 1977.
de Ste. Croix, G.E.M., 'Greek and Roman Accounting', in *Studies in the History of Accounting*, edited by A.C.Littleton and B.S.Yamey, p.14.
Garbutt, Douglas, 'The Origins of Accounting and Writing', *The Accounting Historians Notebook*, Fall 1981, p.10.
Garbutt, Douglas, 'The Significance of Ancient Mesopotamia in Accounting History', *The Accounting Historians Journal*, Spring 1984, p.83.
Hain, H.P., 'Accounting Control in the Zenon Papyri', *The Accounting Review*, October 1966, p.699.
Jacobsen, Lyle E., 'Use of Knotted String Accounting Records in Old Hawaii and Ancient China', *The Accounting Historians Journal*, Fall 1983, p.53.

Keister, Orville R., 'The Incan Quipu', *The Accounting Review*, April 1964, p.414.
Macve, Richard H., 'Some Glosses on Greek and Roman Accounting', *History of Political Thought*, 1986, p.233.
Most, Kenneth S., 'Accounting and the Invention of Writing', *Accounting Historians Notebook*, Spring 1981, p.4.
Most, Kenneth S., 'Accounting by the Ancients', *The Accountant*, 9 May 1959, p.563.
Stevelinck, Ernest, 'Accounting in Ancient Times', *The Accounting Historians Journal*, Spring 1985, p.1.
Stone, Williard, E., 'Antecedents of the Accounting Profession', *The Accounting Review*, April 1969, p.284.
Woolf, Arthur H., *A Short History of Accountants and Accountancy*, London, Gee, 1912, (reprinted by Garland, New York 1986).
Yamey, B.S., 'Some Reflections on the Writing of a General History of Accounting', *Accounting and Business Research*, Spring 1981, p.127.

Chapter 4

Baxter, William T., 'The Account Charge and Discharge', *The Accounting Historians Journal*, Spring 1980, p.69.
Baxter, W.T., 'Accounting Roots and their Lingering Influence', in *Selected Papers from the Charles Waldo Haskins Accounting History Seminars*, edited by James F.Gaertner, The Academy of Accounting Historians, 1983, p.135.
Chatfield, Michael, *A History of Accounting Thought*, Robert E.Krieger Publishing, New York, 1977.
Eldridge, H.J., *The Evolution of the Science of Book-keeping*, 2nd edn revised by Leonard Frankland, Gee, London, 1954 (reprinted by Nihon Shoseki, Osaka, 1975).
Robert, Rudolph., 'A Short History of Tallies', in *Studies in the History of Accounting*, edited by A.C.Littleton and B.S.Yamey, p.75.
Jack, S.M., 'An Historical Defence of Single-entry Book-keeping', *Abacus*, December 1966, p.137.
Jones, Rowan H., 'Accounting in English Local Government from the Middle Ages to c.1835', *Accounting and Business Research*, Summer 1985, p.197.
Noke, Christopher, 'Accounting for Bailiffship in Thirteenth Century England', *Accounting and Business Research*, Spring 1981, p.137.
Parker, Bob, 'Burning Down Parliament: A Story of Accounting Change', *Accountancy*, 1984, p.80.

Chapter 5

Chatfield, Michael, *A History of Accounting Thought*, Robert E.Krieger Publishing, New York, 1977.
de Roover, Raymond, 'The Development of Accounting Prior to Luca Pacioli according to the Account-books of Medieval Merchants' in *Studies in the History of Accounting*, edited by A.C.Littleton and B.S.Yamey, p.114.
de Ste. Croix, G.E.M., 'Greek and Roman Accounting', in *Studies in the History of Accounting*, edited by A.C.Littleton and B.S.Yamey, p.14.

Hatfield, Henry Rand, 'An Historical Defence of Bookkeeping', in *Studies in Accounting*, edited by W.T.Baxter, Sweet & Maxwell, London, 1950, p.1.
Hoskin, Keith W., and Richard H. Macve, 'Accounting and the Examination; a Genealogy of Disciplinary Power', *Accounting, Organizations and Society*, 1986, p.105.
Lall Nigam, B.M., 'Bahi-Khata: The Pre-Pacioli Indian Double-entry System of Bookkeeping', *Abacus*, September 1986, p.148.
Lee, G.A., *Modern Financial Accounting*, 2nd edn, Nelson, London 1976, pp.6–13.
Lee, Geoffrey, A., 'The Coming of Age of Double Entry: The Giovanni Farolfi Ledger of 1299–1300', *The Accounting Historians Journal*, Fall 1977, p.79.
Littleton, A.C., *Accounting Evolution to 1900*, American Institute Publishing Co., New York, 1933 (reprinted by Russel & Russel, New York, 1966).
Nobes, Christopher, 'Pacioli – the first academic accountant?', *Accountancy*, September 1979, p.66.
Pacioli, Frater Luca, *Summa de Arithmetica, Geometria, Proportioni et Proportionalita*, translated by Pietro Crivelli, Institute of Book-keepers, London, 1939.
Parker, Robert, 'From the Abacus to the Computer', *Australian Accountant*, August 1986, p.81.
Stone, Williard E., 'Abacists versus Algorists', *Journal of Accounting Research*, Autumn 1972, p.345.
Sugden, Keith F., 'A History of the Abacus', *The Accounting Historians Journal*, Fall 1981, p.1.
Williams, John J., 'A New Perspective on the Evolution of Double-entry Bookkeeping', *The Accounting Historians Journal*, Spring 1978, p.29.
Yamey, B.S., 'Some Topics in the the History of Financial Accounting in England, 1500–1900', in *Studies in Accounting*, edited by W.T.Baxter and Sidney Davidson, ICAEW, London, 1977, p.11.

Chapter 6

Boys, Peter G., 'A Spectator of Accounting History', *The Accounting Historians Notebook*, Academy of Accounting Historians, Fall 1987, p.1.
Baladouni, Vahe, 'Financial Reporting in the Early Years of The East India Company', *The Accounting Historians Journal*, Spring 1986, p.19.
Chatfield, Michael, *A History of Accounting Thought*, Robert E.Krieger Publishing, New York, 1977.
Hatfield, Henry Rand, 'An Historical Defence of Bookkeeping', in *Studies in Accounting*, edited by W.T.Baxter, Sweet & Maxwell, London, 1950, p.1.
Heaton, Herbert, *Economic History of Europe*, Harper, New York, 1948.
Hopwood, Anthony G. and H. Thomas Johnson, 'Accounting History's claim to Legitimacy', *The International Journal of Accounting*, Spring 1986, p.37.
Jones, Haydn, *Accounting, Costing and Cost Estimation*, University of Wales Press, Cardiff, 1985.
Lisle, George, 'Balance Sheets' in *Encyclopaedia of Accounting, Vol.1*, edited by George Lisle, William Green, Edinburgh, 1903, p.203.

Lister, Roger J., 'Accounting as History', *The International Journal of Accounting*, Spring 1983, p.49.
Littleton A.C. and V.K.Zimmerman, *Accounting Theory: Continuity and Change*, Prentice-Hall, Englewood Cliffs, N.J., 1962.
Macve, Richard H., 'Some Glosses on Greek and Roman Accounting', *History of Political Thought*, 1986, p.233.
Most, Kenneth S, 'Sombart on Accounting History', in *The Academy of Accounting Historians Working Paper Series, Vol. 2*, edited by Edward N. Coffman, 1979, p.244.
Nobes, Christopher W., 'The Gallerani Account Book of 1305–08', *The Accounting Review*, April 1982, p.303.
Pacioli, Frater Luca, *Summa de Arithmetica, Geometria, Proportioni et Proportionalita*, translated by Pietro Crivelli, Institute of Book-keepers, London, 1939.
Parker, R.H., *Macmillan Dictionary of Accounting*, Macmillan, London, 1984.
Peragallo, Edward, 'Origin of the Trial Balance', in *Studies in the History of Accounting*, edited by A.C.Littleton and B.S.Yamey, p.215.
Pollard, Sidney, 'Capital Accounting in the Industrial Revolution', *Yorkshire Bulletin of Economic and Social Research*, November 1963, p.75.
Pollard, Sidney, *The Genesis of Modern Management, a Study of the Industrial Revolution in Great Britain*, Arnold, London 1965.
Sombart, Werner, *Der Moderne Kapitalismus*, ('Modern Capitalism') Duncker & Humblot, Leipzig, 1919 (a translation of the accounting history section of this book appears in Most, pp.247–59).
ten Have, O, 'Simon Stevin of Bruges' , in *Studies in the History of Accounting*, edited by A.C.Littleton and B.S.Yamey, p.236.
Winjum, James Ole, *The Role of Accounting in the Economic Development of England: 1500–1750*, Center for International Education and Research in Accounting, Board of Trustees of the University of Illinois, 1972.
Yamey, B.S., 'Scientific Bookkeeping and the Rise of Capitalism', *The Economic History Review*, 1949, p.99.
Yamey, B.S., 'Accounting and the Rise of Capitalism, further notes on a theme by Sombart', *Journal of Accounting Research*, Autumn 1964, p.117.
Yamey, B.S., 'Closing the Ledger', *Accounting and Business Research*, Winter 1970, p.71.
Yamey, B.S., 'Some Topics in the the History of Financial Accounting in England, 1500–1900', in *Studies in Accounting*, edited by W.T.Baxter and Sidney Davidson, ICAEW, London, 1977, p.11.
Yamey, B.S., 'Early Views on the Origins and Development of Bookkeeping and Accounting', *Accounting and Business Research*, Special Accounting History Issue, 1980, p.81.
Yamey, B.S., 'Some Reflections on the Writing of a General History of Accounting', *Accounting and Business Research*, Spring 1981, p.127.
Yamey, B.S., 'Two Seventeenth Century Accounting Statements', *Accounting and Business Research*, Spring 1982, p.111.
Yamey, B.S., H.C.Edey, and Hugh W.Thomson, *Accounting in England and Scotland: 1543–1800*, Sweet & Maxwell, London, 1963 (reprinted by Garland, New York, 1982).

Chapter 7

Canning, John B., *The Economics of Accountancy*, Ronald Press, New York, 1929 (reprinted by Arno Press, New York, 1978).
Chatfield, Michael, *A History of Accounting Thought*, Robert E.Krieger Publishing, New York, 1977.
Coomber, R.R., 'Hugh Oldcastle and John Mellis', in *Studies in the History of Accounting*, edited by A.C.Littleton and B.S.Yamey, p.206.
Eldridge, H.J., *The Evolution of the Science of Book-keeping*, 2nd edn revised by Leonard Frankland, Gee, London, 1954 (reprinted by Nihon Shoseki, Osaka, 1975).
Emmett Taylor, R., 'Luca Pacioli', in *Studies in the History of Accounting*, edited by A.C.Littleton and B.S.Yamey, p.175.
Etor, J.R., 'Some Problems in Accounting History, 1830–1900', *Business Archives*, 1973, p.38.
Jackson, J.G.C., 'The History of Methods of Exposition of Double-entry Book-keeping in England', in *Studies in the History of Accounting*, edited by A.C.Littleton and B.S.Yamey, p.288.
Jones, Edward Thomas, *Jones's English System of Book-keeping*, Bristol, 1796 (reprinted by Arno Press, New York, 1978).
Littleton A.C. and V.K.Zimmerman, *Accounting Theory: Continuity and Change*, Prentice-Hall, Englewood Cliffs, N.J., 1962.
McMickle, Peter L., '*Young Man's Companion* of 1737: America's First Book on Accounting?', *Abacus*, June 1984, p.34.
Pacioli, Frater Luca, *Summa de Arithmetica, Geometria, Proportioni et Proportionalita*, translated by Pietro Crivelli, Institute of Book-keepers, London, 1939.
Peragallo, Edward, *Origin and Evolution of Double Entry Bookkeeping*, American Institute Publishing Co., New York, 1938.
Sheldahl, Terry K., 'America's Earliest Recorded Text in Accounting: Sargeant's 1789 Book', *The Accounting Historians Journal*, Fall 1985, p.27.
Yamey, Basil S., 'Edward Jones's English System of Bookkeeping', *The Accounting Review*, October 1944, p.407.
Yamey, B.S., 'Edward Jones and the Reform of Book-keeping, 1795–1810', in *Studies in the History of Accounting*, edited by A.C.Littleton and B.S.Yamey, p.313.
Yamey, B.S., 'Oldcastle, Peele and Mellis: A Case of Plagiarism in the Sixteenth Century', *Accounting and Business Research*, Summer 1979, p.209.
Yamey, B.S., 'Early Views on the Origins and Development of Book-keeping and Accounting', *Accounting and Business Research*, Special Accounting History Issue, 1980, p.81.
Yamey, B.S., H.C.Edey, and Hugh W.Thomson, *Accounting in England and Scotland: 1543–1800*, Sweet & Maxwell, London, 1963 (reprinted by Garland, New York, 1982).

Chapter 8

Cannan, Edwin, 'Early History of the Term Capital', in *Quarterly Journal of Economics*, 1921, p.469.
Chandler, Alfred D., *The Visible Hand*, Harvard University Press, Cambridge, Massachusetts and London, 1977.

Chatfield, Michael, *A History of Accounting Thought*, Robert E.Krieger Publishing, New York, 1977.
de Roover, Raymond, 'The Development of Accounting Prior to Luca Pacioli according to the Account-books of Medieval Merchants' in *Studies in the History of Accounting*, edited by A.C.Littleton and B.S.Yamey, p.114.
Edwards, J.R. and C.Baber, 'Dowlais Iron Company: Accounting Policies and Procedures for Profit Measurement and Reporting Purposes', *Accounting and Business Research*, Spring 1979, p.139.
Jones, Haydn, *Accounting, Costing and Cost Estimation*, University of Wales Press, Cardiff 1985.
Lee, G.A., 'The Concept of Profit in British Accounting, 1760–1900', *Business History Review*, Spring 1975, p.6.
Littleton, A.C., *Accounting Evolution to 1900*, American Institute Publishing Co., New York, 1933 (reprinted by Russel & Russel, New York, 1966).
Macve, Richard H., 'Some Glosses on Greek and Roman Accounting', *History of Political Thought*, 1986, p.233.
McKendrick, Neil, 'Josiah Wedgwood and Cost Accounting in the Industrial Revolution', *The Economic History Review*, April 1970, p.45.
Nobes, Christopher W., 'The Pre-Pacioli Indian Double-entry System of Bookkeeping: A Comment', *Abacus*, September 1987, p.182.
Noke Christopher, 'Accounting for Bailiffship in Thirteenth Century England', *Accounting and Business Research*, Spring 1981, p.137.
Parker, R.H., 'Lower of Cost and Market in Britain and the United States: An Historical Survey', *Abacus*, 1965, p.156.
Parker, R.H., 'The First Scottish Book on Accounting: Robert Colinson's *Idea Rationaria (1683)*', *The Accountant's Magazine*, September 1974, p.358.
Pollard, Sidney, *The Genesis of Modern Management, a Study of the Industrial Revolution in Great Britain*, Arnold, London 1965.
Smith, Adam, *An Inquiry into the Nature and Causes of the Wealth of Nations*, P.Nelson & Sons, Edinburgh, 1873 reprint.
Stone, E., 'Profit-and-Loss Accountancy at Norwich Cathedral Priory', *Transactions of The Royal Historical Society*, London, 1962, p.25.
Stone, Williard E., 'An Early English Cotton Mill Cost Accounting System: Charlton Mills, 1810–1889', *Accounting and Business Research*, Winter 1973, p.71.
Tucker, G.F.L., *Progress and Profits in British Economic Thought 1650–1850*, The University Press, Cambridge, 1960.
Winjum, James Ole, *The Role of Accounting in the Economic Development of England: 1500–1750*, Center for International Education and Research in Accounting, Board of Trustees of the University of Illinois, 1972.
Yamey, B.S., 'Some Topics in the the History of Financial Accounting in England, 1500–1900', in *Studies in Accounting*, edited by W.T.Baxter and Sidney Davidson, ICAEW , 1977, p.11.
Yamey, B.S., H.C.Edey, and Hugh W.Thomson, *Accounting in England and Scotland: 1543–1800*, Sweet & Maxwell, London, 1963 (reprinted by Garland, New York, 1982).

Chapter 9

Alderman, Geoffrey, *Modern Britain 1700–1983*, Croom Helm, London, 1986.
Baladouni, Vahe, 'Accounting in the Early Years of the East India

Company', *The Accounting Historians Journal*, Fall 1983, p.63.
Baladouni, Vahe, 'Financial Reporting in the Early Years of The East India Company', *The Accounting Historians Journal*, Spring 1986, p.19.
Clapham, J.H., *An Economic History of Modern Britain, the Early Railway Age, 1820–1850*, 2nd edn, University Press, Cambridge 1964.
Davies, K.G., 'Joint-Stock Investment in the Later Seventeenth Century', *The Economic History Review*, 1952, p.283.
DuBois, Armand Budington, *The English Business Company after the Bubble Act 1720–1800*, Octagon Books, New York, 1971.
Formoy, Ronald, Ralph, *The Historical Foundations of Modern Company Law*, Sweet & Maxwell, London, 1923.
Gower, L.C.B., *The Principles of Modern Company Law*, 4th edn, Stevens, London, 1979, ch.2 & 3.
Hein, Leonard William., *The British Companies Acts and the Practice of Accountancy 1844–1962*, Arno Press, New York, 1978, ch.3.
Hunt, Bishop Carleton, *The Development of the Business Corporation in England 1800–1867*, Harvard University Press, Cambridge, Massachusetts, 1936 (reprinted by Russell & Russell, New York 1969).
Irish, R.A., 'The Evolution of Corporate Accounting', in *Contemporary Studies in the Evolution of Accounting Thought*, edited by Michael Chatfield, Dickenson Publishing, Belmont, California, 1968, p.57.
Littleton, A.C., *Accounting Evolution to 1900*, American Institute Publishing Co., New York, 1933 (reprinted by Russel & Russel, New York, 1966).
Parker, R.H., *The Development of the Accountancy Profession in Britain to the Early Twentieth Century'*, The Academy of Accounting Historians, 1986.
Smith, Adam, *An Inquiry into the Nature and Causes of the Wealth of Nations*, P.Nelson & Sons, Edinburgh, 1873 reprint.
Worthington, Beresford, *Professional Accountants*, Gee, London, 1895 (reprinted by Arno Press, New York, 1978).

Chapter 10

Brief, Richard P., 'Nineteenth Century Accounting Error', *Journal of Accounting Research*, Spring 1965, p.12.
Brief, Richard P, 'The Origin and Evolution of Nineteenth Century Asset Accounting', *Business History Review*, Spring 1966, p.1.
Brief, Richard P., 'Valuation, Matching and Earnings; the Continuing Debate', in *Selected Papers from the Charles Waldo Haskins Accounting History Seminars*, edited by James F.Gaertner, the Academy of Accounting Historians, 1983, p.15.
Dickinson, Arthur Lowes, 'The Profits of a Corporation', *Proceedings of the First International Congress of Accountants* , New York, 1904, p.171.
Dicksee, Lawrence R., *Depreciation Reserves, and Reserve Funds*, Gee, London 1903 (reprinted by Arno Press, New York, 1976).
Edwards, J.R. and C.Baber, 'Dowlais Iron Company: Accounting Policies and Procedures for Profit Measurement and Reporting Purposes', *Accounting and Business Research*, Spring 1979, p.139.
Edwards, J.R., 'British Capital Accounting Practices and Business Finance

1852–1919. An Exemplification', *Accounting and Business Research*, Spring 1980, p.241.

Edwards, J.R. and K.Webb, 'The Influence of Company Law on Corporate Reporting Procedures, 1865–1929: An Exemplification', *Business History*, November 1982, p.259.

Edwards, J.R., 'Depreciation and Fixed Asset Valuation in Railway Company Accounts to 1911, *Accounting and Business Research*, Summer 1986a, p.251.

Edwards, J.R. (ed.), *Reporting Fixed Assets in Nineteenth-Century Company Accounts*, Garland Publishing, New York & London, 1986b.

Garcke, Emile and J.M.Fells, *Factory Accounts*, 4th edn, Crosby Lockwood, London, 1893.

Hill, N.K., 'Accountancy Developments in A Public Utility Company in the Nineteenth Century', *Accounting Research*, October 1955, p.382.

Litherland, D.A., 'Fixed Asset Replacement A Half Century Ago', *The Accounting Review*, October 1951, p.475.

Littleton, A.C., *Accounting Evolution to 1900*, American Institute Publishing Co., New York, 1933 (reprinted by Russel & Russel, New York, 1966).

Montgomery, Hartford H., 'Depreciation of Buildings, Machinery, and Plant, in Reference to Accounts and Income-Tax', *Accountants' Magazine*, 1908, p.313.

Matheson, Ewing, *The Depreciation of Factories*, 2nd edn, E & F.N.Spon, 1893.

Parker, R.H., 'Lower of Cost and Market in Britain and the United States: An Historical Survey', *Abacus*, 1965, p.156.

Pixley, Francis W., *Accountancy*, Pitman, London, 1908.

Pollins, Horold, 'Aspects of Railway Accounting Before 1868', in *Reporting Fixed Assets in Nineteenth-Century Company Accounts*, edited by J.R.Edwards, Garland Publishing, New York & London, 1986, p.312.

Roberts, Roydon, 'The Published Accounts of the Northampton Gas Light Company 1823–1900', in *Reporting Fixed Assets in Nineteenth-Century Company Accounts*, edited by J.R.Edwards, Garland Publishing, New York & London, 1986, p.336.

Yamey, B.S., 'The Development of Company Accounting Conventions', *Three Banks Review*, September 1960, p.3.

Chapter 11

Dickinson, Sir Arthur Lowes, 'Publicity in Industrial Accounts. With a Comparison of English and American Methods', *Accountant*, 1924, p.469.

Edwards, J.R., 'The Accounting Profession and Disclosure in Published Reports, 1925–1935', *Accounting and Business Research*, Autumn 1976, p.289.

Edwards, J.R., 'British Capital Accounting Practices and Business Finance 1852–1919. An Exemplification', *Accounting and Business Research*, Spring 1980, p.241.

Edwards, J.R., *Company Legislation and Changing Patterns of Disclosure in British Company Accounts, 1900–1940*, ICAEW, London, 1981.

Irish, R.A., 'The Evolution of Corporate Accounting', in *Contemporary Studies in the Evolution of Accounting Thought*, edited by Michael Chatfield, Dickenson Publishing, Belmont, California, 1968, p.57.

Jones, Rowan, H., 'Accruals Accounting in Local Government; Some Historical Context to Continuing Controversies', *Financial Accountability and Management*, Winter 1985, p.145.

Kitchen, J., 'The accounts of British holding company groups: development and attitudes to disclosure in the early years', *Accounting and Business Research*, Spring 1972, p.114.

Leake, P.D., *Depreciation and Wasting Assets, and their Treatment in Computing Annual Profit and Loss*, 5th edn, Gee, London, 1948

Chapter 12

Brooks, Collin, *The Royal Mail Case*, Canada Law Book Company, Toronto, 1933 (reprinted by Arno Press, New York, 1980).

Bircher, Paul, 'Company Law Reform and the Board of Trade, 1929–1943', *Accounting and Business Research*, Spring 1988, p.107.

Dicksee, Lawrence R., *Published Balance Sheets and Window Dressing*, Gee, London, 1927 (reprinted by Arno Press, New York, 1980).

Edwards, J.R., 'The Accounting Profession and Disclosure in Published Reports, 1925–1935', *Accounting and Business Research*, Autumn 1976, p.289.

Edwards, J.R., 'William Plender, Lord Plender of Sundridge, Kent, (1869–1946) Accountant', in David J.Jeremy (ed.) *Dictionary of Business Biography, Vol.4 (M–R)*, Butterworth 1985, p.736.

Forbes, R.N., 'Some Contemporary Reactions to a Banking Failure', *The Three Banks Review*, March 1979, p.48.

French, E.A., *Unlimited Liability: the Case of the City of Glasgow Bank*, Certified Accountant Publications Ltd., London, 1985.

Green, Edwin, and Michael Moss, *A Business of National Importance, The Royal Mail Shipping Group 1902–1937*, Methuen, London, 1982.

Hastings, Sir Patrick, 'The Case of the Royal Mail', in *Studies in Accounting Theory*, edited by W.T.Baxter and S.Davidson, Sweet & Maxwell, London, 1962, p.452.

Samuel, Horace B., *Shareholders' Money*, Pitman, London, 1933 (reprinted by Garland Publishing, New York & London, 1982).

Tyson, R.E., 'The Failure of the City of Glasgow Bank and the Rise of Independent Auditing', *The Accountant's Magazine*, April 1974, p.126.

Worthington, Beresford, *Professional Accountants*, Gee, London, 1895 (reprinted by Arno Press, New York, 1978).

Chapter 13

Alderman, Geoffrey, *The Railway Interest*, Leicester University Press, Leicester 1973.

Cutforth, A.E., *Audits*, 8th edn, Gee, London, 1931.

Edwards, John Richard, 'The Origins and Evolution of the Double Account System: An Example of Accounting Innovation', *Abacus*, March 1985, p.19.

Edwards, J.R. (ed.), 'Introduction' to *Legal Regulation of British Company Accounts 1836–1900*, Garland Publishing, New York & London, 1986.

Roberts, Roydon, 'The Published Accounts of the Northampton Gas Light Company 1823–1900', in *Reporting Fixed Assets in Nineteenth-Century Company Accounts*, edited by J.R.Edwards, Garland Publishing, New York & London, 1986, p.336.

Chapter 14

Brief, Richard P, 'The Origin and Evolution of Nineteenth Century Asset Accounting', *Business History Review*, Spring 1966, p.1.

DuBois, Armand Budington, *The English Business Company after the Bubble Act 1720–1800*, Octagon Books, New York, 1971.

French, E.A., 'The Evolution of the Dividend Law of England', in *Studies in Accounting*, edited by W.T.Baxter and Sidney Davidson, ICAEW, London, 1977, p.306.

Gower, L.C.B., *The Principles of Modern Company Law*, 4th edn, Stevens, London, 1979, ch. 10.

Morris, Richard D., 'Lee v. Neuchatel Asphalte Company (1889) and Depreciation Accounting: Two Empirical Studies', *Accounting and Business Research*, Winter 1986, p.71.

Reid, Jean Margo, *Law and Accounting. Pre-1889 British Legal Cases*, Garland Publishing, New York & London, 1986.

Reid, Jean Margot, 'Judicial Views on Accounting in Britain before 1889', *Accounting and Business Research*, Summer 1987, p.247.

Yamey B.S., 'Aspects of the Law Relating to Company Dividends', in *Studies in Accounting*, edited by W.T.Baxter, Sweet & Maxwell, London, 1950, p.59

Chapter 15

Alderman, Geoffrey, *Modern Britain 1700–1983*, Croom Helm, London, 1986.

Edwards, J.R. and K.M.Webb, 'Use of Table A by Companies Registering Under the Companies Act 1862', *Accounting and Business Research*, Summer 1985, p.177.

Edey, H.C. and Prot. Panitpakdi, 'British Company Accounting and the Law 1844–1900', in *Studies in the History of Accounting*, edited by A.C.Littleton and B.S.Yamey, p.356.

Taylor Arthur J., *Laissez-faire and State Intervention in Nineteenth-century Britain*, Macmillan, London, 1972.

Watts, Ross L., and Jerold L.Zimmerman, 'The Demand for and Supply of Accounting Theories,: The Market for Excuses', *The Accounting Review*, April 1979, p.273.

Chapter 16

Arayana, Nissim, 'The Influence of Pressure Groups on Financial Statements in Britain', *Abacus*, June 1974, p.3.

Bircher, Paul, 'Company Law Reform and the Board of Trade, 1929–1943', *Accounting and Business Research*, Spring 1988, p.107.

Dicksee, Lawrence R., *Published Balance Sheets and Window Dressing*, Gee, London, 1927 (reprinted by Arno Press, New York, 1980).

Edey, H.C. and Prot. Panitpakdi, 'British Company Accounting and the Law 1844–1900', in *Studies in the History of Accounting,* edited by A.C.Littleton and B.S.Yamey, p.356.

Edwards, J.R. (ed.), *British Company Legislation and Company Accounts, 1844–1976*, Arno Press, New York, 1980.

Edwards, J.R. (ed.), *Legal Regulation of British Company Accounts*, Garland Publishing, New York & London, 1986.

Howitt, Sir Harold., *The History of the Institute of Chartered Accountants in England and Wales 1880–1965, and its founder accountancy bodies 1870–1880*, Heinemann, London, 1966 (reprinted by Garland Publishing, New York, 1984).

Watts, Ross L., and Jerold L.Zimmerman, 'The Demand for and Supply of Accounting Theories,: The Market for Excuses', *The Accounting Review*, April 1979, p.273.

Chapter 17

Edey, H.C. and Prot.Panitpakdi, 'British Company Accounting and the Law 1844–1900', in *Studies in the History of Accounting,* edited by A.C.Littleton and B.S.Yamey, p.356.

Edwards, J.R., 'Standardisation of Accounts: A look back at changing attitudes', *Certified Accountant*, 1981, p.229.

Hein, Leonard William., *The British Companies Acts and the Practice of Accountancy 1844–1962*, Arno Press, New York, 1978, chapter 8.

Hodgkins, Peter, 'Unilever – The First 21 Years', in *The Evolution of Corporate Financial Reporting*, edited by T.A.Lee and R.H.Parker, Nelson, Middlesex, 1979 (reprinted by Garland Publishing, New York & London, 1984) p.40.

Nobes, C.W., 'The Evolution of the Harmonising Provisions of the 1980 and 1981 Companies Acts', *Accounting and Business Research*, Winter 1983, p.43.

Parker, R.H., 'The Want of Uniformity in Accounts: A Nineteenth Century Debate', in *Essays in Honour of Trevor R.Johnston,* edited by D.M.Emanuel and I.C.Stewart, University of Auckland, 1980, p.201.

Chapter 18

Edwards, J.R. and K.M.Webb, 'The Development of Group Accounting in the United Kingdom to 1933', *The Accounting Historians Journal,* Spring 1984, p.31.

Garnsey, Sir Gilbert, *Holding Companies and their Published Accounts*, Gee, London, 1923 (reprinted by Garland Publishing, New York & London, 1982).

Garnsey, Sir Gilbert, *Holding Companies and their Published Accounts*, 2nd edn, Gee, London, 1931.

Hannah, Leslie, *The Rise of the Corporate Economy*, Methuen, London, 1983.

Kitchen, J., 'The accounts of British holding company groups: development and attitudes to disclosure in the early years', *Accounting and Business Research,* Spring 1972, p.114.

Parker, R.H., 'Explaining National Differences in Consolidated Accounts', *Accounting and Business Research*, Summer 1977, p.203.

Payne, P.L., 'The Emergance of the Large Scale Company in Great Britain 1870–1914', *Economic History Review*, 1967, p.519.
Walker, R.G., *Consolidated Statements*, Arno Press, New York, 1978.
Watts, Ross L. and Jerold L.Zimmerman, 'The Demand for and Supply of Accounting Theories: The Market for Excuses', *The Accounting Review*, April 1979, p.273.

Chapter 19

Accounting Standards Committee, 'Review of the Standard Setting Process', *Accountancy*, July 1983, p.115.
Accounting Standards Committee, *Accounting for the Effects of Changing Prices: A Handbook*, ASC, London, 1986.
Accounting Standards Steering Committee, *The Corporate Report*, ASSC, London, 1975.
Baxter, W.T., *Studies in Accounting*, Sweet & Maxwell, London, 1950.
Baxter, W.T., 'Recommendations on Accounting Theory', *The Accountant*, 10 October 1953, p.405.
Baxter, William, *Collected Papers in Accounting*, Arno Press, New York, 1978.
Baxter, W.T., *Inflation Accounting*, Philip Allan, Oxford, 1984.
Bonbright, J.C., *The Valuation of Property*, Michie, Charlottesville, 1937.
Canning, J.B., *The Economics of Accountancy*, Ronald Press, New York, 1929.
Chambers, R.J., 'Financial Information and the Securities Market', *Abacus*, September 1965, p.3.
Chambers, Raymond J., *Accounting, Evaluation and Economic Behavior*, Prentice-Hall, Englewood Cliffs, N.J., 1966.
Dev, Susan, *Accounting and the L.S.E. Tradition*, the London School of Economics and Political Science, London, 1980.
Edey, Harold C., 'Accounting Standards in the British Isles', in *Studies in Accounting*, edited by W.T.Baxter and Sidney Davidson, Sweet & Maxwell, London, 1977, p.294.
Edey, Harold, C., *Accounting Queries*, Garland Publishing, New York & London, 1982.
Edwards, E.O. and P.W.Bell, *The Theory and Measurement of Business Income*, University of California Press, Stanford, 1961.
FASB, *Scope and Implications of the Conceptual Framwework Project*, Stamford, Connecticut, 1976.
FASB, Statement of Financial Accounting Concepts 5, Recognition and Measurement in Financial Statements of Business Enterprises, Stamford, Connecticut, 1984.
ICAEW, *Accounting for Stewardship in a Period of Inflation*, 1968.
ICAEW, 'Statement of Intent on Accounting Standards in the 1970's', *Accountancy*, January 1970, p.2.
Kitchen, J. and R.H.Parker, *Accounting Thought and Education: Six English Pioneers*, ICAEW, London, 1980 (reprinted by Garland Publishing, New York & London, 1984).
Leach, Sir Ronald, 'The Birth of Accounting Standards', in *British Accounting Standards. The First 10 Years*, edited by Sir Ronald Leach and Professor Edward Stamp, Woodhead Faulkener, Cambridge, 1981, p.3.
Lee, T.A., 'Cash Flow Accounting and Corporate Financial Reporting', in Essays in British Accounting Research, edited by Michael Bromwich

and Anthony Hopwood, Pitman, London, 1981, p.63.
Macdonald, N.C.L., 'Depreciation and Revaluations of Fixed Assets', in *Financial Reporting 1986–87: A Survey of UK Reporting Practice*, edited by D.J.Tonkin and L.C.L.Skerratt, ICAEW, London, 1987.
Macve, Richard, *A Conceptual Framework for Financial Accounting and Reporting: the Possibilities of an Agreed Structure*, ICAEW, London, 1981.
Morpeth, D.S., 'Developing a Current Cost Accounting Standard', in *British Accounting Standards. The First 10 Years*, edited by Sir Ronald Leach and Professor Edward Stamp, Woodhead Faulkener, Cambridge, 1981, p.41.
Mumford, M.J., 'The 1952 Study, Accounting for Inflation. A Review Article', *Accounting and Business Research*, Winter 1983, p.71.
Peasnell, K.V., 'The Function of a Conceptual Framework for Corporate Financial Reporting', *Accounting and Business Research*, Autumn 1982, p.243.
Solomons, David, *Studies in Costing*, Sweet & Maxwell, London, 1952.
Stamp, Edward, and Christopher Marley, *Accounting Principles and the City Code: The Case for Reform*, Butterworths, London, 1970.
Sweeney, H.W., *Stabilized Accounting*, Harper, New York, 1936.
Tweedie, David and Geoffrey Whittington, *The Debate on Inflation Accounting*, Cambridge University Press, Cambridge, 1984.
Wells, M.C., 'A Revolution in Accounting Thought?', *The Accounting Review*, July 1976, p.471.
Zeff, Stephen A., *Forging Accounting Principles in Five Countries: a History and an Analysis of Trends*, Stipes Publishing, Illinois, 1972.
Zeff, Stephen A., '*Truth in Accounting:* The Ordeal of Kenneth MacNeal', *The Accounting Review*, July 1982, p.528.

Chapter 20

Anyon, James T., *Recollections of the Early Days of American Accountancy 1883–1893*, privately printed, 1925 (reprinted by Nihon Shoseki, Osaka, Japan, 1974).
Cooper, E., *Fifty-Seven Years in an Accountant's Office*, Gee, London, 1921 (reprinted by Arno Press, New York, 1976).
De Paula, F.R.M., 'Fifty Years', *Accounting Research*, November 1948, p.20.
Dicksee, Lawrence R, *Auditing: A Practical Manual for Auditors*, Gee, London, 1892 (reprinted by Arno Press, New York, 1976).
Edwards, John Richard, 'The Origins and Evolution of the Double Account System: An Example of Accounting Innovation', *Abacus*, March 1985a, p.19.
Edwards, J.R., 'Sir Gilbert Francis Garnsey (1883–1932), Accountant', in David J.Jeremy (ed.), *Dictionary of Business Biography, Vol.2 (D–G)*, Butterworths, 1985b, p.487.
Edwards, J.R., 'Edwin Waterhouse (1841–1917), Accountant', in David J.Jeremy (ed.) *Dictionary of Business Biography, Vol 5 (S–Z)*, Butterworths, 1986, p.674.
Jones, Edgar, *Accountancy and the British Economy 1840–1980. The Evolution of Ernst & Whinney*, Batsford, London, 1981.
Kettle, Sir Russell, *Deloitte & Co. 1845–1956*, University Press, Oxford, 1957.
Lee, T.A., *Company Auditing: Concepts and Practices*, Gee, London, 1972.
Parker, R.H. (ed.), *British Accountants: A Biographical Sourcebook*, Arno Press, New York, 1980.

Parker, R.H., *The Development of the Accountancy Profession in Britain to the Early Twentieth Century'*, The Academy of Accounting Historians, 1986.
Pixley, Francis W., *The Profession of a Chartered Accountant*, Good, London, 1897 (reprinted by Arno Press, New York, 1978).
Solomons, David, *Studies in Costing*, Sweet & Maxwell, London, 1952.
Spicer, Ernest Evan and Ernest C.Pegler, *Practical Auditing*, 6th edn edited by Walter W.Bigg, H.F.L., London, 1933.
Spicer, Ernest Evan and Ernest C.Pegler, *Practical Auditing*, seventh 7th edn edited by Walter W.Bigg, H.F.L., London, 1936.
Stewart, Jas. C., *Pioneers of a Profession*, The Institute of Chartered Accountants of Scotland, Edinburgh, 1977.
Wilson, Charles, *The History of Unilever: A Study in Economic Growth and Social Change*, Cassell, London, 1954.
Worthington, Beresford, *Professional Accountants*, Gee, London, 1895 (reprinted by Arno Press, New York, 1978).

Chapter 21

Freear, John, 'The Final Examinations of the Institute of Chartered Accountants in England and Wales, 1882–1981', *The Accounting Historians Journal*, Spring 1982, p.53.
Howitt, Sir Harold, *The History of the Institute of Chartered Accountants in England and Wales 1880–1965, and its founder accountancy bodies 1870–1880*, Heinemann, London, 1966 (reprinted by Garland Publishing, New York & London, 1984).
Locke, Robert R., 'New Insights from Cost Accounting into British Entrepreneurial Performance Circa 1914', *The Accounting Historians Journal*, Spring 1979, p.17.
Loft, Anne, 'Towards a Critical Understanding of Accounting: The Case of Cost Accounting in the UK, 1914–1925', *Accounting, Organizations and Society*, 1986, p.137.
Parker, R.H., 'British Men of Account', *Abacus*, June 1978, p.53.
Parker, R.H., *The Development of the Accountancy Profession in Britain to the Early Twentieth Century'*, The Academy of Accounting Historians, 1986.
Renshall, Michael, 'A Short Survey of the Accounting Profession', in *Current Issues in Accounting*, 2nd edn edited by Bryan Carsberg and Tony Hope, Phillip Allan, 1984. p.23.
Stacey, Nicholas A.H., *English Accountancy 1800–1954*, Gee, London, 1954.
Stewart, Jas. C., *Pioneers of a Profession*, The Institute of Chartered Accountants of Scotland, Edinburgh, 1977.
Willmott, Hugh, 'Organising the Profession: a Theoretical and Historical Examination of the Development of the Major Accountancy Bodies in the UK', *Accounting, Organizations and Society*, 1986, p.555.
Woolf, Emile, *Auditing Today*, 3rd edn, Prentice-Hall, Englewood Cliffs, N.J., 1986.
Worthington, Beresford, *Professional Accountants*, Gee, London, 1895 (reprinted by Arno Press, New York, 1978).
Zeff, Stephen A., 'The Business of Being a CPA', *Accountancy*, February 1988, p.110.

Index

For Product Safety Concerns and Information please contact our EU representative GPSR@taylorandfrancis.com Taylor & Francis Verlag GmbH, Kaufingerstraße 24, 80331 München, Germany

Batch number: 10726294

Printed by Printforce, the Netherlands